CLUBBIE

JULIE,

ENJOY MY WACKY STORIES
FROM MY BASEBALL DAYS!

10/11/22

CLUBBIE

A MINOR LEAGUE BASEBALL MEMOIR

GREG LARSON

University of Nebraska Press · LINCOLN

Parts of chapter 3 previously appeared in *Switchback* 11, no. 22
(Fall 2015).

Library of Congress Cataloging-in-Publication Data
Names: Larson, Greg, 1988– author.
Title: Clubbie: a minor league baseball memoir / Greg Larson.
Description: Lincoln: University of Nebraska Press, 2021.
Identifiers: LCCN 2020029688
ISBN 9781496224293 (hardback)
ISBN 9781496226334 (epub)
ISBN 9781496226341 (mobi)
ISBN 9781496226358 (pdf)
Subjects: LCSH: Larson, Greg, 1988– | Aberdeen IronBirds
(Baseball team) | Minor league baseball—United States. |
Baseball fans—United States—Biography.
Classification: LCC GV865.L324 A3 2021 | DDC
796.357/640973—dc23
LC record available at https://lccn.loc.gov/2020029688

Set in Arno Pro by Laura Buis.

For my dad, Ricky T.

Contents

CLUBBIE

PART 1

1

A Shooting Star

I wiped the rain from my brow as I entered the lobby of Ed Smith Stadium, the Baltimore Orioles' spring training home. My '97 Cadillac Deville had somehow survived. It was only seventy-five miles from my parents' retirement community to the stadium in Sarasota, but the check engine light flashed Oriole orange the whole way. "Nice," I thought. "The sonofabitch is still alive."

I stood in the lobby awkwardly as Florida thunder clapped outside. Jake Parker, the man I was here to meet, eventually grabbed me. He wore a black Nike Orioles shirt that hung loose on his muscle-bound torso. He was attentive—polite, even—despite being brusque. He walked with speed and expected me to keep up.

The downpour seemed to worsen, leaving players and coaches to wander the stadium, half-dressed and bored.

"You look just like your YouTube videos," Jake said as we walked.

"Oh? Which ones did you watch?"

"Stand-up routine. Said Winthrop University, I think."

"Oh, god."

"No, it was good. You were kinda funny."

We walked into his "office," which was an empty classroom with a cluttered desk against the wall. He told me everything I needed to know for my new job: how to do laundry as quickly as possible, how much food to put out for pregame meals, how to swing deals with the stadium beer supplier. Jake had worked his way from being

3

the IronBirds clubbie to his current position: equipment manager for the Orioles' Minor League teams. So he knew his shit.

He alluded to me buying groceries for team meals.

"That money comes out of my pocket?" I said.

He nodded.

"And I use their dues to pay for it?"

"Don't worry. If you do it right, you'll have plenty of cash left-over. What're you charging, six a day?"

"Seven, actually." During my phone interview, my new boss had mentioned something odd: that players would pay me dues for feeding them. He suggested I go with seven dollars per home game. It seemed as good as any other number, so I agreed.

"Hmm. That's a lot at your level—I think guys get like $1,200 a month there—but you should be good to go. You've basically included your tip in the dues, which is fine, but don't expect anything extra on top of it. Plus you're new, so the respect factor isn't there yet. In professional baseball, respect is earned not given." He eyed my chest. "You look like you might work out. A little bit."

I shrugged. I stayed in shape but I wasn't very muscular—about six foot, 185 pounds.

"You might wanna start lifting weights once you get to Aberdeen—helps to maintain order in the clubhouse. I used to be a teaching sub for a middle school. That's how you gotta treat these guys: just like middle schoolers, because that's what most of 'em are. Last week I wrestled one of the players because he said he could take me. Were we joking? Sure, of course. But was it a little serious too? Abso-fucking-lutely. These guys have to know you're not afraid of them. If they come up giving you an attitude, trying to get extra equipment they don't need or causing problems in the clubhouse, you cut a fuckin' muscle in 'em and let 'em know who's in charge." He flexed his bicep at me and nodded as if to say, "Capisce?"

He took me to the laundry room. I asked him how much he made when he worked for the IronBirds.

He looked past my shoulder like we were about to make a drug deal.

"I'm only telling you this because we're part of the same fraternity now, okay? My last two years in Aberdeen I made $19,000 a summer. Net."

"Holy shit."

"Don't get too excited. You won't make that much at first, but you'll still do well. You don't show it, though. You live like you're fucking poor. The second guys start seeing you're making hand over fist, that's when the tips go down and you lose the clubhouse."

"Shouldn't be a problem," I thought. I already had a flip phone. Nothing said poor like a flip phone.

He put on a pair of surgeon's rubber gloves and snapped them over his wrists. He grabbed a pile of dirty, orange and black athletic clothes and threw them into an industrial washer.

"You use gloves when you did laundry for Winthrop?"

I shook my head.

"Start using 'em. You don't know where some of these guys have been. Especially the coños."

"The what?"

"Coños," he said. "Dominicans. Try to split up their lockers, too. Just so they have to talk to the American guys. And don't give them any end lockers—they never tip."

As I tried to process what the hell I'd just heard, a player walked into the laundry room.

"Ah, perfect," Jake said. "Greg, this is Alex Schmarzoo."

"It's Schmarzo," the player said.

"Schmarzoo!" Jake said again, with kazoo-like inflection at the end.

I shook his hand. "Greg Larson," I said. He looked at me and smiled all the way up to his eyes. He had a huge puff of brown hair on his head, which flowed into a mullet hanging down the back, a style that hadn't been cool since—well, never.

"You have any nicknames?" Schmarzo said.

"I dunno. People sometimes call me G-lar."

"Eh. We'll just call you G."

"And is it Schmarzo or Schmarzoo?"

"It's Schmarzo. Jake, being the very serious clubbie that he is, decided to pin an extra 'o' on my nameplate—what was that, two weeks ago? Nobody told me, so I walked around with guys calling me Schmarzoo all day, wondering what the fuck was going on. Luckily I didn't pitch."

"No," Jake said seriously, "I would've never done that shit if you were slated to pitch."

Schmarzo thought for a moment. "Although, it might've been better. That way if I gave up five runs the Orioles would've said, 'Let's get rid of this Schmarzoo character,' and I could still stick around."

We laughed.

"You gotta keep these guys loose," Jake said to me. "That's why I was glad to see your stand-up video—as a clubbie, you can't be scared to pull some practical jokes. Especially on dirtbags like Schmarzoo. All seriousness, though? This is the best guy I've met in sixteen years working in professional baseball. He'll be your number one in Aberdeen."

"Aw, shucks," Schmarzo said.

"Okay, see that? He's acting bashful because he wants something."

"You're good," Schmarzo said. "No, yeah, I can't find my warm-up shirt. I'm pretty sure the guys took it to fuck with me, but they won't budge."

"What about the extra one I gave you last week?"

Schmarzo cringed.

"Here, Greg: this is perfect practice. You're the clubbie and Schmarzo's asking you for gear."

"Greg—G-baby—I need a shirt."

"You're wearing one," I said.

Jake nodded his approval. "Good."

"Well, I need a different one. My grandma died and—"

"I don't care."

"Damn," Jake said. "Maybe a bit much."

"No," Schmarzo said. "Guys pull that shit all the time. Don't let 'em play the dead grandma card."

"Okay," Jake said. "Not bad."

"But really, I just need something for the day. I'll give it right back. I won't even sweat in it."

Jake eyed him sideways for a moment. "Here," he said, and he led us both to a storage room full of gear. He grabbed a black shirt with the smiling cartoon Oriole on the breast.

"Is he really gonna return that shirt?" I said when Schmarzo left.

"Oh, absolutely. I wasn't lying when I said he's the best guy I've met in baseball. Come on, let's go meet some of your staff. If we can find 'em."

We walked past players moving lazily in the hallways. I guessed that meant it was still raining. "Let's take a quick detour," Jake said, guiding us into the locker room. I knew that Minor Leaguers and Major Leaguers all played spring training games at the same complex, and it seemed like there were a lot of common areas where they could intermingle, but the locker rooms were separate.

The Minor League locker room had a county jail vibe. The lockers were cage-like with metal intermeshed on the sides like thick chain-link fences. Hot shower mist made it humid like a Vietnam War jungle. Half-naked young men walked around talking and laughing loudly, booming with confidence—just a mass movement of skin and testosterone. Jake introduced me to a few players who'd be up in Aberdeen with me. He grabbed a canvas laundry cart as we walked out. When we passed the laundry room, he released the bin with expert precision and it wheeled its way right next to the washers.

"Trek will be the trainer in Aberdeen. He's good, as long as you keep him happy."

"Okay," I said. "How do I do that?"

"Lots of Diet Mountain Dew and Budweiser. Don't worry—I'll put you in touch with my beer guy in Aberdeen. He'll hook you up.

And Ripken pays for all the Gatorades and sodas for the coaches. Ellie Ripken, up in the front office—just give her the receipts and she'll reimburse you. She checks that shit, too, so don't try to sneak anything by her."

"Oh, no, I wouldn't—"

"But let's say you want some Red Bull? Just buy that shit on the same receipt and it's all yours. Oh, and before I forget: make the coaches plates after the game."

"Plates? Like from the meal?"

"Yeah. God forbid, if you run out of food, you wanna make sure the coaches eat before the players. But don't you dare run out of food. Nobody gives a shit if you wash a stain from their pants or clean their warm-up shorts. The only thing that matters in this job is food. That's where all your tips come from." He took a hard turn into the trainers' office. "Okay, I think Trek's in here."

Trek looked like he was in his midforties, with a widow's peak pointing down his forehead to a matching pointy nose. His ears were like butterfly wings flaring out.

"Trek, this is Greg, your new clubbie in Aberdeen."

"This the new kid?" He spit a brown glob into an empty Diet Mountain Dew bottle. Then he stood up from his desk to shake my hand.

"Tell him where you're from," Jake said to me.

"Elk River, Minnesota?"

"Oh, yeah?" Trek said. "I'm from Warren."

"Where's that?"

"Northwest. Closest cities are Grand Forks and Thief River Falls."

Jake nodded, satisfied. "Alright, I gotta move some laundry over. You got a few minutes, Trek?"

"Yeah, that's fine," he said, and Jake walked out. "So, I'm sure he told you, but I like two-liter bottles of Diet Mountain Dew for road trips and a few extras laying around for emergencies. Just keep a few cases at the bottom of your locker and I'll grab 'em from there."

I nodded.

"And he told you about beer? I like Bud Heavy. I don't know what anyone else drinks."

I nodded. Silence. I looked around for something to talk about.

"Things are a little slow around here. Doesn't look like anyone's doing much of anything." I forced a chuckle.

"Don't ever say that. It might *look* slow because we're waiting for this rain to pass, but we got work up to our fuckin' elbows in here. We got about a half dozen Major League guys we're trying to heal right now, so . . . yeah. Don't go saying it doesn't look busy, because it is."

Jake finally came back to grab me. "How'd that go?" he said as we walked out.

"Pretty good. Just a couple of Minnesota boys."

• • •

Baseball taught me how to love.

The game made sense to me, and spending time with it felt more like an obsessive relationship than a simple want. From the first moment I started to uncover the infinite mysteries of baseball—like why players chose to wear certain numbers, what the brown stuff in players' mouths was, and just what the hell a balk entailed—I was hooked.

I grew up in Minnesota, before my parents made Florida their permanent home. When I was a teenager, Fort Myers was a tropical paradise we only visited in winter. A place we'd go to see my Minnesota Twins do early spring training workouts. My dad used to drop me off at Hammond Stadium in the morning—before anyone else arrived—glove on my left hand, jersey on my back, and five-dollar bill in my pocket to buy a bratwurst for lunch. The only thing that could've made me happier on those February days was getting on the field with my heroes. "In a few years," I said to myself, "I'll be one of them."

I stood near the locker room entrance, already hot in the early Florida sun. I said hello to all of my favorite players as they walked sleepily into the stadium. "Good morning, Mr. Hunter! Hello, Mr. Mauer! Good morning, Mr. Morneau!" And they acknowledged me, every one of them. They sounded a bit surprised, though, because spring training games wouldn't start for another week and I was the only person at the stadium who wasn't paid to be there.

They took batting practice on the back fields. I watched from right-field foul territory with my cap turned backward so I could stick my freckled nose through the chain links. I was nearly close enough to smell their sunscreen and sweat. Over at the bullpen, I gripped my clawed fingers through the fence. More fans might show up after lunchtime, but for the moment it was just the pitcher, catcher, coach, and me. Quietly I strained to hear the conversation between coach and player on the mound. I could see myself in that same place: wearing the jersey of my favorite team, having a coach put his hand on my shoulder and whisper those same mystical secrets to me.

The day's workouts eventually ended and, long after the other fans had left, I said goodbye to the players as they exited the complex. They each said goodbye back to me.

A photographer from the Fort Myers *News-Press* took a picture of me staring through the fence one time. He asked where I was from so he could put my hometown underneath the photo. "Elk River, Minnesota," I said. "You look like you want to be out there with them," he said, pointing with his pen. He showed me the picture on his digital camera and I could see my mouth wide open, gaping in awe.

The cameraman must've heard me wrong. When I found the picture on the *News-Press* website, the caption said I was a young fan from Oak River, Minnesota, a place that doesn't exist.

Baseball taught me how to have my heart broken.

As a high schooler I struggled to establish myself as a star player in a state that's more known for hockey, lakes, and snow than it is for baseball. The main problem, I'd come to discover, was that Major League scouts didn't show up to high school baseball games to see the backup shortstop. "My god," they would've said, "that young man has his ass planted squarely on the dugout bench more perfectly than any baseball player I've ever seen!"

"But I love baseball," I would've told the scouts, "and I'll work harder than anyone if I get a chance." No such luck. I was relegated to watch the 8-13 Elk River Elks from the pine.

My .091 batting average my senior year was good enough to earn me a tryout with the Hamline University Pipers baseball team (granted, the lowly Saint Paul–based Division III team would've let your uncle try out if he was a tuition-paying student). After a week of embarrassing practices, I was cut.

When my parents made their move to Florida after that freshman year of college, I decided there was nothing keeping me in the "Land of 10,000 Lakes." I escaped the cold and went down to Winthrop in South Carolina.

I eventually got a scholarship with the baseball team, but not for the reasons I'd hoped. I became an equipment manager for the Winthrop Eagles. I looked after the baseballs and washed jockstraps. I was still a long way from hitting home runs.

But washing jockstraps was the extent of my job experience out of college, and I could do worse than working in professional baseball. So in the spring of 2012, I applied online to be a Minor League clubhouse attendant (or clubbie) for the Aberdeen IronBirds— single-A affiliate for the Baltimore Orioles—and I got the job. By chance, my parents' condo in Fort Myers (where I lived at the time) was just south of the Orioles' spring training complex. So on my drive up to Aberdeen, Maryland, my new boss suggested I stop at the complex and meet Jake for some tips.

What I didn't realize was that working for the IronBirds would change me and my perception of baseball forever.

• • •

Jake pulled me into a conference room where a half-dozen coaches shuffled papers and talked seriously.

"Muggsy, this is Greg. He'll be your clubbie up in Aberdeen."

Gary Allenson (who went by Muggsy, I guessed) shook my hand from his seat, assessed me with his light blue eyes, and tongued tobacco at the front of his mouth, which wiggled his brown mustache. He looked back at his sheet.

"Don't worry, slick," he said, spitting into his Dixie cup, "I don't bite."

Jake brought me into another training room to meet Alan Mills, the pitching coach. When I walked in, he was holding court for a handful of Major Leaguers.

To my dismay, Jake walked right into the middle of the circle to introduce me to Mills. I was thankful, in that moment, that I was working in the Orioles' organization and not the Twins'—if I'd recognized any of those guys, I would've been petrified by a forced suppression of my adoration.

"Millsy, this is Greg, your new clubbie up in Aberdeen."

I reached my hand out, but he didn't take it.

He was bigger than the pictures I'd seen online. I looked Mills up and found out he'd pitched in the Majors for more than ten years. I also read that he once punched out Darryl Strawberry in a famous brawl. Mills, the forty-five-year-old, took up a lot of space with his energy and movements.

He started talking to me in Spanish, his accent flawless.

Everyone laughed.

"¿Puedes hablar inglés?" I said quietly.

"What's up, meat? What're you looking for—you need autographs from these guys? Autograph time's not for twenty minutes. Come back then."

"I'm the clubbie in Aberdeen."

"Oh, shit. You're the clubbie? Man, I feel sorry for you. Thankless job. Good luck, meat, really. That shit ain't easy." He shook my hand. "Good to meet you—what'd you say?"

"Greg," I said.

"We'll get you loosened up in Aberdeen, meat."

"So that's Alan Mills," Jake said as we walked out.

I looked at him and he smiled.

"He'll take good care of you," he said, and I guessed that meant he would tip well. "So, you've got a long way to drive. You're not going all the way up there today are you?"

"No, no. I'm stopping to see my girlfriend in Georgia then going the rest of the way in a few days."

"Okay, good," he said as we walked. "You got a living situation up there yet? I used to share a little apartment with, like, four other guys, I think it was. Sounds like a lot, but when they hit the road I had the place to myself.

"Then one summer I lived in the clubhouse. Think about that one—you don't pay utilities: free water, free electricity, free AC, free internet. You don't have to buy food—you just eat the leftover spreads from the previous home stand. And you don't pay for fucking rent. I made bank that summer. I just put down a blanket on the clubhouse couch and I was good to go."

"Oh, yeah, the team is putting me up in an apartment. Town called White Marsh?"

He stopped walking. "For free?"

"Yeah."

He squinted at me, thinking. "Interesting." He started speed walking again, continuing on to the cafeteria, where a handful of players ate.

"You want some pizza?" He called out to the guy behind the food counter to put a few slices in Saran Wrap. "What do you want— bananas, apples?"

"Oh, no," I said, "I have some food in the car."

He turned and studied me gravely. "Listen, when someone offers you something in this game you smile, say thank you, and accept it."

He handed me the Saran-wrapped plate with a loose orange and banana.

"Thank you," I said.

"You're welcome. How much would you pay for a meal on the road: ten, twelve bucks? You just got lunch for free. That's money in your pocket. You seem like a polite young man, and that's good, but don't be so polite that you lose money."

He walked me to the lobby. Heavy rain bounced against the glass doors like a swarm of locusts. Jake asked the receptionist to give me a poncho. She reached under her desk and produced a slim packet. I clumsily tried to carry it all.

"Okay," Jake said. "You're all set?"

"I think so, yeah."

"You'll be fine. Just keep the guys well fed and everything will work out. Alright, I gotta get back to it. I'll let you know when your first shipment of game balls is on its way. Other than that, just text me if you need advice."

He slapped me on the back before speed walking away.

I stood in the lobby, staring at the storm. After a few moments, I slipped the plastic poncho over me and thanked the receptionist.

She smiled back. "Drive safe."

I ran into the churning, gray Florida afternoon and laughed—my chest swelling with the beating of my nervous heart—all the way to my car, which twinkled with droplets of rain beading on its golden body.

2

The Bottom Rung

Ripken Stadium's address was 873 Long Drive, Aberdeen, Maryland. The numbers represented owner Cal Ripken Jr.'s former jersey number, eight; the deceased Cal Sr.'s number, seven; and brother Billy's number, three. The Long Drive part—well, that was just one of those Minor League Baseball puns, representing the 431 long drives Cal Jr. hit in his twenty-one-year career with Baltimore.

The stadium was oddly secluded in the woods when I approached it in the Caddie, despite the map showing I-95 no more than a few hundred feet beyond the right-field foul pole. A brick façade with a green roof arched over the home-plate entrance to Ripken Stadium—solid, new, and sturdy.

My new boss, Jason, met me in the front office and introduced me to people whose names I forgot the moment I heard them. The office was cluttered with boxes of programs, foam fingers leaning on the corners of cubicles, and old bobbleheads and player figurines on people's desks.

He walked me through the stadium concourse. White letters spelled out "Welcome to Ripken Stadium" as we faced the field, where dirt cutouts made walkways in the grass between each dugout and home plate—as close to a red carpet as a guy might find on a baseball field. A video board rose up beyond the fence in right-center—above the green, padded wall—topped with a "Ripken Stadium" logo.

"Looks amazing," I said.

"The field looks like shit," Jason said. "It's all torn up from high school kids playing tournaments on it all summer."

Jason asked me about the apartment and I told him it was great. I'd slept on my air mattress the night before. I didn't have a television or any furniture other than my desk, so the living room sat empty. I also discovered an unsecured Wi-Fi network from an unsuspecting neighbor, so there'd be no need for me to get internet service, either.

That first night I ate a bag of Taco Bell chalupas at my desk before passing out from a long day of driving. I'd spent the past few days visiting my girlfriend, Nicole, in Georgia. She'd been living with her folks in her hometown of Augusta ever since her graduation the month before. She had an English degree, just like me. In fact, that's how we met in college: we had a poetry workshop together, and I asked her out with a poem. We dated long distance for a year while I lived with my parents in Florida and she finished her degree.

It was still summer, of course, but in the fall she'd be teaching English and coaching volleyball at a small private high school in the middle of a peach field in Johnston, South Carolina, just southwest of "Where the hell are we?" They'd pay her $24,000 a year with no benefits, which, with the 2012 economy still in the crapper, sounded like real adult money to me—the kind of salary that allowed someone to provide for themselves without leaning on their parents, something I only dreamed of.

Our plan was for her to stay at her parents' place until the Iron-Birds' season finished in September, then I'd go down south and we'd move in together. We'd spent part of my visit looking for houses to rent, but nothing caught our eye in our very low price range ($800 a month was the limit). She promised to keep looking over the summer; both of us excited to finally start our lives together with no more long distance.

I thought of Nicole my first night in the new apartment, in those lonely hours between life and sleep. Only the night before she'd been lying naked next to me in her childhood bedroom in Georgia; now her absence felt like a sinking misstep over a cliff. I took familiar comfort underneath my Minnesota Twins blanket, which my mom had made me a few years before. I flipped it so the team logos faced my body and only showed red to the world. My boss, Jason, said a few players might live with me—I didn't want guys in the Orioles' organization to see my Twins blanket.

Jason and I continued walking up the Ripken Stadium concourse, along the first base line.

"Do you know when the players will be moving in with me?"

"As far as I know," he said, "there won't be anyone else in your apartment. But if you want a roommate for company, go ahead and ask a couple guys on the team to live with you. There'll probably be someone who can't find a host family."

"I might just stay there by myself, if it's all the same to you."

"Yeah, you can do that if you want—it's your place." Jason's eyes got big. "Or, you could consider the ethics of having guys stay with you and asking them to pay for it."

We walked on level with the field now, passing the batting cages placed side-by-side like a double-barreled shotgun. The yellow right-field foul pole stood near the clubhouse entrance. On we walked, into the clubhouse, which looked like a long, one-story, brick rambler. The words "Home Clubhouse" were written in plastic, white letters above the door.

The manager's office was immediately to the left inside the entrance, with its own couch, desk, fridge, and bathroom. Next door was the coaches' office, with a tile floor, a few wooden lockers, and a bathroom with two shower stalls. A right turn at the clubhouse entrance brought us into the locker room area, where tan wooden lockers lined the walls. The harsh fluorescent lights reminded me of an office building. On one wall was the IronBirds' logo painted on white concrete.

The logo was a cartoon airplane with eyes, a smiling mouth, and the number eight on the fin in honor of Cal Jr. The IronBirds—in their ten-season history to that point—had one winning season, one .500 season, and eight losing seasons, failing to live up to the standard of greatness set by their owner. Cal Jr. held one of baseball's most hallowed records: 2,632 consecutive games played. It was Lou Gehrig's record before it was his, and the feat had granted Cal the nickname Iron Man. The IronBirds were named in honor of him and his tie to the Orioles (who were nicknamed "the Birds"), as well as a nod to the Aberdeen Proving Ground just east of Ripken Stadium, where the fighter jets were nicknamed ironbirds.

"We'll get some couches and a fridge in here for you," Jason said.

There was a main bathroom with showers like a high school locker room. And to its left, near the back entrance, was the laundry room, with two huge industrial washers and dryers. On the other end of the locker room, a hallway led through the training room. White, black, and putrid-green, square tiles lined the ice bath area. Up above the treatment tables another logo adorned the wall: "Orioles" written in cursive with a realistic black-and-orange oriole bird perched on the "i" and a baseball diamond in the background. Beyond the training tables sat Trek's tiny office. If he faced his office door from his desk and looked right, he'd peer through a square cutout in the wall to the weight room, which housed a few racks of rusty dumbbells and some old multiuse gym machines that looked like they'd been shipped directly from the USSR courtesy of Ivan Drago.

"These are Cal's personal weightlifting machines," Jason said. "Hopefully we'll get these outta here and the O's will get us some new equipment, but I'm not holding my breath."

On the left side of the weight room were white, metal double doors with a little placard on the wall that said "Equipment Closet."

"Don't mind the boxes," he said when we entered. "Those are the jerseys and stuff we'll get hung up tomorrow. And we got new pants this season, so we'll have to figure out what to do with all these old ones." He opened a box and baseball pants popped out the top like fake snakes springing from a can of nuts. "Give 'em to some high school or something, I don't know."

The tiny room was lined on all sides with solid wood shelves extending several feet from the walls, each one holding a mess of equipment. Batting helmets were strewn about on one sad shelf, like decapitated heads of former players. Some random bats gathered here and there, most of them broken. Jason found an old box of sunflower seeds that expired the year before.

He peered into the box. "Looks like you're good on seeds for a bit," he said.

Old mustard and ketchup bottles sat on a shelf, along with a tub of Utz Pub Mix, half-empty like someone had their arm in elbow deep and thought, "You know what? Fuck this," then walked away from this place and never returned. Behind the door was a big brick number eight, about as tall as my chest and a few bricks thick.

"What's this?" I said.

"Yeah, that was a gift to Cal and we can't figure out where to put it. They wanted to stand it on the plaza entrance, but I said, 'You know what'll happen if we do that? Some kid is gonna climb up onto that thing, knock it over, and kill someone.'"

I envisioned the bloody splat of a child crushed by this symbol of Cal's legacy.

"It's pretty fucking heavy too," he said, "so we have it down here because where else would it go? Actually, I'd be surprised if anyone knows this thing exists. This is a good place to work, and you made the right decision, but you'll find that a lot of shit here falls to the bottom rung of the ladder. Guess who that is?"

I pointed my thumb to my chest.

"Yeah," he said. "And me."

"What is your job, exactly?"

"I'm the video production manager and I oversee game entertainment. Basically, if you see any of the between-inning stuff on the field or on the video board during the game, I'm in charge of it."

"So then—not to sound weird—but why are you my boss?"

"It doesn't make much sense, does it? I kind of like overseeing the clubbie, but that's just another one of those things that fell to me."

I looked up to a top shelf where old Crock-Pots and hot plates looked like they'd been piled together, unwashed. "Jesus," I thought, "how fancy did Jake and other clubbies get when they made meals for the team? I wasn't planning on making a whole goddamn turkey dinner—maybe some deli meat and PB&Js."

"Well," Jason said, "what do you think? This'll be your home for the summer."

"Looks pretty good," I said, suddenly homesick for nowhere in particular.

He nodded, staring off at something on the other side of the room. He stepped over piles of loose pants and started rifling through some small boxes on a shelf.

"You look like you have a decent-sized head," Jason said. "You think you wear a large? I guess it really doesn't matter—this is all that's left. Here."

He pulled out a blue stretch-fit cap with orange trim on the bill and an orange, cursive capital "A" for Aberdeen on the crown. He slapped it onto my head. The bill sagged halfway over my eyes and I could see only his feet.

"There," he said. "Now you look like a clubbie."

3

Lottery Ticket Odds

stepped onto the scale at my new apartment's community weight room: 172 pounds, already 13 pounds lighter than when I came to Maryland. My stomach knotted thinking about the soon-to-arrive players. I already felt anxious meeting new people; the last thing I wanted was to add physical intimidation on top of it. Jake had suggested I stay strong, so I got a workout in before a long day of preparation.

The players drove or flew up from the Ed Smith Stadium complex in Sarasota for a week of workouts in Aberdeen before the season started on June 18. Jake had given me a suggested locker order based on relationships between players, positions, who tipped the best, and, despite my inner protests, ethnicities. But as the reporting day approached, Trek kept sending me new players who signed from the draft. I wrote everyone's last names on athletic tape and stuck them on the little name slots above their lockers (including "Schmarzoo" for Alex Schmarzo).

I sat on the couch in the middle of the locker room, waiting for the players to arrive in the early afternoon like a kid waiting for his first-ever date. When I heard the laughing groups approaching the back door near the laundry room, I sprung up and escaped to the equipment closet, convincing myself that something there needed my immediate attention. "Yep, the pants are still in order.

Got enough hats? Check. Are all of the new bats still in their boxes? Okay, good, they are."

But eventually the players sniffed me out and they started pouring in to get geared up. The guys were all very polite and cordial, most of them eager to get their first taste of professional baseball out of the draft. They didn't strike me as bullying muscle-bros—they were just a bunch of guys who happened to be athletic.

"What size pants do you wear?" I said.

Some guys looked at me like, "I thought you were supposed to know that."

But I could recognize the veterans pretty quickly: they knew the answer to every question.

"What size pants do you wear?"

"Thirty-six long."

"Cap?"

"Seven and a quarter."

"You a pitcher?"

"No."

"What kind of bat do you use?"

"Got any one-thirteens?"

I'd check. "Looks like it, yeah."

"Let me get a thirty-four-inch."

The new draftee guys seemed more keen to grab a bat and chop a few fake swings with it, or stand with it in batting position and look at their reflection in the equipment closet refrigerator's window. They'd ask to see three or four different models and sizes.

Then I'd say, "What size cap do you wear?"

They'd say, "Ah, what do you have?"

"Anywhere from seven to eight."

"Let me try an eight."

A size eight would've made a nice lid for a watermelon. They'd wiggle their head and feel the cap swinging around, then we'd narrow it down until we got the right size.

When Schmarzo walked in it felt like seeing an old friend. He'd grown a Fu Manchu since I saw him in Sarasota, which, along with his thick brown mullet, made him look like a player from the late '80s.

"G-baby," he said, giving me a one-armed bro-hug. "What's good with the Crapperdeen IronTurds?"

"Nothing much. Just gear day."

"Anyone trying to snag extras off of you?"

"Not yet, no."

"They will," he said. "Just give it time. They'll get comfortable and start trying to scam shit from you. All these new guys are scared outta their wits right now—I know I was when I first got here."

"Last year?"

"I wish. This is my third season in Aberdeen—not good, G, not good at all. I'm like the resident senior citizen of fucking short-season baseball."

I didn't know what to say. "What was the team like last year?"

"We sucked," he said, "but we had a good group in here."

"How'd you do?"

"I pitched better than my ERA," he said.

Someone had taped a Schmarzo baseball card from 2011 on the side of the laundry room dryers. In the picture, Schmarzo was looking out of frame, his brown glove in front of his face—index finger peeking out—with his right hand reaching into the mitt. He looked, in the picture, like he'd been clean shaven precisely two days before, save for thick sideburns that reached down to the bottom of his ear lobes. I could tell he was trying to make his eyes thin and intense, but instead he just looked sleepy. There was nothing intimidating about Schmarzo, not even when he hammed it up for the photographer. On the back it said:

Height: 6'3"	Weight: 200
Bats: Right	Throws: Right

Born: 2/28/89 Cincinnati OH
Acquired: 48th round selection, 2010 draft

The card only had his stats from 2010. I had to look up his pro-file on MiLB.com to see his 2011 numbers: 0-2 with a 6.69 ERA in 36.1 innings with no saves and one spot start. I sure hoped he'd pitched better than that ERA.

• • •

A lot of that first day was focused on nonbaseball nuts and bolts. Trek handed out housing information. The list had names, numbers, addresses, and short descriptions of host families. Host families were local families who offered to take in ballplayers for the season. Appar-ently, some of them asked for token rent, something like ten bucks a day, but a lot of them seemed to do it out of the kindness of their hearts and love for the team. I didn't see my apartment listed on Trek's sheets.

I asked Schmarzo if he had a spot.

"Thanks, but me, Slime, and a couple other guys got an apart-ment together. I bet some of the new guys could use a spot—there's not shit for host families this year."

One of the newly signed players overheard our conversation and asked if he could stay with me. His name was Sam Kimmel, an eighteenth-round draft pick out of Stetson University in DeLand, Florida. He had black eyebrows, black stubble on his shaved head, and brown eyes, seemingly squinting at all times. He was my height, almost six feet tall, but still stout, like the catcher he was. He spoke in a monotone, and his absent-minded smile made you wonder if he was constantly high.

He said the host families were all taken.

I said it was no problem—he could definitely crash in my apartment.

Kimmel asked me how much he'd owe for rent.

I had to decide in that moment: *Do I charge this guy rent like my boss, Jason, suggested, or do I let it slide, even if I could already see Jake in Sarasota, shaking his head saying, "That's money in your pocket."*

"You take care of utilities," I said, "but don't worry about rent."

"No, really," Kimmel said, "what will I owe you?"

"Just utilities. I promise."

I didn't make the choice because of some inherent kindness in my heart—I simply didn't have the guts to pull off the scam. I took the easy (and inadvertently polite) way out, and it was already costing me money.

The coaches were the last ones to get gear that day. Muggsy came marching into the equipment closet, halfway through his sentence before he was in the door.

"Get me some thirty-eights, slick."

I flipped through the piles of pants. My stomach hit the floor—I was out of pants with a thirty-eight-inch waist. I continued shuffling, praying that I had accidentally misplaced a pair in the thirty-six or forty pile. He stood there watching me, making this closed-mouth clicking noise in the back of his sinuses, like he was trying to knock loose a stuck piece of phlegm.

I said, almost to myself, "It looks like—I don't think we have any more thirty-eights."

"You don't have what?" he said.

"Any size thirty-eight pants."

He stared me down for seconds. "Here's a tip: you always make sure the manager has a pair of pants his size. Give me whatever the next size down is."

He put on a pair of thirty-sixes with the elastic at the bottom so tight they stopped about three inches short of his shoe tops.

"How does that look?" he said.

"Not the best."

"I look like a goddamn JV coach."

I got him fitted with the team caps: the blue BP cap (the same kind I wore), the black home cap with the cartoon airplane logo in front of a gray cursive "A," and the gray road cap with the same IronBirds' logo and a black bill (Muggsy's had an unusually high crown, which made him look like a goddamn train conductor).

I quickly learned how to cut the elastic band at the bottom of his pants without ruining them, and how to unobtrusively remove the hard fabric layer inside the front of a baseball cap (the key was to make the first gentle cut from the inside without piercing through the outer cloth. From there I just worked my way along the edges and plucked the thick, black, fish-bone-like threads that popped out along the way).

I thought my trouble was over until Alan Mills came in.

"Hello, Mr. Mills," I said.

"Don't call me that," he said. "That's my father's name."

"Oh, sorry."

"Don't worry about it, meat. So, what? You gotta get me a jersey or something? Let's go."

He'd requested to have number seventy-five, but our numbers only went up to sixty-five.

"I'm sorry," I said.

"Doesn't matter. I'm not a player—I don't wear a jersey. I grew up in Florida heat, so I'd just cover it up with a jacket anyway."

"What size cap do you wear?" I said. I glanced up at his shiny, bald head. "Seven and three-eighths?"

"Shit, my head ain't that big, meat. Get me seven and a quarter."

He swiped the cap from my hand without trying it on and walked out.

I sighed, but he stopped before getting all the way out of the equipment closet.

"Oh, and another thing," he said. "My pitchers need baseballs. How many can I get every week?"

"Well, I don't know," I said. "I'll have to ask."

"You're the clubbie, aren't you? Don't you have the balls to give me what I need? Pitchers at this level, they need new baseballs."

"I know in the Majors guys need new balls every at bat, but here—"

"Well, this isn't the Majors," he said, slowing down his speech so I could understand. "I. Just. Need. Baseballs."

I put my hands up and shrugged. He let the silence linger, longer than most people would—longer than what any social situation ever called for. He stared at me, too, trying to figure me out.

He finally broke the silence, still speaking slowly. "How old are you?"

"I'm twenty-three."

"See, you're twenty-three now. I've been in professional baseball for as many years as you've been alive. We need baseballs, that's all there is to it. This is baseball—you'll learn."

• • •

In the quiet afternoon hours prior to the first official team meeting, I wanted to prove to everyone that I was willing to lay down the law. Jake said to cut a muscle into anyone who tried me, so that's what I did. One player came into my closet asking for bats. This was my chance. I speed walked out to his locker and made a scene.

"You already have bats," I said. "No shot."

He looked at me like I was dumb.

I sat in the equipment closet after that, proud for holding a steady fist over the clubhouse. Schmarzo knocked on the door and walked in.

"Hey, man. How's it going?" he said, scratching his Fu Manchu. "You know, it's okay to give these guys bats. You probably don't need to be so strict about giving those out."

"Oh, yeah, I just didn't want—"

"No, I get it. You don't want these guys taking advantage of you, and I don't blame you. But yeah, you can give them bats."

I nodded.

"By the way, you're doing a hell of a job today. This shit can be stressful, and I've seen clubbies with a lot more experience handle it worse than you."

We walked out together for the team meeting. I sat alongside the coaches, which wasn't natural for me—I felt more like a player than a coach. The players all lined up against one side of the locker room, facing us. The experienced guys listened absently, maybe twirling a bat in their hands or bending the leather of their mitt.

The new guys listened intently, peeking around someone's head so they could make eye contact with the coaches as they spoke.

Muggsy talked about team rules: everything from clothing policies (no items with logos from other teams) to tobacco use (tobacco was not allowed in the clubhouse, he said, so keep your cans in your locker cubby just in case MLB's dip police, as he called them, came sniffing around).

"And the Orioles have a mustache-only facial hair policy," he said, looking down at the player handbook. "Mustache to the corner of the lips, and sideburns to the bottom of the earlobe."

I made eye contact with Schmarzo then glanced at his full, brown Fu Manchu. He had to bury his head smiling.

Muggsy turned to me. "You got something you wanna say?"

I panicked at first, thinking he was reprimanding me for laughing. Then I realized he wanted me to lay down the laws for the clubhouse.

I jumped up and spoke from prepared notes like I was giving a class speech.

"As some of you may know, my name is Greg Larson, the new clubbie. I'm twenty-three years old, from Elk River, Minnes—"

"You got a nickname?" Muggsy said. "You don't wanna go around hearing 'Greg' all season."

"Uh, yeah, call me G or anything like that." I told them about dues, gear policies, and even proper chewing gum protocol ("don't leave gum in your game pants—it'll make a mess in the dryer")—the least of their worries on a day that was for many of them their first in professional baseball. "I'm excited for the season," I concluded.

Muggsy gave me a look that said, "You're the only one in that boat, slick."

After the meeting, I sat in the coaches' office before workouts on the field. The coaches' office set me on edge, despite the fact that I had my own locker in there. I felt like I was one wrong look from being reprimanded. Muggsy and Mills sat talking in front of

Mills's locker, where a Darth Vader action figure stood on the top shelf, red lightsaber in hand.

"Hey, meat," Mills said to me. "Come here. I wanna show you something." He was inspecting a baseball in his hands. "What'd you hear about those baseballs?"

"I still have to ask," I said.

"I've been in professional baseball eighteen seasons," Muggsy said. "Mills was in the Majors for twelve. I don't know how many games that is, but it's a lot, and we needed baseballs to play in every one of 'em."

"Well, yeah," I said. "Of course we'll have game balls."

"See," Mills said, "look at this ball here." He tossed it to me. I could feel them analyzing me—trying to gauge how I handled the baseball. I remembered a scene from *The Rookie* that I'd watched with my dad. Dennis Quaid, acting as real-life pitcher Jim Morris, stood on the mound with his glove under his armpit when a scout tossed him a baseball. Quaid caught the ball with both hands like a child cupping a firefly. He then held the ball with his full palm and threw it into his mitt. "Look at that," my dad said, "he doesn't even hold the ball like ballplayer." I didn't know why exactly, but my dad was right—you can intuit when someone's not a player, the same way you can tell which jersey numbers are good and which ones aren't.

I caught the ball in my right hand and tried to hold it as though it was meant for me—born from my hand, like a pearl embedded in the soft tissue of a clam.

"See that scuff there?" Mills said. I twisted it to find a patch of road rash with bits of leather flying away. "That scuff makes the ball move off path. See, a pitcher knows what the ball is gonna do if it's a clean ball, but a scuff will fuck up its path. I don't know if you've ever played baseball before, but if you're throwing with a scuffed ball it's gonna tail from you. If pitchers practice with a ball like that for long enough they'll expect everything to move like that. Then what happens? They get in a game, they're using new balls, and it doesn't tail the same way they're used to. Then they walk the batter and we lose the game. Do you know why?"

I shook my head.

"Because the damn clubbie didn't give them any baseballs."

Mills eventually asked me for the information to contact Rawlings, the company that made the baseballs, so he could order some himself. I asked Jake for the number, but when I told him why, he sent back: "Just make Mills happy—it's not worth it."

The team went out to the field for practice. Alone now in the clubhouse, I picked up one of the manuals in the locker room that said "Baltimore Orioles Player Development: Minor League Player Information & Guidelines." What I found inside shocked me.

It wasn't the dress code, facial hair policy, or any of those other inane, seemingly antiquated guidelines that surprised me—it was the salary scale. Look, I didn't think Minor Leaguers made Alex Rodriguez money ($30 million a year), but I had no understanding of the astronomical difference between Major League and Minor League salaries. The chart looked like this:

Salary Scale

GCL
  1st year: $1,100 per month
  2nd year: $1,150 per month
  3rd year: $1,200 per month

Aberdeen
  1st year: $1,100/$1,200 per month
  2nd year: $1,250 per month
  3rd year: $1,300 per month

Delmarva/Frederick
  1st year: $1,400 per month
  2nd year: $1,500 per month
  3rd year: $1,600 per month

Bowie
> 1st year: $1,800 per month
> 2nd year: $1,900 per month
> 3rd year: $2,100 per month

Norfolk
> 1st year: $2,500 per month
> 2nd year: $2,800 per month
> 3rd year: $3,200 per month

(The Orioles even made a careful effort to insert dollar signs and commas on each number, as if to say, "This is *four* figures we're talking here.")

I hadn't quite memorized the Orioles' organizational ladder yet, but it was easy enough to figure that GCL meant Gulf Coast League (all the guys who were left behind in the Sarasota complex for "extended spring training" played in the GCL), Aberdeen was short-season single-A, Delmarva was low-A, Frederick was high-A, Bowie was double-A, and Norfolk was triple-A.

So, what, this meant the guys at Ripken Stadium were making fourteen, maybe fifteen thousand dollars a year? Yeah, at the time I would've been overjoyed to make that much money, but I wasn't a professional athlete. I thought about what Jake had told me: that he'd made nineteen grand one summer working in the clubhouse. The dude washing jockstraps made more in one summer than the players made in *one year*? That sure as hell didn't make sense to me. I asked Schmarzo about it when the players came in.

He laughed as he put his glove in his top cubby. "I wish it was that good," he said. "We only get paid during the season."

"Holy shit," I said. "So you're making what, if you don't mind me asking?"

"Less than four grand. Way less."

"A year?"

"With the Orioles, yeah. I teach some clinics in the off-season, but that won't exactly put my kids through college. Oh, by the way, before I forget, what do we owe for dues during workouts?"

"Oh, yeah. Fourteen—it's just two bucks a day for laundry since I'm not putting out a spread."

One player nearby piped up. "Then what're dues during the season?" he said.

"Seven a day," I said.

"Seven?" He looked at his neighbor in disbelief.

Schmarzo pulled a twenty out of his wallet. "Keep it," he said.

• • •

In November 2006, during Alex Schmarzo's senior year at California's Palo Alto High, the six-foot-three-inch, 180-pound right-hander signed a letter of intent to pitch on scholarship at Saint Mary's College of California, only an hour drive north across the San Francisco Bay from his hometown. In early 2007, at an alumni game for his high school, Alex reared back to throw a 3-2 fastball and heard a pop in his right arm. Two of his fingers went numb. He didn't know it at the time, but he had micro tears in the ulnar collateral ligament in his elbow, an injury that usually requires Tommy John surgery.

After a week with no improvement in his arm, Alex called the head baseball coach at St. Mary's College. Alex told him about the injury, letting the coach know that if he didn't want to waste a scholarship on damaged goods, he didn't have to. However, the coach stuck with Alex and gave him the scholarship he was promised.

Three seasons passed at St. Mary's. By June of 2010, Alex had built a 5.34 career ERA with a 2-6 record. In that junior season, though, he had an improved 4.50 ERA in sixteen innings out of the bullpen. He worked as a closer most of his college career, and his scouting report read: "Not a slam dunk to be picked as a junior, but with an 88–91 mph fastball, and changeup that is average at times, he has a chance to develop in pro ball. Has some deception in the delivery but struggles to repeat it, and he'll have to develop a better breaking ball."

The Baltimore Orioles had been in contact with Alex leading up to the 2010 draft, saying they'd pick him anywhere from the seventh round to the twentieth round, along with a $100,000 signing bonus and a promise to pay for his last year of college (since he would give up his St. Mary's scholarship to play in the Orioles organization). But bad luck struck again: one day before the draft, Alex broke the pinky on his throwing hand playing pickup basketball. Once again, he was open and honest with the people taking a chance on him.

He told the Orioles and other interested teams about the broken pinky. The Orioles rewarded his honesty by dropping the expected offer to a $75,000 signing bonus with his last year of school still paid for. As the first day of the draft went by, nobody chose Alex. The number lowered: $50,000 and school; $40,000 with no school; then $20,000 and no school. At that point, Alex told the Orioles that he'd just go back to St. Mary's and finish his senior year if that was their best offer. The number jumped up a few thousand and the Orioles selected Alex on the third and final day of the draft with the 1,438th pick. (He still went back to finish his degree in the off-season.)

At spring training that year, a time when forty-eighth rounders were put together with top prospects, Orioles first round draft pick Manny Machado showed Alex a tattoo on his inner bicep. The design was a stylized M3M: signifying Machado's initials split with a "3" and representing his place as the third overall choice in the 2010 draft.

"I thought about getting 'A1438s' tattooed on my bicep," Alex told Machado, "but it just didn't have the same ring to it."

• • •

Schmarzo, now 200 pounds, sat in front of his locker in the IronBirds' clubhouse, where everyone was taking a quick break before going back into the sun (we were just a few days into preseason workouts). He ran his hand through his thick brown hair. Spit shot out of his mouth as he stared a hole through the carpet, eyes pulsing ever so slightly.

"What's going on?" I said.

He clicked his head to the right. "I'm leaving," he said. "Just look at all these guys." He gestured around the packed clubhouse full of players enjoying themselves, despite the fact that some of them would inevitably get released in a matter of days. We had more than forty players in there—so many that I had to bring in portable lockers and double up a few guys.

Schmarzo had already cried wolf about quitting baseball at least twice since he drove up from Sarasota. Yet here he was.

"I'm too fucking old to be here, man. What am I even doing?"

I shook my head and decided against making a joke about his 6.69 ERA for the IronBirds last year.

"They'd be doing me a favor if they cut me, really. But what the fuck am I gonna do? Maybe three guys in this clubhouse have college degrees, and I'm one of 'em. And even I'm fucked. Some of these guys—Jimenez, Rivera, Nivar—they never got out of elementary school. These kids drafted out of high school, you think they know how to take care of themselves? Hell no. They've had people like you to feed them, do their laundry, and clean up after them their whole lives. Straight up, I have no idea what I'd be doing if I wasn't playing baseball. It's our identity, man."

It was the first time in my postgraduate life that I felt a sense of superiority for having my degree.

Petersime—a tall, blond, lanky pitcher—reached past me to grab something from his locker.

"Slime," Schmarzo said, "what would you be doing if you weren't playing baseball?"

He looked at Schmarzo like the premise of the question was so unlikely that it couldn't be answered. Schmarzo might as well have asked *What would you do if you were born on Mars instead of Earth?* "I have no idea," Slime said, and he walked away.

"See what I mean?" Schmarzo said. "This life fucks with you, man. I always say it's like scratching lottery tickets: when you have enough guys together playing the lottery—buying scratch-offs—of course one or two of them is gonna win big. It's inevitable. But they win and you're just left sitting there scratching away. You throw your money and time away one dollar and one day at a time. But those guys won, right? Maybe I can too. So we keep coming back for more until we realize we're broke and out of time." He leaned forward, elbows on his knees, and got to work staring another hole through the floor. "That's what it's like to play single-A baseball."

Later on, I told Nicole about my conversation with Schmarzo.

"It's validation," she said on the phone. "It's like seeing what would've happened if your dreams of being drafted had come true."

Nicole and Schmarzo were both right—I knew that. But still, I couldn't help wishing to be in his position, even if I'd only have lottery ticket odds.

• • •

Jake had told me to keep things light and loose with practical jokes, so I decided to write a fake fan letter to Schmarzo. I pulled his 2011 card off the dryer. So far, in the piles of mail I brought from the front office to the clubhouse, I'd only seen fan mail for the coaches: letters with self-addressed, stamped envelopes inside and baseball cards of glory days long past.

(On the first day of workouts, I'd asked Schmarzo to sign his card. "Absolutely not," he'd said, laughing. "That thing wouldn't be worth the cardboard it's printed on." I'd had no intention to sell it, but I suspected he'd known as much.)

I wrote a note in looping girl's handwriting:

Dear Alex,

I'm a thirteen-year-old girl and I found your card in a box of tampons. Your icy stare and Zen-like focus penetrated me like only three men have before. Could you please sign your card?

Love,
Susie

I took a solid ten minutes coming up with that note, hoping desperately that it would make him and the other guys laugh. I wrote his name with hearts and stars on the envelope and put it in his locker when no one was looking.

Eventually, after waiting in giddy anticipation, the pitchers came in from pitchers' fielding practice, sweaty and huffing.

"Schmarzo," I said, "you have fan mail in your locker."

His face lifted for only a moment before he forced it back down. "No I don't."

"Okay," I said, shrugging. I walked away to the trainer's room to fold towels just beyond its open door, out of sight but within earshot of the locker room.

"Someone's messing with me," Schmarzo said to the guys. "Look, no return address. There's a clue."

He read it out loud and they laughed at all the right parts. I smiled as I folded towels.

"Hey, G!" Schmarzo called out.

"Yeah?"

"Did Slime do this?"

I walked out to the locker room. "I don't know what you're talking about. It looks like it's from a fan."

He smirked and flicked the letter into his locker, pretending that he didn't care. But I could see the look on his face when I said "you have fan mail," and there was no faking the pure childlike joy. His smiles at other times seemed forced, wrinkled, like he was trying to convince everyone else that things were dandy, and in doing so he might believe it too. But there was no faking the bright, expectant dreamer that flashed on his face in that moment, happy at the reminder: "Oh yeah," his face had said, "that's why we do this." Because he couldn't help himself. He couldn't help but dream, just for a moment, even if he might walk away the next.

I worried that Schmarzo might throw the card away, so, in a quiet moment later on, I plucked it out of his locker and taped it against the side of the dryer, back where it belonged.

4

Shadowboxing

Orioles pitcher Armando Benitez came set on the mound. It was May 19, 1998, and the Orioles were battling the Yankees in the Bronx. Benitez had just given up a towering three-run home run to Bernie Williams to put the Yankees up 7–5 in the bottom of the eighth.

Benitez delivered and plunked Yankees star Tino Martinez in the back with a fastball (his fastball had been recorded at one hundred miles per hour on at least one occasion). The pitch hit Martinez square between the number two and four, and he arched his back and neck like someone just dropped an ice cube down his jersey. The home plate umpire stood up and emphatically threw Benitez from the game, much to the pleasure of the packed Yankee Stadium.

Martinez had been plagued with back issues that season, so his Yankee teammates were especially eager to protect their injured star. The benches cleared in what looked like nothing more than a show, a play that any Major League team has acted out many times before. The script usually goes like this:

The benches clear quickly as players run to the mound to defend their respective teammates. The bullpen pitchers run in through the outfield. A few choice words are shared—*cocksucker, pussy, coward* among them. Ultimately, most of these "altercations" end without a single punch being thrown.

But on that night, a balmy eighty-four-degree mid-May evening, the Yankees and Orioles did not act according to the script.

As the benches cleared, the pitcher, Benitez, raised his hands as if to say, "Whatchu gonna do about it?" to the Yankees, who spilled onto the field in front of 31,311 screaming fans. A staggering number of superstars stood on the field at that moment: a twenty-four-year-old Derek Jeter flashed a smile as he held back Yankees star outfielder Darryl Strawberry from going after Benitez; future Hall of Famer Cal Ripken Jr., who was playing in his 2,522nd consecutive game, stood with an umpire, apart from the scuffling teams, like a star pupil commiserating with a teacher; future Hall of Fame manager Joe Torre tried to calm down his Yankees; veteran superstar and Orioles first baseman Rafael Palmeiro tried to maintain peace in the infield as well; future Hall of Famer Roberto Alomar jogged from second base position toward the crowd at the pitcher's mound, but he maintained his distance.

Things looked relatively benign.

Then the dam broke.

One of the Yankees got loose and went after Benitez, who started throwing counter punches like wild fastballs at anyone within striking distance. In the chaos, the mob shuffled toward the Yankee dugout until they were abutting the concrete dugout steps. Their common sense kicked in: they seemed to realize that a slip of their spikes could result in a career-ending cracked skull or worse. So the mob made every attempt to stay on the field.

The combined effort to keep the scuffle out of the dugout looked like it had squelched the fire. Orioles and Yankees continued to hold onto each other as the umpires regained control and doled out ejections.

But Tino Martinez remained hot—Benitez didn't get his proper comeuppance for the cheap shot on Tino's injured back. The crowd jeered as Tino tried to break free to attack Benitez like a dog at the end of his leash. Orioles relief pitcher Alan Mills shouted into Tino's face. As Tino and Mills jawed, Darryl Strawberry, who looked like he was waiting for an opportunity to strike, came around the side of the huddle and took a cheap shot at Benitez, which knocked Armando back into the dugout. The crowd roared its approval.

Alan Mills, who had extensive martial arts training, descended upon Darryl Strawberry. One punch knocked Strawberry to the concrete floor of the dugout. Mills reared back for another.

Millsy stood before me, his left hand gripping Darryl Strawberry fourteen years before, his right hand cocked back, ready to lay another blow to the imaginary man on the floor. He paused as he told me the story in the coaches' office at Ripken Stadium, named after his teammate on that May night in New York. Mills's eyes bulged wide open, frighteningly white, as he remembered.

"I'm standing over him," Mills said, "and I wake up." He dropped his fist and released the windbreaker on the ghost of Darryl Strawberry.

"What do you mean you wake up?"

"I mean I looked down and saw this dude, and I realized if I took another swing I'd really hurt him." He thought for a moment as he sat down.

I'd only asked him if his Wikipedia page was right—if he'd really punched Darryl Strawberry.

"Changed my life," he said. "I used to be a bad dude, you know? But after that, I never threw my weight around again. At least I tried not to." He laughed. "I realized I could kill somebody."

• • •

Guys dealt with the tension in different ways. The purpose of that workout week was to make difficult choices: who to move up, who to release, and who to keep pat. The way I understood it, the same thing was happening at all of the Orioles affiliates.

Some of the players stuck to themselves in the clubhouse, staring intently as they taped the handle of their bat, silent except for that muffled cloth rip of white athletic tape. Others played poker and laughed with each other.

Schmarzo was one of the poker guys. Except sometimes, instead of laughing like his teammates, he'd yield a quick "fuck!" when a hand didn't go his way. He'd then cover it with a forced smile, as if to say, "Don't worry, guys, I'm just kidding." When nobody else wanted to play, he'd deal himself a game of FreeCell and sit, hand on his forehead, wondering how the hell he'd get out of this one.

The man making the decisions that dominated Schmarzo's and the other players' thoughts was not team owner Cal Ripken Jr.; it was Brian Graham, the coordinator of Minor League Instruction for the Baltimore Orioles. He'd been hanging around the clubhouse and watching intently on the field during preseason workouts.

"God, I hate seeing him," Schmarzo said one afternoon. "That dude is the grim fucking reaper."

Schmarzo, twenty-three years old in a clubhouse full of new draft picks, could feel death rattles building in his lungs every time Graham floated into his presence. I chose to despise the grim reaper in Schmarzo's honor.

Graham, who went by B.G., only made it to double-A as a player in the '80s. He went to UCLA for four years, setting school records for hits, stolen bases, and runs. He played five seasons in the Minors with the Athletics, Indians, Tigers, and Brewers, compiling a .253 average as a utility player. But he became a much better coach than player, leading every Minor League team he managed to a winning record (and winning Carolina League and American Association championships in the process).

From 2002 to 2007, he served as the Pirates' director of player development. In that time the Pirates produced the second-highest total of homegrown Major Leaguers, ranked fourth in Minor League winning percentage, and were awarded the 2002 Topps Organization of the year. In 2007 Graham served as the interim GM of the Pirates. The next year the Orioles brought him on as the grim reaper, and there he remained in 2012.

The only thing that made me detest B.G. more than Schmarzo's aversion was interacting with the man myself.

It was one of the last days of workouts. I brushed aside Schmarzo's deck of cards to eat my lunch at the fold-up table. I'd packed a homemade turkey sandwich and chips in the cloth Rachael Ray lunch bag my mom had given me.

B.G. halted in his tracks when he saw me eating, as though my consumption of calories was a potent expression of disrespect to him.

"Come here," he said.

I forced myself to stand straight and breathe as I approached. He had this way of looking down his long nose at you—head tilted back ever so slightly—like you should be honored to be the subject of his analysis. His narrow mouth and steely, almost marble-like, eyes reminded me of Ty Cobb.

"This is your first year here?" he said. "I know you weren't the clubbie before, but is this your first job in a clubhouse?"

"Yeah, it's my first year, but I used to be a clubbie in college."

"I'm not talking about college. I'm talking about professional baseball."

"Yes," I said.

"How'd you get this job—do you know someone?"

Muggsy walked past from behind me and I used it as an excuse to break eye contact. "No," I said. "I applied through a job board online."

"Nice," Muggsy said as he marched by.

"So you're new at this," B.G. said.

I refused to nod.

"Answer a question for me: Why don't you have a meal spread for these guys?"

"'Cause I'm only charging them for laundry during workouts, not meals."

"Who told you to do that?"

"Jake."

He said, with an executive calm, "Do me a favor: the next time you talk to Jake, tell him to take that idea and shove it up his ass. Let him know I said so."

"Okay," I said.

"How many fuckin' guys you got in here," he said. "Forty?"

I nodded.

"So charge them an extra three bucks a day and get them a post-BP spread. These guys are dying in that heat and they're here all day. Then they have to wake up tomorrow and do it again. Do you know what happens when they don't get proper nutrition? They get hurt. Most of these guys don't have cars to get food, and they're too stupid to pack a lunch for the day.

"You seem like a smart enough kid. What's three times forty?"

I paused. "One twenty," I said.

"Would it cost you one hundred and twenty bucks to get some meat, cheese, and bread?"

"No," I said.

"No. How much would it cost you?"

"I don't know, fifty, sixty bucks for all these guys."

"Not even. Do me a favor. Go out to that little grocery store here on 22, what's it called? Go there and buy these guys a spread."

I did just as B.G. told me. I strongly considered whether to send Jake a text telling him to shove his idea up his ass ("Will B.G. find out if I don't?" I wondered), but I never did send it, which gave me a false sense of victory over the grim reaper.

• • •

I'd once heard war described as long periods of boredom punctuated by moments of sheer terror. There seemed to be something similar going on in the IronBirds' clubhouse. Baseball was full of those long stretches of boredom, and pitchers, more than anybody, were masters of filling that time. Why? Because pitchers, even the best pitchers in the world, sit and watch the game go by for innings, maybe days at a time, before getting into the action.

In one of those dead moments during workouts, a handful of guys struck up a typical pitchers' bullshit session—they discussed how they wanted to die.

One of the tall surfer-looking guys from Cali said he'd like to die drowning in the ocean.

"At what age?" I said.

"I don't know," he said, "maybe fifty or something."

A few guys looked at each other.

"Why so young, man?" I said.

Kimmel (my roommate) said, "That seems pretty old to me."

"Old?" I said. "You think fifty is old to die?"

"I don't know," Kimmel said in his monotone voice.

Someone else chimed in. "Well, fuck, Kimmel, how d'you wanna go?"

"Probably thirty-one or something."

"Not *when*, dumbass, *how*."

"Wait, thirty-one?" the Cali surfer said.

"Yeah," Kimmel said. "What, is that old too?"

Everyone erupted in laughter. Kimmel was twenty-two and dead serious: he had no idea how he wanted to die, just that he expected to live only nine more years.

"I want to go at sixty-three," another guy said, "coaching for a Minor League team. Nothing too high like triple-A, but not the fuckin' GCL either. Something right in that sweet spot like high-A or double-A. I'll be throwing batting practice without an L-screen and boom! Line drive to the skull. Game over."

At that moment, Schmarzo walked in from Trek's training room. I could tell by the look on his face that he'd been considering a mortality of a different sort. He smiled but didn't say anything as he sat down at his locker amid our laughter.

"What about you, Schmarzo?" another pitcher said as his tongue performed routine maintenance on the stray tobacco flecks on his lips.

"What about what? I just sat down, how the fuck should I know what you're talking about?"

"How do you wanna die, Schmarzo?" I said.

He stood up like he sat on a bee. "Fuck that. Fuck no."

"Dude, what?" we said.

Schmarzo started walking away. "No. I can't think about that shit or you're gonna depress me even more."

• • •

I finally gathered the courage to go outside on the last day of work-out week.

I leaned against a waist-high strip of padded wall in right-field foul territory—between the field and the clubhouse—just watching practice. Mills, who was chatting with his pitchers near the right-field fence, noticed me and walked closer, slowly. He asked me if I had his warm-up jacket yet. The team seamstress was making special jackets for the whole coaching staff because they'd seen that Trek, from his previous years with Aberdeen, had a blue, three-quarter-sleeve, polyester warm-up jacket with a cursive "A" over the heart. Mills asked about it every day, like a child waiting for his toy in the mail.

"A couple more days," I said. "But I'm sure you'll keep asking about it until then."

He kinda laughed. "See, you might think I'm arrogant or cocky or something. I don't know that I am. You know what I am, though? I'm a pitcher. And pitchers have to be arrogant if they're gonna be successful." A few pitchers gathered around as he spoke, as if by instinct. "Pitcher's the only position in sports that's higher on the playing field than everyone else. Batters, fielders, coaches—everyone else is on the ground, but pitchers stand on a mound, closer to God than anyone. People say pitchers are arrogant like it's a bad thing or a choice, but how could you not be, meat?"

It got me thinking about Schmarzo again, who was about as arrogant as a monk. That evening, I went into Muggsy's office to grab his dirty clothes. On his desk was a handwritten, annotated roster. It said they needed to get down to twenty-five players (from forty) and they could only have three guys over the age of twenty-three on the team.

"Damn," I thought. "Schmarzo's twenty-three."

Muggsy had written Schmarzo's name on the side, separate from the rest of the team, with a circled "R" next to it. What the hell did that "R" mean? Released? Rookie ball? I put the sheet down before someone could find me, even though the place had cleared for the day. Now I'd have to lie when Schmarzo asked me for information ("I know you have the inside scoop," he once told me. "The clubbie always knows").

By the time B.G. left at the end of the week, they'd moved up a handful of guys to low-A Delmarva and high-A Frederick, and they released four players.

Schmarzo was not one of them.

B.G.'s work in Aberdeen was done . . . for now. As he walked out the door, he approached me—Orioles bag in tow, wet hair, wearing street clothes. He must've just hopped out of the shower. I remembered the previous day: as I walked through the coaches' office to check their towel supply, B.G. had stepped out of the shower behind me, towel draped around his waist.

He said, "Hey, Greg, I got some hairs on my back. Do you mind shaving 'em for me?"

The coaches all laughed.

Someone said, "It must be June in Aberdeen."

I didn't know what made me angrier: that B.G. actually knew my name, that he'd humiliated me, or that I damn near considered shaving his back.

Now, freshly showered and leaving Aberdeen, he handed me a check as he passed by.

"Buy yourself some lunch," he said with a hard slap on my shoulder.

I looked down to see that the Orioles' executive had written me a check for ten dollars. I tore it into confetti and threw it in the trash.

• • •

When B.G. and Muggsy released guys, they worded it like this: "We're giving you your release." We're *giving you* your release—as though dashing your dreams was a gift. But who knows, maybe they were doing you a favor by ending the Minor League grind. You could go out to your friends in the locker room, and they'd be shocked and indignant on your behalf.

"That's bullshit," they'd tell you. "Fuckin' half the guys here could've gone just as easily. Me included."

They'd laugh, and when they did, it would mark the exact moment that the game forgot you existed. You'd pretend not to notice.

They'd have the luxury of saying, "Hey, stay in touch, kid."

And you could say, "For sure, man. I'll come see a game or two this season."

You could pack up your stuff calmly, as though you'd be back tomorrow. You'd tell them it was actually a relief to finally have an answer. You wouldn't let anyone know about the fear in the pit of your belly. How it feels to discover that everything you've ever known about yourself is wrong—that you can no longer do the only thing you know: play baseball. You could get on an airplane. Somewhere between Aberdeen and home you'd allow yourself to cry, and you wouldn't stop for weeks or months.

And then finally, mercifully, life could begin—without baseball.

5

On a Train Bound for Nowhere

I t wasn't part of my job to travel with the team. So instead of getting on the bus to Hudson Valley for their first road trip, I just watched the game's play-by-play in my apartment (at least whenever I could catch my neighbor's internet signal). I ate Taco Bell chalupas as little circles popped up to symbolize pitches on the game day website.

Even with an underutilized kitchen and a lack of furniture, my apartment already felt like home. To boot, there was something comforting about getting in late and tiptoeing over Kimmel's sleeping body. Sometimes I'd be surprised to see a new player or two on air mattresses next to him (nobody ever claimed the spare bedroom).

And, after a few nights of Kimmel staying in my living room, I took the risk of flipping my Minnesota Twins blanket so the logos faced the world. Nobody cared if I was a fan of a team other than the Orioles. In fact, it seemed like players were seen as nerds if they changed their team allegiances. One afternoon, I heard a few pitchers bullshitting about their favorite teams. "I grew up watching the Padres," one guy said, "but now I'm liking the O's too." Another pitcher put on a nasally voice and said, "I like the Orioles because I play for them." Growing up, I thought all players would be loyal to their team and their team only. Not so, apparently.

The IronBirds split their first two at Hudson Valley before coming back to Aberdeen for the home opener. On a high from the mediocre road trip, Schmarzo bet me that they'd go 10-5 in the first fifteen games. If they did, I'd have to roast the team, like one of those Comedy Central specials.

"We're gonna be good this year," Schmarzo told me. "I know everyone says that every year, but we looked pretty fucking solid in Hudson Valley.

"Fifteen games brings us to, what, early July? Oh yeah, you'll have plenty of dirt on these guys by then."

I think he made the bet for the same reason he paid his dues as quickly as possible during workouts: to convince himself that he'd stick around. "If I pay my dues through workouts," said his subconscious, "then I'll be here through workouts. If I make a fifteen-game bet, then I'll be here at least fifteen games." I took the deal, wondering how I'd ever muster the balls to roast the team. Their 1-1 record was fine by me: I wanted them to play well, but not to win so much that they'd make good on Schmarzo's wager—staying at .500 was excitement enough.

More exciting, though, was the influx of cash I got after workouts ended. As B.G. instructed, I put out little spreads with sandwich fixings, animal crackers, and orange slices every day. It was full-on eleven-year-old-soccer-practice style, but they seemed to enjoy it nevertheless.

• • •

The old clubbie handled postgame spreads like a dog owner feeding table scraps to his mutt: in the last few innings of each game he'd slide into the VIP-level kitchen, slip the staff a few bucks, and they'd let him take the leftovers. He'd then feed the IronBirds this lukewarm food that had been sitting out under heat lamps for hours and picked at by Ripken Stadium's elite.

The head of food services (a guy named Barkley) wanted to do something different with me.

We met in his office behind the first base concessions.

"So we're thinking about three bucks a head," Barkley said to me across his cluttered desk, "and we make you a fresh meal every night."

"I don't know if that's gonna work for me," I said. "I make my money off of dues. If that gets cut then I might not make anything."

"So what're you charging these guys, six a day?"

"Seven."

"Seven? You must be making a killing."

"I don't know. This is my first year as a clubbie."

He looked at me like a lion eyeing its prey. "So we get three per home game. That still leaves you with four bucks a day—per player—going in your pocket."

"Well, I still have to buy pregame."

"And does it cost you four dollars per player to buy pregame?"

"Well, no."

"Great," he said. "We'll get you guys taken care of. No more leftovers, either. And if we do give you leftovers, we won't charge you for all that. We'll get you a menu set up every game and I'll give you an invoice at the end of each month—it'll work out great. Sound good?" He stood up to shake my hand.

I shook it out of instinct.

"Let me know if there's anything else you need."

When I told Jake about it, he said they were trying to screw me. "Food services always tries to squeeze the clubbie. They know we have money and they all want their cut."

I didn't have money though. The three hundred some bucks I'd made in dues hardly covered the up-front costs of meal spreads, OxiClean, and drinks, let alone the cost of moving up there. I'd been promised that the front office would reimburse me for all sorts of stuff I hadn't seen checks for yet, and I was starting to get worried. I didn't take the gamble of moving to Maryland expecting to make bank, but I didn't expect to *lose* money either. A broken promise here and there would be the difference between failure and success for me in Minor League Baseball.

• • •

On the afternoon before the home opener, the pitchers invited me to play poker with them. I had laundry to do and produce to cut, but I couldn't pass up the opportunity to bond with the team. The game was Texas Hold'em and each poker chip was worth a quarter. I sat down and Schmarzo counted out a stack and slid it my way.

I bluffed on nearly every hand just because playing for quarters seemed silly to me, but this was no joke to them. Two guys might get sucked into a long, drawn-out hand; then someone would silently count the chips and say, without irony, "There's more than ten bucks in that pot right now."

My bluffing worked for a while, until I was finally knocked out when the guys got wise to my ways.

"What was the buy-in?" I asked as I stood up.

"It was ten," Schmarzo said, shuffling, "but you're good."

"No, I want to," I said. I opened my wallet.

"No, really. Don't worry about it, G."

I wanted to say, "Please take my money. I know you guys are being polite—you're just letting me know that I belong—but can't you see it's having the opposite effect? Let me give you my stupid ten dollars. Let me gamble with you. We're in this together, aren't we?"

Schmarzo dealt two cards per player and they placed their bets. I put my wallet into my back pocket, walked to the equipment closet, and got back to work cutting oranges, wondering if I was really a part of this thing after all.

6

The Baseball Gallows

Bunting adorned Ripken Stadium for opening night. The Kids Zone in left-field foul territory looked like a mini carnival, with a bouncy castle, an inflatable slide, and a pitch-speed game.

Early in the afternoon—hours before game time—the grounds crew got to work watering the infield dirt. If they left the dirt too dry, it would cut up players' legs on slides and cause nasty hops on ground balls. If they got the dirt too wet, it would clump in the players' cleats and make them slip all over the infield like drunken ice skaters. As game time drew nearer, the grounds crew made last minute trimmings to the grass and sprinkled down the lime for the batters' boxes.

The gray bird mascots, Ripcord and Ferrous, walked around waving team flags and high-fiving little kids. The day was clear, hot—perfect for baseball.

By game time, the stadium pulsed with the energy of more than 6,500 fans. The PA announcer introduced the starting lineup for the IronBirds as their pictures flashed on the video board and the crowd cheered at this team of strangers. Like all Minor League teams, this year's iteration was completely different from last year's.

Cal Jr. took the microphone at home plate, looking tanned, tall, and a little chubby.

"I want to thank all of you for your support in the first ten years," he said, referring to the IronBirds' ten-year anniversary. "It's been a wonderful ten years. As you can see, we've made some changes in the food. We've got a lot more different options. I know we're very proud of the changes we've made."

A single person yelled out "Woo!" in response. The electric crowd had grown silent as Cal talked about the new concession options at Ripken Stadium. I guess you gotta talk about *something* if you've only had one winning season and no postseason appearances as a team.

His mom, Violet, threw out the first pitch from halfway between the rubber and home plate. Cal caught the ball (a strike down the middle) and gave his short white-haired mom a kiss and a hug.

A little more than a month later, Violet would be abducted at gunpoint from her Aberdeen home. The abductor would tie her hands behind her back and drive her around for hours before taking her back home the next morning. Cal would offer $100,000 for any information that would lead to the suspect, but the reward would yield no clues—he wouldn't even discover the motivation for the kidnapping.

The way that summer was about to go for Violet and the Iron-Birds, her throwing the home opener's first pitch would turn out to be a perfect symbol of the chaos ahead.

• • •

The Hudson Valley Renegades got out to an early 3–0 lead against IronBirds starter Jorge Rivera, a lefty from the Dominican Republic. In the top of the sixth, the Birds rallied to tie the game, 3–3. It stayed knotted that way until the top of the ninth, when the Renegades scored two more runs. The IronBirds went quietly in the ninth to lose that home opener 5–3.

I hadn't watched any of the action, though, as I was running upstairs to the VIP-level kitchen to grab the team's postgame food. Barkley hadn't set up a menu for the home stand like he said he would, so all I got were a few half-eaten trays of chicken with already-congealed sauce, limp and soggy green beans, and dried-out potatoes.

It dawned on me that I was charging these guys money to eat scraps. It was like sending the family dog an invoice at the end of every month for the privilege of licking my plate clean.

The players filtered in. My stomach sank as I realized just how many we had—there were more than a dozen nonroster players who were just along for the ride, waiting for the Orioles to officially place them on the roster or let them go. One such player was Schmarzo.

"Go easy on the spread, guys," he said when he walked in. "There's not a lot of food."

I wheeled the already-full laundry carts—which had been stolen long before I arrived, from the Aberdeen ShopRite—into the laundry room to get the washes going. I didn't yet have a system in place for laundry, so I was in for a long night. I'd been on my feet all day. The insides of my shoes squished with sweat. The backs of my knees and ankles ached. Blisters had bubbled on my toes and heels. I didn't eat all day. Not because I wasn't hungry, but because I didn't want to take from the spread if players weren't getting enough food.

I could hear the boom of fireworks bursting over the stadium. I never went outside to watch. Instead, I stood there scrubbing pants, contemplating the cosmic distance between the glory of baseball as I knew it in childhood and the spot where I found myself just then.

How could I do this for one more day, let alone the rest of the summer and beyond?

• • •

"Hey, meat!" Mills yelled.

I kept walking. It had been a long night, and I wasn't eager for an a.m. talking-to from Mills.

"Greg," Muggsy said.

I stopped and looked back.

"Come here," Mills said, pointing in front of him.

I obeyed.

"Muggsy and me—we went out to eat after the game last night."

"Where'd you go?" I said.

"See, that part doesn't matter. You're the clubbie, right? Your first question should be, 'Why didn't you eat the spread?'"

I let the silence sit for a moment. "Why didn't you eat the spread?"

"We got reports to write. After every game I gotta sit my ass down and write a report on our pitchers and send it to Baltimore. Muggsy and the other coaches all do the same thing."

"I'm sorry. We ran out of food."

"Do I wear a jersey?" Mills said.

"What? No."

"No. I wear a jacket. Where is that new jacket by the way? Is it coming in yet?"

"It'll be here soon."

"Mhmm. You said that last week. But I'm not worried about that right now. I wear a jacket, right, not a jersey. Because I'm not a player."

Muggsy chimed in. "We don't want to cut players off in line because they need their nutrition more than we do. I mean look at Millsy—he's already a fat fuck."

"So you want me to set aside food for you guys after the games?"

"I'm not saying you have to do all that," Mills said. "I'm just saying we didn't get any of the spread last night."

I had to keep reminding myself, "These guys aren't your bosses— you could disobey every single thing they tell you and they still couldn't fire you." I realized that Mills and Muggsy were both former Major Leaguers. They'd probably been taken care of by people like me their whole lives—someone else made their copies, fed them, did their laundry, and so on. I tried to imagine Trek asking me to make him a dinner plate in such a roundabout way, but I just couldn't see it. Trek wasn't a baseball guy, he was just a guy, and he was perfectly capable of taking care of himself. I stewed thinking about it. It wasn't my fault they couldn't do anything but coach baseball. It wasn't my fault they couldn't take care of themselves. It wasn't my fault even Mills, who had twelve years in the Majors, was a failure.

My bitterness simmered all day. I hid away in the equipment closet most of the afternoon while the clubhouse filled with players. I couldn't stay back there forever—eventually I'd have to bring out the pregame spread and make the daily trips back and forth to the front office. I finally left the equipment closet and walked past the coaches' office out the front door. Mills spotted me.

"Hey, come here!"

I continued walking.

"I know you heard me, meat."

I stormed back into the coaches' room and walked up to him. "I'm not a dog, man. What do you want?"

He looked taken aback. "Nothing," he said. "It's alright."

Before I could derive any false sense of satisfaction from standing up to Mills, our hitting coach whistled and said, "Here, Fido," as I walked out the door.

Just before the game, when everyone else was out on the field stretching and throwing, Mills and I sat in front of our lockers, alone in silence together. He put on his white uniform pants with a blue stripe running along the outside of each thigh. The dark blue cage jackets had arrived that afternoon, so he slipped his on as I pretended to diddle on my phone.

His eyes were down as he tied his shoes. "You're an ornery fucker, you know that?"

"Oh, really?"

"Yeah, really. And I'll tell you something: it's hard to be angry in baseball. I don't care if you're the clubbie, a pitcher, the GM— whoever—this game will eventually eat you up if you take this shit too seriously. It's a long season, meat. They call this short season, but it's still a long season. And you know what?" He laughed. "I'm gonna wear your ass out."

"Just ease back some. I'm not always in the mood for it. Sometimes I got a lot of shit to do."

"I know you do. I used to be a clubbie when I played."

"*While* you played?"

"Mhmm. I'd have to go out and find laundromats during road trips and collect dues from my teammates—it was tough. But I needed the extra money, so I did it. I'll tell you what—I learned something being a clubbie and a player: this game doesn't care what kinda mood you're in. And I'll tell you something else, Greg: nobody in this clubhouse does either."

• • •

The IronBirds were down 3–1 going into the bottom of the ninth. Then our second baseman led off with a double. "God damn it," I said as I watched from right-field foul territory. The game had already taken three hours and I just wanted it to end so I could get going on laundry. Luckily, the next three IronBirds batters grounded out in succession to end the game, dropping Aberdeen to a 1-3 record.

We were only four games into the season, but I was already running schemes like a veteran clubbie. I sold sodas for a dollar a can even though I got them for free. The Conrad's Crab truck, which supplied the stadium with blue crabs, sat outside of Muggsy's office, steaming up tasty crabs every afternoon. I slipped the Conrad's guy a baseball and a shirt every once in a while, and he hooked me up with blue crabs for the coaches, who tipped better when they were full of crabs. When I was scrambling to get the spread set up one night after a quick game, a couple of pitchers helped me, so I gave them (and only them) Chick-fil-A sandwiches I'd gotten for free from the concessions people. One night I had a lot of chicken leftover, so I packaged it, put it in the fridge, and cut it up for team salads the next day. My favorite money-saving move was taking the leftovers I couldn't disguise or repurpose (like pasta) and giving them to the visiting team. The other team would be well fed, happily pay their three-dollar-a-day dues, and I'd pocket that 100 percent profit.

Adding together that home stand's dues, tips, and my first pay-check from the front office, I had the first disposable income of my adult life.

Nicole came to visit me during the team's first long road trip. I took her out to restaurants on Baltimore's Inner Harbor, look-ing out over docked sailboats and a rainbow of two-person pad-dleboats crisscrossing the water. We went to a vineyard ten miles north of my apartment and drank wine like we knew what the fuck we were talking about ("Sort of an oaky afterbirth," we'd say after a long sip, quoting from *The Office*).

All the while, though, I could tell her mind was elsewhere, even in the midst of a wonderful visit. Yes, she'd been struggling to find a home for us within driving distance of her new teaching job in Johnston, South Carolina, but something else was bothering her (besides sleeping on my air mattress over the previous week). She stared through me as we ate dinner in my apartment (standing at the counter, since I didn't have furniture).

"What's wrong?"

She shook her head and remained silent. Finally, she said, "I'm nervous to live with you."

"That's understandable. I'm nervous about it too. But I'm really excited. We can finally start our lives together, remember?"

She shook her head. "I'm nervous because—nothing."

"No, what?"

"You're the same."

"The same as what?"

"I don't know."

"Yes, you do."

She shook her head.

"Just tell me."

She chewed her tongue as she formulated what to say. "You're the same as when you were in Florida."

I forced a laugh. I'd been directionless while I lived in Florida. I had been jobless, friendless, and aimless, living in my parents' retirement community. But that time, when I had lost all confidence and hope, was a million miles away.

I pressed my belly into hers and embraced her as fully as I could. I knew she wasn't right—I'd actually changed a lot since becoming a clubbie. But, in due time, I'd realize I was changing more than I preferred to admit.

. . .

We went to an Orioles game at Camden Yards during her visit. We got to the stadium early and drank Natty Bohs, a Baltimore favorite, at Pickles, Sliders, and the Bullpen bars. We were full-on drunk by the first pitch as we watched from the right-field bleachers.

Baseball plays that I'd seen hundreds of times before had a new effect on me. I looked at each player and wondered how many nameless Minor Leaguers had fallen away to make his existence on that field possible. I couldn't help but cringe every time a player slid into a bag. "That's another five minutes of work for their clubbie," I thought. I wondered what their clubbie was doing at that moment—if he even gave a shit that he got to interact with Major Leaguers every day. Or did he feel like me on most days at the park: just waiting for the next out so the game could finish already and we could all go home? It didn't matter to me who won or lost at Ripken Stadium—or Camden Yards for that matter. An out was an out, whether IronBird or otherwise, and each one brought me closer to the end of the game, the end of the home stand, and the end of the season.

I'd been to Camden Yards one time before, in 2009, with two Orioles-supporting college friends. Back then the Orioles were cellar dwellers and the stadium was empty enough that you could walk from your cheap outfield seats to sit behind home plate if you wanted to. When we visited, I was a sophomore in college, a year removed from being cut by the Hamline Pipers Division III baseball team and a year into my time at Division I Winthrop University in South Carolina, where I had a baseball scholarship as an equipment manager (basically a clubbie).

Back then, I'd stood in those same right-field bleachers and heckled Atlanta Braves players during their afternoon batting practice. I'd point to the sky and yell "heads up!" and we'd watch the players duck for the nonexistent baseball. My buddies laughed every time. Jeff Bennett, a pitcher for the visiting Atlanta Braves, came over to talk to me.

"You know," he said, "it's actually pretty dangerous when we're out here trying to shag fly balls. They can hurt us if we're not paying attention."

I pointed up to the sky as he spoke and said, "Ball!"

He flinched instinctively, but then realized that there was no baseball. He walked away, dismissing me as hopeless.

I high-fived my laughing friends. There was this deep need for a reaction from the players, even if something on my surface harbored an odd contempt for them. I suppose I wanted to be on the field so badly that a simple conversation was validating, even if Bennett admonished me.

Now it was 2012. The Orioles were suddenly a first-place team, the stands were a bit fuller, and the Orioles won a back-and-forth game with the Indians, 9–8.

The game these Major Leaguers played was a baseball of precision. Even when they made mistakes, they were so good at minimizing them (with a scoop here or a swipe there) that it rendered the misfires moot. It looked so different from the mistake-filled games at Ripken Stadium. I'd already seen guys on the IronBirds get sent to the baseball gallows—how many more drops of the guillotine would they have to survive before they made it to Baltimore? If that Orioles game was any indication, the boys in Aberdeen didn't have very good odds: none of the Orioles on the field at Camden Yards that night had ever played for the IronBirds.

After the game, the stadium went dark and the PA announcer told fans to gather behind home plate for fireworks. Bursts of rainbow lights shot out of center field in coordination with music. I didn't care a lick about fireworks, but it was the most incredible display

I'd ever seen. All the while, the grounds crew went to work tamping down home plate and raking the infield. The Orioles' clubbie was probably getting the first load of laundry going. Probably none of them—the clubbie or the grounds crew—could give less of a shit about the fireworks in center field. I sat with my arm around Nicole as she smiled and squealed with glee as the bursts of light reflected in her wide-open green eyes.

I knew in that moment that I'd never see baseball the same way again.

7

The Boatload Mentality

Schmarzo lost our bet on June 25, when the IronBirds fell to 2-6. At that point, it was mathematically impossible for the team to go 10-5 in their first fifteen games, so I wouldn't be roasting the players Comedy Central style. The event passed without comment from Schmarzo. Maybe he just forgot about it. He did have more important matters on his mind:

The Orioles had finally placed him on the official IronBirds roster.

He got his first action against the Brooklyn Cyclones on June 30, a road game in front of eight thousand fans, a monstrous turnout in the New York–Penn League.

Lefty reliever Enrico Jimenez had come on in relief to pitch scoreless fifth and sixth innings before giving up a leadoff double in the bottom of the seventh. With the game tied 2–2, Muggsy replaced Jimenez, the lefty, with Schmarzo, the righty. After all that worrying about getting released and the talk of quitting baseball, here he was, finally on the mound in front of a capacity crowd in a tie game.

The IronBirds' twenty-three-year-old veteran faced the New York Mets' first-round draft pick from that year (the Cyclones were a Mets affiliate) with a man on second. Schmarzo coaxed a ground-out to short that moved the runner to third. With the infield in to keep the go-ahead run from scoring, Schmarzo got another ground ball to the shortstop, who checked the runner on third then threw to first for the second out of the inning.

It looked like Schmarzo might work out of the jam. But he proceeded to walk the next two batters, loading the bases for the Cyclones. Schmarzo needed a first-pitch strike after the back-to-back walks, so he started the next batter with a fastball. The batter lined Schmarzo's pitch over the left-field fence for a grand slam. Schmarzo gave up a single to the next batter before getting a pop-up to end the inning. The loss technically belonged to Jimenez, who gave up the leadoff double that scored the go-ahead run for the Cyclones, but Schmarzo felt every bit of that losing pain.

"I'm done," he said to me when the team bus arrived back in Aberdeen. "I can't stick around with an ERA of fucking twenty-seven, you know?" He forced one of those manic, wrinkled smiles—*it's just a joke, see?*—before shaking his head in disgust.

I didn't give him the reaction he was secretly hoping for: telling him that he sucked, that he was a worthless piece-of-shit pitcher and human being, that he should clear out his locker and give it to someone who could play worth a damn. Schmarzo needed someone to hurt him so badly that he'd walk away with no regrets. But I didn't give him that gift because how could I? How does anyone do that in the moment, even if you know it's what your friend needs?

He walked out the back door of the clubhouse into the summer night. When he talked like this during preseason workouts, Slime (his best friend on the team) would say, "He always says he's leaving. He'll be back." But now Slime was gone, moved up to Delmarva, and there was nobody to assure me that Schmarzo would actually return. I took solace in the sight of Schmarzo's unpacked locker, the one closest to the rear exit of the clubhouse.

Something brushed against my arm.

"Here," Trek said. He handed me the bat bag I packed before every road trip. "We broke a lot this trip."

I'd stuffed it with almost forty toothpicks, but there were only a few lonely bats left, barely enough to start a campfire. Maybe I could get that fire going before Schmarzo drove home. Maybe let him take the number thirteen jersey off his back and throw it into the flame—let him forget this place ever existed.

· · ·

They say that the true fireballers can throw a baseball so fast that when a batter fouls it straight back he can put the bat up to his nose and smell the wood burning. This only happens when someone just misses crushing the ball—it spins so ferociously that the momentary friction of the leather and seams against the grain of the bat creates a burn. On July 3, Enrico Jimenez didn't light any bats on fire.

Jimenez came off the mound to a chorus of boos from the record-breaking Ripken Stadium crowd of 6,904, many of whom were— let's be honest—only in attendance to see the postgame fireworks rather than the 5-10 IronBirds. Despite Jimenez's performance (three earned runs in two innings), the IronBirds pulled out a 21–7 victory, setting a team record for runs scored.

The quick clicks of cleats against the concrete between the field and the clubhouse signaled the flood of players coming in after the game.

"Pants and jerseys in the carts before you eat!" I shouted to the locker room.

Rivera yelled, "Take a shower for you hands!" I'd finally discovered the meaning of this phrase: the American players didn't think the Dominicans valued cleanliness enough, so they told the "coños" to shower their dirty hands before dipping them into the communal spread.

The hiss of hot showers echoed through the bathrooms. The stink of sweaty, dirt-stained jerseys climbed up my nostrils as players threw them into the carts before dishing up. Jimenez came lumbering in from the field, not eager to eat like his teammates. He pulled off his white home jersey and threw it into his locker with the most speed and accuracy he'd displayed all night. He screamed "fuck!" and punched his solid wood locker with his most valuable asset. The outburst startled me as I sorted through the dirty jerseys, but nobody else seemed to care; they went on eating and disrobing around him as though throwing a temper tantrum was business as usual. A few guys grabbed plates and stood outside the clubhouse to watch the fireworks—barefoot, shirtless, pants undone. Rivera turned on the speakers above his locker and blasted his fast-paced, heavy-bass Spanish music. Some other Dominicans immediately danced their naked bodies to the beat, as some Americans shook their heads—some laughing, some not.

Jimenez, after sulking against his locker for minutes, finally took off his clothes and hit the showers. His birth certificate said he was born on February 7, 1989, which made him twenty-three at the time, same as Schmarzo. And sure, twenty-three was old for short-season single-A, but I couldn't help but notice the way he walked with that arched back, cartoonishly sticking out his potbelly—his mouth framed on either side by deep wrinkles that led up to his high, perpetually sweaty cheeks. If he were a position player, he'd probably walk around using a baseball bat like a cane. I'd even heard the coaches say that Jimenez was one of those Dominicans who'd forged their birth certificate when they were first signed, the better to increase their potential value to a team (Muggsy estimated Jimenez's age at being somewhere around forty fuckin' years old, give or take).

I could hear the boom of fireworks through the concrete clubhouse walls, and outside the smell of sulfur must have dominated the air. It was July 3, and Enrico's American dream was falling through his fingers like powdered rosin.

Although July 3 was the beginning of the end for Enrico Jimenez, for many young baseball players just like him down in the Dominican Republic, early July was a time of hope and anticipation. July 2 of every year was the day Major League Baseball opened up its international signing period. Unlike American players—who were selected in the draft—international players were signed exclusively as free agents. The Dominican Republic was home to only ten million people at the time, about 3 percent of America's population, yet

Dominican players made up more than 11 percent of Major League rosters at the start of that 2012 season and more than 25 percent of Minor League rosters. This discrepancy was due in large part to MLB's more lax rules regarding Dominican players. Whereas Americans had to wait until they turned eighteen and graduated from high school to sign with a Major League team, Dominicans could sign as young as sixteen years old—sometimes for millions of dollars, sometimes for just a few thousand. An executive for an MLB team once said, "Instead of signing four American guys at $25,000 each, we sign twenty Dominican guys for $5,000 each." This was known as the boatload mentality: sign a bunch of cheap Dominicans for less than they're worth, then if only one or two of them becomes a Major Leaguer, the team's investment has more than paid off.

These rules that allowed teams to sign sixteen-year-olds starting on July 2 created a Dominican talent-scouting environment much different from America's. They were called *buscones*, and they hunted the island in search of children, sometimes as young as thirteen, who they thought could someday be stars. These buscones (from the Spanish *buscar*, to search) were men who had no affiliation with any Major League team. They gave young boys instruction on dusty fields and often used busted-lace baseballs and tied-up car tires to chop against for batting practice. Buscones even gave the boys equipment, food, and transportation if they needed it; all in the hopes that they'd sign a fat contract on the July 2 after their sixteenth birthday. Then the buscones took a cut of that signing bonus, usually around 35 percent (as compared to about 5 percent with most American agents), or, if a player didn't develop as the buscones thought, they dropped the boy like a bad habit, and he hoped to be picked up by someone else. These boys often left school at a young age to chase this dream—sometimes as young as second grade, which was the case for several Dominican players on the IronBirds.

But players who signed professional baseball contracts didn't go straight to the highest level: they went from being the stud at their college or high school to being a nobody in the Minor Leagues. For Dominicans, though, coming to America was like jumping straight into Las Mayores: bright lights, clean water, air-conditioning, and a shot at the dream. It's a dream that, unfortunately, Jimenez never achieved.

• • •

Jorge Rivera's scouting report said he was a six-foot-tall, two-hundred-pound lefty. Under the "school" category, it said Dominican Republic. "Deceptive lefty who sits 90–94 mph and can touch 95 on his good days. Average breaking ball. Good arm speed. Effectiveness will be based on command of fastball and control of secondary pitches." What his scouting report didn't say, however, was that Jorge Rivera was stealing baseball bats from the team bag. It turned out he was the reason Trek came back from that road trip with nothing more than a few pieces of kindling.

I approached Trek in his training room office in early July. He stared at his computer as he spit tobacco juice into an empty Diet Mountain Dew bottle.

"I've been meaning to ask you," I said, "how'd we use so many bats this last road trip?"

"Greg, I don't make them turn in their broken bats to get a new one. If they need a new bat, I give 'em one. This is baseball—you need bats and balls to play."

"It's just that Jake's gonna chew my ass about it."

"If Jake has a problem with how I do something, then he can talk to me—he doesn't need to go bothering you. And if he starts giving you a hard time about it you tell him to call me."

At the time, I had no idea Rivera was the one pilfering from me, I just knew my supply was depleting. The IronBirds, too, were fading fast in the standings and tensions in the clubhouse were building between the American and Dominican factions. The petty disagreements extended all the way to music choice—whether to play American or Dominican music seemed more important than wins and losses.

Schmarzo came to me one afternoon before a home game in mid-July as I threw a load of towels in the wash.

"Hey, man, you don't happen to have a screwdriver do ya?"

I reached into my fanny pack and pulled out a Leatherman. "This work?"

"Fuckin' A, G, what don't you have in there?"

"Probably a decent fastball."

"Shit. That makes two of us. I'll bring it right back."

"Anything I should be worried about?" I called after him as he walked away.

He clicked his head to the right. "We'll see."

I slammed the door of the industrial washer and turned the latch.

An hour later I unlatched the door and pulled out an armful of clean wet towels. (Underneath the detergent scent was always this faint smell of sweat that never disappeared, like a wet dog.) It turned out I should've been worried when Schmarzo asked me for a screwdriver. Apparently, some Americans had gotten so fed up listening to Rivera's music that Schmarzo finally unscrewed the outlet above Rivera's locker to put an end to it (I was happy Schmarzo didn't electrocute himself in the process).

How Rivera eventually got the outlet working again I had no idea, but he did, and he turned up his thumping music even louder than before. Blackmar, his locker neighbor, finally had enough. He reached up to the outlet above Rivera's locker and yanked the plug out of the wall.

Rivera screamed something in Spanish, his anger betraying the boyishness of his face—red accentuating the dark freckles on his light skin. He unfolded his metal fold-up chair (which had his name "Jorge" written in permanent marker on the bottom), stood on it, and plugged the music back in, bass thumping. He got down off the chair and stared down Blackmar.

"No," Blackmar said, "no more of this."

One more round of unplugging and plugging back in.

"Hey," Rivera said, "you turn it off again—"

Without hesitation, Blackmar yanked the cord out for a final time. Rivera's face turned even redder and he dug into his bag, pulled out a bat, and reared back to swing at Blackmar. By this point the whole clubhouse was watching, even perpetually injured catcher Pedro Perez, who had anticipated his friend's move. Perez quickly limped up from the couch, just a few feet away, and made two hops before tackling Rivera into his locker.

"I hope you hit me, Jorge," Mark said as the other two wrestled over the bat. "I hope you hit me and go to jail."

Perez took the bat and limped over to his locker to deposit it, away from Rivera. Blackmar sat down, but before he knew it Rivera pulled another bat from his bag and was about to take a swing again. Hollers came from all around the clubhouse.

"Watch out!"

"Ayyyy, coño!"

"Blackmar, he's got another one!"

Then one final shout from Alan Mills, who had stomped into the clubhouse at the right time: "Shut the fuck up!" Everyone froze and turned to Mills, standing there with a bat of his own and his nineties-style sunglasses on his sweaty face. "You think you're gonna take a swing at him, meat?"

Rivera tried to plead his case in broken English, but Mills cut him off.

In the middle of a game a few days later, alone in the clubhouse, I climbed onto Rivera's chair to look in the bag atop his locker. I pulled out one bat. Then another. Then another. All told there were more than ten bats up there, which would've been a lot even for a position player. I took them back to the equipment closet.

Rivera, realizing his stash was gone, cornered me the next day as I cut up oranges in a cloud of citrusy sweetness. He entered the equipment closet with Cesar, one of the coaches, acting as translator. Cesar told me that Rivera had gotten those bats as a gift and I'd stolen them from him. I knew this was false because the stolen bats were the brittle ash wood Rawlings brand that I issued the team—bats so bad that nobody would be mean enough to give them as a gift.

Cesar put his hands up. "I don't know if what he sayin' is true. I just telling you what he says."

All the while Rivera stared at me through his eyebrows.

"I—I can't. He's a pitcher, you know?" I gestured to Rivera. "Why would he need all those bats?"

Cesar translated what I'd said for Rivera, who fumed to him in Spanish and angrily pointed at me until Cesar finally shoved him out of the equipment closet.

If I had to guess, I would've said that Rivera planned on bringing those bats home to the Dominican Republic to sell them in the off-season, but I didn't know for sure. All I knew was that the Iron-Birds—on the field and in the clubhouse—had broken on contact like a busted-cover baseball, falling apart midair before dying on the grass in a heap of leather and string.

• • •

On July 22 the IronBirds were 11-22 overall and in the middle of an 8–2 loss to the Hudson Valley Renegades.

After not pitching for seven straight days and building an 0-2 record with a 5.63 ERA, Enrico Jimenez walked out in the middle of the game. He was sitting in the bullpen when Mills made a call to get another lefty hot. This was the breaking point for Jimenez, who was a lefty himself. He stood up and made the short walk from the bullpen behind the right-field fence to the clubhouse. Rivera followed his friend and came back to tell the rest of the bullpen that Jimenez was packing up his shit to leave.

"Whatever," they said back to him. "Where's he gonna go?"

The next inning Mills made another call. "Get Jimenez loose."

"He's not here right now," the backup catcher said.

Mills hung up, probably assuming Jimenez was in the clubhouse taking a dump or something.

An inning later another call came from Mills. "Get Jimenez loose."

"He's still not here," the catcher said, fighting back laughter.

"The fuck you mean he's not there? What're you talking about?"

"Dude, he left."

Mills hung up the phone and stormed up the right-field line toward the bullpen in the middle of the inning. Hometown fans who'd watched Mills in his years as an Oriole begged for his attention as they all bathed in the electric light of the Aberdeen evening.

"Mr. Mills! Can I have a ball?"

"Millsy!"

Usually eager to talk to anyone, Mills continued walking, occasionally turning his back to make sure he wasn't hit by a ball in play.

He opened the padded fence door of the bullpen. "Where the fuck is Jimenez?"

Schmarzo, ever the diplomat, spoke on everyone's behalf. "He's gone, Millsy, he left a couple innings ago."

"How the fuck you lose someone, meat?"

Everyone tried to stifle laughter.

"We didn't lose him," Schmarzo said. "He pulled a Mota." Jose Mota, a Dominican, was Schmarzo's old friend and roommate who'd escaped in the middle of a game once he caught wind that he was going to be released.

Mills leaned in close. "Listen. If the Orioles start hearing that I'm losing pitchers, I'm gonna get my ass fired. I know y'all don't like me, but you can't go pulling this shit when I need pitchers to pitch in the fuckin' game."

"I mean, let's be frank," Schmarzo said, "the only guy you should be mad at just left."

After the game, when the position players heard about Jimenez's disappearance, the clubhouse buzzed with gleeful laughter from some of the Americans. A solemnity palled over the Dominicans. I hustled around, cleaning and getting uniforms into the wash.

Muggsy stopped me dead in my tracks as he walked toward me—
always on a straight line, always upright, always pissed. He was all
mustache and beady, penetrating blue eyes.

"Were you in here when Jimenez left?" he said.

"Yeah, but I was—"

"You see that happen again, you come down to the dugout and
tell one of us."

"*Again*?" I thought.

"He's gonna hop on a train up to New York and disappear. Then
the Orioles will be out a visa."

I didn't realize it at the time, but Muggsy was making an out-
dated reference to the limited H-2B visas that Dominican Minor
Leaguers needed to play ball in the U.S. By 2012, though, international Minor Leaguers could use a P-1 visa just like the Major
Leaguers, which allowed teams to give out as many visas as they
wanted. Either way, losing a player didn't look good for a coaching staff that had just turned their record to 11-23.

I heard a couple guys joking about Jimenez as they got ready
to shower.

"Does he even have a car?"

"No, dude, he's a Dominican. He's probably gonna try to bike
back to the DR."

• • •

The next morning, Enrico Jimenez biked to Ripken Stadium
from his host family's house. He readied himself to catch the bus
to Brooklyn—where the IronBirds had a road series against the
Cyclones—going about his business as if the night before had
never happened. As I walked around, marking guys off my sheet as
they paid dues, I heard whispers that Jimenez had a friend in New
York. Apparently, he was just trying to catch a free ride to escape
before getting released and sent back to the Dominican. Instead,
the Orioles suspended him, which kept him in Aberdeen for a week
before they released him. I got anxious as I waited to hear his fate:

we had a few new players coming in and I had to assign them jerseys and lockers. Jimenez's number twenty-six was a popular size and I needed to know when I could give it away to an incoming replacement.

Eventually, Jimenez's picture was taken down from his player page on the official Minor League Baseball website, leaving a blank silhouette where his headshot used to be—nothing left but a shadow.

In a quiet moment, as we folded towels in the training room, I asked Trek what took so long for the front office to release a player who'd walked out in the middle of a game.

"That's a good fuckin' question, Greg. Welcome to the Baltimore Orioles."

I went back to folding towels. "You know where any of these guys go when they get released?"

"I don't know, Greg. If a guy's here, I'll worry about him and give him the treatment he needs." He stowed a pile of towels and swiped his hands clean. "If they're not here, I'm not worried about 'em."

8

Alexander the Great

egend has it that Alexander the Great wore a breastplate with the image of Medusa facing out toward his enemies. The beheaded Medusa, who turned anyone who looked in her eyes to stone, represented a slain foe to Alexander's enemies—proof that he had conquered the unique fear that her image could induce in men. I think Alex Schmarzo wore the number thirteen for the same reason. I didn't assign him that number like I did with many other players; he requested it before the season started. It seemed like an effort on Schmarzo's part to prove to his enemies and (perhaps more importantly) to himself that he'd conquered a superstitious aversion to the unlucky thirteen.

In late July a writer for the *Baltimore Sun* posted a column online titled "Interviewing Athletes Is Easy, Just Follow These Instructions." He ended it with this: "The other night, when I was interviewing IronBird reliever Alex Schmarzo, I pointed out that he had not allowed an earned run in about three weeks, and he said, 'Well, that's gone now because you just jinxed it, thanks!' He wasn't entirely serious, but I sure hope I didn't jinx him by mentioning his recent success."

I knew Schmarzo by then. I knew the face he made when he said that line to the newspaperman: the wry smile that told you he was just joking around. Weeks before that conversation with the *Baltimore Sun*, Mills called Schmarzo into the coaches' office after he'd given up that grand slam in his first outing. Mills shut the door behind them and let the silence linger for a moment.

"You're gonna die one day," he said.

"What the hell are you talking about, Millsy?"

"You're gonna die, meat. And you know what? There's nothing you can do to avoid it. Same thing with your baseball career. You're gonna stop playing one day—maybe it's tomorrow, maybe it's when you're forty—but it's gonna come eventually. If you keep spending your time worrying about when that day's coming, then you're sure as hell not gonna enjoy the days you got now."

Something clicked in Schmarzo. He thought, "Holy shit, he's right. Fuck this stupid game."

The IronBirds continued to drop games, losing by scores like 10–0 and 13–3, but since that conversation, Schmarzo hadn't given up a single run.

• • •

A sold-out crowd surrounded us on a cool Saturday night in late July—seventy-six degrees, with a light drizzle. My arms hung over the dugout rails as I talked to Cam Edman, one of our catchers. Cam liked to sit alone at his locker after games, praying over his meal while other guys cussed and screamed around him. He thanked me for the food every single night and tipped modestly when he paid his dues.

On the rare occasions that I watched the games, I usually sat in the bullpen, but Schmarzo was getting warmed up and I'd never seen him pitch before, so I came down to the dugout instead.

After warming up the infielders between half innings, our first baseman turned to us in the dugout. He wagged the baseball to get someone's attention, and fans above the dugout thought it was for them. He ignored the fans, instead throwing it on one hop to a teammate near the steps. Another player intercepted it, just for something to do. At the end of that half inning, the first baseman put his glove up as he jogged in from the field and the player flipped it back to him, foregoing a simple handoff in the dugout. This small ritual gave the person in the dugout a job, something to do to replace the profound boredom of being a benchwarmer in baseball.

Cam had warmed the bench all season.

"Got the laundry done already?" Cam said.

"Nah, just taking a break to watch a little baseball for once."

In moments between pitches, quiet moments, I could feel the fans' gazes drifting down, wondering what players talk about in the dugout, maybe even speculating about that nonuniformed person and his status on the team—the kind of thoughts I would've had as a baseball fan.

"Look at that guy with a fanny pack and little crustache," I imagined someone in the stands saying, "probably wishes he was one of the players."

"Jock-sniffer by the looks of him," their friend would say.

I wanted to prove them wrong and show that I was indeed welcome in this group.

Our pitcher threw a wild curveball and the runner moved to second.

"Muy inteligente aquí," Mills yelled to his pitcher. It would likely be his last inning.

"Have you had an at bat yet?" I asked Cam.

His eyes flashed over to me for a moment before looking back to the game. "No," he said.

Another pitch.

"How does it feel to not get any playing time?" I said.

"It doesn't feel good," he said. "It feels pretty shitty to be honest with you."

I'd never heard him swear before. He moved down to the other end of the dugout, hanging on the fence near the camera well. There was suddenly a two-person space on either side of me. Now what did the fans think of the kid with the black shirt, fanny pack, and frayed cargo shorts held up with an elastic baseball belt?

Schmarzo came in to start the top of the seventh, the IronBirds leading 3–1. I'd looked forward to watching him pitch all season.

I never knew he did this little wiggle with his right arm when he looked in for the signs—I didn't know he only worked from the stretch either. Number thirteen's brown hair curled out the back of his cap and his thick sideburns still ran down to the tips of his ear-lobes, but the Fu Manchu was gone. Grizzly Wintergreen would've bulged his bottom lip if he weren't worried about getting fined—or maybe it was there and I just couldn't see it. He nodded, came to the set, delivered, and snatched each throw back from the catcher with his dark brown Rawlings glove. He looked like he was made to exist on that mound. He was a natural phenomenon, sprung up through the dirt, like lava cracking the rumbling crust of a volcano. This was the only place Alex Schmarzo could possibly be: on the mound at Ripken Stadium. His delivery was wild and inconsistent, sometimes falling over toward first base on his follow through, but everything down to the wiggle of his arm screamed confidence. Even his nervous head ticks were like preparatory cracks of the neck before destroying another man. This was not the Schmarzo I knew in the clubhouse—this guy was absolutely dealing.

He pitched a clean seventh inning and worked out of a jam in the eighth. He clicked his head to the right as he sauntered off the field, sighing in relief. Then I saw something just as he walked, head down, toward the dugout: the man who wore thirteen, the unluckiest number, still made a point of stepping over the white chalk line, an eternal aversion to bad luck.

Jonathan, my batboy, tapped me on the shoulder.

"We're low on baseballs," he said. He opened up the black cloth bag to show me the half dozen he had left from the six dozen we'd started with.

"The rain?" I said.

He nodded.

I ran up the right-field line toward the clubhouse. I kept a secret stash of leftover game balls in the equipment closet for situations like this. Or sometimes Jonathan would let me know which umpires were less liberal about using damaged baseballs and I could pack a few extras before the game. (I told Jonathan that Alan Mills must never discover that secret supply of baseballs, which he never did.)

I waited for a stoppage in play to run back down the right-field foul line with reinforcements.

Some grown man yelled, "Heyyyyy, ball boy!"

A child said, "Can I have a ball?"

Whenever kids asked me for baseballs I'd think to myself, "I'm the equipment manager—there's no person in this stadium less inclined to give away baseballs than me."

The team got the baseballs they needed, just enough for someone to relieve Schmarzo and give up the game in the ninth, yielding a 4–3 IronBirds loss.

The team went on a road trip to Brooklyn, and Schmarzo gave up a single run in three innings of work on July 24, breaking his three-week streak of scoreless outings. He pitched well enough, though, to earn the save—his first save or win in three years of pro ball. He also got into an altercation during the game, a tiff that, to his surprise, did not result in an ejection. He came back from the road trip with a 1.89 ERA and the expectation that he'd be suspended for the fight. Instead, he was only slapped with a fifty-dollar fine from the New York–Penn League.

While the team was on the road, I dyed the crustache I'd been growing black. The guys told me it was the most disgusting thing they'd ever seen. I grew my sideburns as well, down to the bottoms of my earlobes, where they looked singed with an orange tint (the brown hair on my head naturally yields to ginger facial hair). I'd started dipping too. The brown flakes buzzing inside my bottom lip helped me stay focused during those long hours of late-night laundry.

By then, I'd started crashing in the clubhouse some nights just to catch a few extra hours of sleep. I'd blow up an air mattress in the equipment closet and pass out for the night rather than make the hour-long round trip to my apartment in White Marsh. Whenever I did sleep at home, though, seeing my roommate Kimmel's air mattress and little pile of clothes in the corner of my living room comforted me—it meant I wasn't all alone. I wished we could actually hang out—maybe have a drink together—but whenever I was at the apartment it meant that Kimmel and the team were on the road. So instead I'd grab a beer from our otherwise barren fridge and sit in my bedroom drinking by myself during road trips.

. . .

Schmarzo pitched one and a third innings of scoreless ball in a loss to the Vermont Lake Monsters on July 28. After the game, Muggsy called him into his office. Schmarzo was moving up to the Delmarva Shorebirds. Genuine excitement permeated the clubhouse. Sometimes when a player moved up, a few guys might say their goodbyes with a phony smile and an awkward hug, secretly thinking, "That should be me moving up." But Schmarzo was different. Guys whooped in his honor, embracing him as their friend and wishing him luck.

"It's probably just a temporary thing," he said. "If I had to guess, I'd say I'll be back before August first."

Schmarzo always said that his dream was to be the "player to be named later" in a trade between Major League teams. People would laugh when he said that, but we knew his real dream was getting called up from the IronBirds and eventually making the Majors. He got one step closer to his dream that night when he packed his things for Delmarva. There he would join the Shorebirds, the Orioles' low-A affiliate, where he would make $1,400 a month instead of $1,300.

He almost walked out the back of the clubhouse, right past the laundry room, without saying a thing to me, like he forgot that he wouldn't be back the next day.

"Schmarzo!" I said.

"Oh shit, G. I don't have any cash on me. I'll have to drop my dues at the front office before I leave tomorrow."

"No, not that." I grabbed his baseball card from the side of the dryer, where it'd been taped all season, and gave him a Sharpie out of my fanny pack.

His hand shook slightly as he signed the card.

"You know it was me who did the fake fan letter, right?"

"I figured," he said.

He handed me the card and we hugged before he pulled away and stopped for a moment. Silence. He held his palms up saying "I don't know what to do with my hands" and smiled that same smile I'd seen before. He didn't make any self-deprecating jokes about the baseball card being devalued now with his signature—thirty-five cents instead of forty.

"You won't get in trouble if I take this, will you?" He held up his white number thirteen jersey with his name on the back.

"No, probably not."

"If you do, just have Jason contact me. He has my number."

I wished I had the guts to tell him, "You're not a Major League pitcher, Alex." To tell him that getting closer to his dream might be the worst thing that ever happened to him. That he should get in his car, drive back to California, and wash himself clean of this whole baseball thing. But he wouldn't stop playing until someone told him he had to.

Alex walked out the door of the clubhouse and into the night behind Ripken Stadium. I took his signed card to the equipment closet, put it up in a safe spot, and stifled the coming tears.

The next day, I went up to the front office to drop off some outgoing envelopes from players and coaches returning fan mail.

"Some outgoing mail," I said to Ginger, the receptionist.

"Thank you. And Alex dropped this off before he left this morning." She pulled out an envelope. "It had one hundred dollars in it. Fifty for you. Fifty for his fine."

Schmarzo had already made the two-and-a-half-hour drive south on the Delmarva Peninsula to the decrepit Perdue Stadium, home of the Delmarva Shorebirds. He would be given the number thirty-seven and make his first appearance on August 2 against the Lakewood BlueClaws.

Schmarzo came in with the Shorebirds down 6–0 in the top of the eighth. He got three quick outs and came back to work the ninth. He gave up a leadoff double. Then a walk. Then a single. Then another single. All told, he gave up four runs and got yanked before recording a single out in the ninth inning. His ERA ballooned to 36.00 after that outing.

Less than two weeks later, Schmarzo pitched again. He got a groundout and two quick strikeouts to end the eighth inning. Once again, he came back in the top of the ninth and the wheels came off. He gave up a leadoff triple to right field and backed it up with a balk, a rookie mistake that scored the runner from third. The next batter singled to left, and two quick pop-outs followed. Another triple sailed out to center, scoring one more run. Schmarzo balked once more to make it two in the same inning, a rare embarrassment for a pitcher at any level. He then got a fly ball to end the inning.

Schmarzo would finish the season with a 6.14 ERA in Delmarva. Come December of that year, he would be back home in California. There he'd work as a children's baseball instructor to make ends meet in the off-season. He slept on a blow-up mattress in the equipment closet upstairs at the training facility (he couldn't afford a one-bedroom apartment where he lived, which would cost him about $1,400—same as his monthly salary had been in Delmarva). On December 23, he got word from the Orioles that he'd been released—Merry Christmas.

One of Schmarzo's friends, who had recently been released from the Colorado Rockies organization, approached him with an offer.

"I'm playing indie ball," his friend said, referring to independent, nonaffiliated baseball, "and you're coming with me."

Schmarzo said he'd think about it.

"Well, fuck," he thought, "I just spent the last four months training like I'll be back next year, I might as well go play a season." But Schmarzo would waffle on the decision, oscillating between bouts of angry motivation—"Fuck this, I'm gonna go play and prove the Orioles wrong"—and depression.

"Aw, screw it," he finally said. "I don't wanna play anymore."

Once next spring rolled around, Schmarzo watched his friends go off to spring training with their various teams while he was left at the facility, working on the pitching mechanics of little kids. Schmarzo ultimately decided that he'd join his friend in indie ball. Maybe he could actually have fun playing baseball for one last year before calling it a career.

Schmarzo spent the first half of his 2013 season pitching for the Alexandria Aces, fighting for his life to get signed by an affiliated team again. The Aces played in Alexandria, Louisiana, calling dilapidated Bringhurst Field their home. The eighty-year-old stadium had sections of the grandstand roped off by the fire chief of Alexandria as a condemned fire hazard (part of the stadium would eventually light on fire in 2014). Schmarzo put together a lackluster 2-2 record and 4.22 ERA before the team ran out of money and the league canceled the rest of the Aces' games. But just as the outfit folded, the Aces paid their bus company with a bad check, prompting their driver to abandon the team in the middle of a road game, leaving the players high and dry somewhere in Texas.

Schmarzo looked at the desert surrounding him and said, "You know what? I'm done playing baseball."

But another team in the league picked him up: the Edinburg Roadrunners. All of a sudden baseball was fun again—he didn't have anyone looking over his shoulder, he wasn't playing for anyone other than himself, and he stopped worrying about getting signed by an affiliated team or being released. He gave up all hope and, of course, in doing so, he became a great pitcher again. Schmarzo ended the second half of that 2013 season with a 0.60 ERA after moving to the Roadrunners. He wouldn't return to any professional team in 2014, 2015, or beyond. Instead, he would find that clubhouse camaraderie and those intense, pressure-filled situations in a different form.

The kid who went to Palo Alto High School, smack dab between the Stanford campus and Google headquarters, would move to the other side of the Bay Area. There, he would follow the necessary steps to become a police officer in Oakland, California, a city with one of the highest violent crime rates in America.

During his senior year of high school at Palo Alto, once he started throwing after rehabbing his injured elbow, Alex talked to a local newspaperman about his return to the mound.

"You're never going to be who you were before if you're afraid to go there again," Alex said. "So I just reared back and chucked it. There's still some discomfort, but it's holding up fine. You can't go anywhere in baseball without confidence."

9

The Dog Star

People often refer to those hottest days of summer as the dog days—when the throbbing heat is so oppressive that it hammers you down in pulsations. Burning waves of sun wash over you incessantly, to the brink of madness. They think those hot days are associated with dogs panting, or going outside themselves and gasping for air like a dog.

The real rationale for the phrase is this: Sirius, the Dog Star (the most prominent star in the Canis Major constellation), makes its first morning appearances in July and August, rising in tandem with the sun. Weeks later, it finally shines as the brightest star in the night sky. It just so happens that the Northern Hemisphere's most intense heat often coincides with those first morning rises of Sirius. But on those dog days in 2012 the IronBirds were not rising. Instead, they slid down the standings, without effort, into the cosmic nothingness of forgotten seasons from meaningless baseball teams. And nobody, it seemed, cared one way or the other.

• • •

Our hitting coach, Brad Komminsk, no longer whistled at me or called me Fido when we crossed paths, like he did after I told Mills I wasn't a dog. In fact, most mornings he ignored me, even when we were the only two people in the clubhouse. I passed him at his locker one August morning just a couple days before the All-Star break.

"Brad," I said, "How's it going?"

"Oh, I'm just doing great."

"Really?"

"What do you think?" he said.

He stared me down for a moment before walking out of the coaches' office. Taped up in his locker was a pocket schedule for the IronBirds. Most of the little squares had been x-ed out in black marker. I was sure he couldn't wait to come in from that night's game, mark that X on August 12, and take his two-day All-Star break to do whatever he pleased.

The first time I'd seen Brad's barrage of Xs I cringed at the open contempt for his time as an IronBird, but I eventually adopted the same habit. Now I carried an x-ed out, tattered pocket calendar of my own in my fanny pack. Each X served as a reminder that I was one day closer to—well, what exactly?

Nicole had found us a rental home in a small town called North Augusta, South Carolina. The house sat just across the Savannah River from her hometown, Augusta, Georgia, and it was a forty-five-minute drive from the school where she'd be teaching. Rent would only be $700, and when I considered that we'd split that major expense, plus utilities, groceries, and so forth, I could potentially last the entire off-season with just the cash I made over the summer. I wouldn't finish in Jake Parker territory, around $19,000, but it looked like I'd be somewhere north of $10,000.

Then I could use my time in the off-season to—again, I wasn't quite sure what. It would be a relief to finally live with Nicole after being long distance for more than a year since I'd graduated college. I knew the novelty of living together might wear off at some point (every couple I'd ever seen, even those deeply in love, grew familiar with one another in time), but I wanted to get to that illusory state of honeymoon bliss as fast as possible. Marking days off the calendar reminded me how much closer I was getting to whatever came after the baseball season ending in just a few short weeks.

I walked out of the coaches' office and saw Kimmel at his locker. Kimmel was one of four IronBirds to make the All-Star team. (The All-Star Game seemed like an odd endeavor at that level—the players had to be good enough to be chosen to represent the team, but not good enough to be moved up in the organization. Kimmel, for example, had a solid .286 batting average but struggled behind the plate as a catcher—on August 7, he allowed eight stolen bases and allowed his eleventh passed ball of the season.) I congratulated him on his selection.

"Thanks," he said with sleepy brown eyes and a smile. "I kinda wish I didn't, just so I could get the days off."

"I don't blame you."

"And I meant to tell you," he said. "I found a host family."

"Just for the few weeks we have left?"

"That drive to White Marsh was brutal. I don't know how you make it every day."

"Really? I like the drive. It's a chance to unwind."

"Sorry," he said. "Just let me know when the electric bill comes in and I'll get you the money."

"Will do. And nothing to be sorry for."

"But I'm sure it was nice having other people in there. I don't know, just for comfort of mind or whatever."

I shrugged. "It's all the same to me."

At one point we had five of us in the apartment (including Nicole during her visit). Not once did anyone use the second bedroom— there would only be little nests in different corners of the living room. Now it would just be me.

• • •

That day's game went by quickly, which afforded me a rare treat: getting home while the sun was still up. Kimmel had already moved his stuff out of the apartment; there was no evidence to suggest that he'd ever been there at all. I opened the fridge, nearly empty except for a few sad inches of milk, a browning head of lettuce, a half loaf of bread, and a container of lunch meat I bought in June. I set down a nice stash of Budweiser from John, the beer supplier for the stadium that Jake put me in contact with. I'd just loaded him up with some signed baseballs, some bats, and a few caps from visiting teams. In return, he gave me three cases of Bud Heavy for Trek, some Fat Tire and Sam Adams for Muggsy, and a few extra cases for me. I shoved the lonely food items to the side and placed Budweiser cans in rows on the refrigerator shelf.

I sat in my little bedroom and drank alone that All-Star break. When I got tired of drinking, I took a can of Grizzly Wintergreen chewing tobacco and snapped it between my thumb and middle finger, popping my loose index finger against the top. I learned this trick from the players: it packed the contents into a nice pinchable pile on one side of the can. Then you could pull out a compact wad of finely shaved tobacco and nestle it against the vulnerable wet tissue of your gums. When I first started dipping, I only did it in secret, when the players and coaches had all left for the day. I didn't want them thinking I was trying to impress them; I could tell myself I needed the nicotine to help me focus on my menial tasks. I'd spit light brown juice into an empty Powerade bottle while I scrubbed jerseys and pants.

I bought my first can during a tobacco run for the players. I opened it up and took a pinch the size of my index fingernail. The wave of electricity washed through me almost instantly. Then that tingle surged up into my head and knocked me woozy. The first time that happened, I had to take it out before I got sick. Once I'd gone through that first can, I went out and bought another, which I was still working through during the All-Star break.

I threw an empty beer into the wastebasket in my bedroom, sounding an aluminum clink against the stack of empties already piling high. The sun had set now. I placed a wad of Grizz Green big enough to bulge my lower lip and reached back to the garbage to fumble for an empty. I spit dark brown juice through the mouth hole at the top. I'd planned on making a trip to Baltimore—maybe walk along the Inner Harbor or go to the library—but I was much more content to sit alone in my apartment on that rare off day, buzzing in nothingness.

• • •

It was August 30 now, two weeks after the All-Star Game. Kimmel's fly ball to right sailed over the Ripken Stadium fence for his second home run of the season and a 1–0 lead over the Staten Island Yankees. The IronBirds went on to win the game, which broke an eight-game losing streak. The celebration in the clubhouse—high fives, smiles, music—was nothing if not completely sarcastic, the players' happiness dripping with irony. Of course guys were always competing for their jobs and trying to advance personally, but it was almost as though this winning team effort was spawned in some idle afternoon poker conversation: "Dude, how ridiculous would it be if we actually won a game tonight." And the pitchers, all with cards in their hands, had looked at each other, shrugged, and said, "Yeah, why not. That might be kinda funny."

There was no champagne, no jumping up and down in celebration, no tarps on the lockers, or beer dripping from the ceiling tiles—just dirty pants and jerseys. I stood there in the laundry room, with the mechanical whir of washers and dryers behind me, scrubbing dirt stains out of the white home pants for the 26-44 Aberdeen IronBirds.

Sometimes die-hard young fans and potbellied eBay poachers would stand out behind the clubhouse waiting for autographs after games. They could watch me scrubbing pants from the darkness outside my laundry-room window. But from the fluorescent light of the laundry room, I saw nobody. I went about my business, pretending that they wouldn't care to watch me, though I was the closest thing to entertainment they had while they waited for their favorite players.

But sometimes, in the a.m. hours—long after the stadium lights had cut off, those autograph seekers had gone, and I was the last person in Ripken Stadium—I randomly looked up from my laundry. I pretended to gaze through the window into the thick trees and bushes between me and I-95, just in case there was another human out there—on the off chance that something existed outside of that little clubhouse. But I'd see nothing but the blurred image of my laundry room reflected back to me.

That night I accidentally caught my own gaze in the window, my color dulled. My hands were clad in pale blue surgical gloves, one holding a pair of dirty pants, the other holding a plastic-bristled brush. The blue stretch-fit cap that I'd worn all season had absorbed every bit of that summer's sweat and unshowered grime—I could almost see the stink emanating from it like Pigpen's cloud. A Powerade bottle sat on my scrubbing table with brown-flecked spit at the bottom. My narrow mustache (trimmed to the corner of the lips, according to team rules) looked absurd: the black dye was wearing off, no longer hiding its patchiness. My neck had thinned—same with my arms. I looked wiry but strong, an effect of never eating enough coupled with hours of low-level physical exertion. My skin, in the reflection, looked sallow, my eyes adorned with bags.

I had to wonder what unique set of circumstances led me to that moment. Not just to the point of having a demeaning job—that I could handle (most of my college friends were still struggling to find good-paying work)—but how was it that baseball of all things had brought me here? If I was working for a hotel doing laundry and scrubbing toilets, I could at least take consolation in the fact that I never grew up wanting to be a hotel manager. I could easily throw my hatred at my bosses, my coworkers—the whole goddamn concept of hotels for all I'd care. But this was baseball. How could I grow to resent baseball?

It felt like finding out your first girlfriend never cared about you, but she didn't mention it until years later, casually dropping it in a catch-up conversation. "You know, it's kind of funny: I never actually loved you." And then you blink and you're rumbling a utility tractor through the sticky darkness behind Ripken Stadium, bumping along on the gravel access road. The headlights cut the night in a cone as you shuttle a load of pants to the extra washer in the visiting clubhouse. You feel the wind drying the beaded sweat on your forehead.

You realize that the sleeping stadium is more beautiful at night, with the unshakable quietus rooting it to the earth. It rests like a graveyard—empty but throbbing all at once. With the pollution of light extinguished, maybe you even see the Dog Star blinking back at you, its appearance consistent in the late summer sky, if impermanent. But compared to mere mortals like you, Sirius is beyond time. And its inevitable return, like baseball after the winter, dares you to come back to the stadium when it rises the next summer.

"I will return next year," the Dog Star says. "Will you?"

But it's just a trick of the eyes—Sirius won't be visible in the night sky for weeks. You've made the same mistake so many of us have: you've taken a smaller star to be something much bigger and closer than it really is.

10

Nightshade

Days during the baseball season don't start with M, T, W, F, or S. They only start with G or O: game day or off day. Some days I'd walk past the restaurants and shops along Baltimore's Inner Harbor or drive around White Marsh and see ghost towns. "Damn," I'd think, "it's an off day—why isn't anyone out and about?" Then I'd remember it was 11:00 a.m. on a Tuesday or some such thing and not everyone in the universe worked on Aberdeen IronBirds time. But pretty soon all of the days would begin with an O: off-season. I was on the fence about whether or not I'd come back the next year—I'd have to see how the job hunt went in North Augusta before I made any decisions.

Prior to the end of the season, my dad, Rick, came up to visit from Florida. My parents' condo in Fort Myers, where I lived for a year after finishing college in 2011, was a long way from where my family grew up in Minnesota. I'd seen pictures of my dad when he was young. We could've been brothers. We had the same blue eyes, the same lanky frame—hell, even the same earlobes too: kind of perky, flaring out to a little point. And we shared the same love for baseball. He was a stud for the Elk River baseball team in high school. I, too, wanted to be a stud ballplayer.

Just northwest of our affluent, rural neighborhood on the outskirts of town were two dusty baseball diamonds, nestled in between cornfields. Some days during the whitewashed winter months of high school, I'd take the long way home just to pass those ball fields. They blended in with the rest of the landscape in January—for all I knew there could've been frozen cornstalks beneath the snow on the other side of those chain-linked fences. But when winter melted and those cornfields sprouted back to life, my dad stood in the dust-spitting wind hitting me ground balls.

He had two rules when it came to us playing ball: he would never say no to a round of grounders if he was physically able, and he would hit to me for as long as he could. Not once in those days of junior high and high school did I ever say stop—I just set up camp at shortstop and gobbled grounders for as long as Dad would hit them. For a starry-eyed kid who had dreams of playing in the Major Leagues, I forced myself to see it as training: *I need to out-work all those kids down south if I'm ever gonna catch up.*

Baseball wasn't just work, though—it was fun for me. There was no single thing in the universe that could compare to diving for a ground ball, catching it, and standing up to toss it back to my dad. Even when I got so mad at a botched play that I'd throw the ball over the fence or attempt to rip my glove in half, my dad would just stand there and let it happen, never scolding or threatening me. Not because he was soft but because he knew how my brain worked. He knew that I would mentally discipline myself and that would do the work for both of us. He stood at home plate, leaning against his bat as I jogged, head down, to the ball I'd chucked over the fence. I picked it up, tossed it over the fence back to him, and assumed my post at shortstop for more. We'd go for hours at a time, over and over until the repetition had lulled me, trance-like, into a false confidence. "I'm gonna be a fucking pro," I'd think. "This is what I'm born to do."

I told him I had dreams of being a Major Leaguer—he knew that about me. But Dad was a baseball guy growing up. He must've known that I had a snowball's chance in hell to make a nickel playing baseball. But he let me chase that dream—in fact, aided me heavily in the pursuit—without reservation.

When I was cut from the Hamline baseball team during my freshman year of college, before I ever stepped foot onto their home field or wore a jersey, I drove the forty minutes north from campus to my childhood home near those dusty baseball fields. I didn't take the long way past the diamonds but went on a direct path from my dorm to our living room in Elk River. Mom and Dad consoled me about being cut from the team. I told them I'd be fine, and they nodded. When they were in the kitchen, I saw my dad's open laptop on the coffee table. He had an article pulled up titled "How to Help Your Child Cope with the Loss of a Loved One."

By 2012 that loved one had returned in the strange form of me being a clubbie for the IronBirds. Dad, wanting to again share this part of my life with me, visited near the end of the season while the IronBirds were on the road. (Since the Birds were out of town, the only baseball we saw was a Nationals game up in DC.)

He could only laugh when he entered my apartment for the first time.

"Not much for furniture," he said.

"No, but I got you set up over here."

I pointed over to a blow-up mattress, the same one Kimmel had used. Dad slept in that little corner near the back sliding door to the tiny patio. I'd thrown out all my empty beer cans before he arrived and refrained from dipping tobacco (except in the shower). And my dad, the sixty-two-year-old, slept like a Minor Leaguer for a few nights.

"Have you gotten any time on the field?" he asked one day.

"Not really," I said.

When he left town he gave me a hug, then pulled away and said, "You just gotta get out there and try to throw the ball around before you leave. Otherwise you're inside washing towels and cleaning up after people. You might as well be working in a hotel."

• • •

On the night of September 1, the Hudson Valley Renegades blanked the IronBirds, 2–0, to win the McNamara Division title. The Renegades bounced and sprayed each other with champagne in Ripken Stadium's left field as the Saturday night fireworks display burst above them in the night sky.

The next day was the IronBirds' last home game. I came in early and only Komminsk and Cesar were in the coaches' office. Cesar sat there watching his little television. Brad's calendar was almost all x-ed out.

Komminsk handed me a hundred-dollar bill. "Got any change?" he said. Dues for that last seven-game marathon home stand were forty-two dollars.

"No," I said, reaching up to hand the bill back.

He thought about it for a second then waved his hand in defeat. "Keep it," he said. "Consider it an end of the year tip."

I could see him roll his eyes at Cesar, who smiled with his mouthful of breakfast sandwich, and went back to watching his TV.

As the day progressed, the clubhouse packed with extra players who'd come up from the Gulf Coast League in Florida. Jake made the trip as well, performing an end-of-the-season inventory on all the Orioles' affiliates. He still looked beefy, strong, but maybe a little smaller than when I'd seen him last. Perhaps even Jake Parker was susceptible to midseason clubbie weight loss.

"Look at that thing," Jake said, referring to my crustache. "Did you lose a bet?"

"Yeah right. More like I won a bet."

"I don't think so. Anyway, you think you could show me around?"

He led me to the equipment room. He inspected the floor and shelves full of gear.

"How often do you sweep in here?" he said.

I looked down at the little chunks of tuna flake, dirt, and rosin dust on the ground. "I don't know. I'd say once a home stand."

"How often do you clean the urinals and the toilets?"

"About the same."

"Hmm. And what's the food situation been? Are you getting the spread from VIP?"

"Yeah, I tip 'em a few bucks and—"

"How much?"

"Usually ten bucks, then I take their leftovers and feed the team."

Silence. "How do you think you did this season?"

"On a scale of one to ten?" I said.

"Sure."

"I'd say an eight and a half. I'm pleased with it, you know, but I could've done a little better."

"Interesting," he said. Silence. "These guys talk to me, your staff—they tell me what's good, what isn't. The players too. One example, I heard about your bat fiasco with Rivera."

"*My* bat fiasco?"

"It happened in *your* clubhouse, right? Then it's your responsibility." Silence again. "Here, come with me." He led us to the locker room and grabbed a few players. He asked them, "What exactly happened with that bat attack in July?"

The guys told the story.

When they finished, Jake shook his head and said, "If your clubbie had any balls, he would've done something about the Dominicans."

"I took Rivera's bats," I said.

"So what? These guys don't care about bats." He turned back to the players. "If he'd come in here and said 'no more music' you guys would've given him a fucking round of applause, wouldn't you?"

They nodded. "Yeah, dude. That shit was kinda ridiculous."

"Tips probably would've gone up too," Jake said.

They nodded again and Jake excused them.

"Everything that happens in this clubhouse is your responsibility. Don't forget that. I know how much free time you have in this job because, remember, I used to be right where you are. This job isn't that tough, man. When I came in here, I went into the coaches' office to take a leak and I almost threw up. All that hair and dried urine—it was fucking disgusting. You have gloves, right? Put on some gloves, squirt the urinal, wipe it down, and you're done. I mean—well, let's go look."

He clubbie-walked us, fast and purposeful, to the coaches' office.

"Look at that," he said, pointing to the urinal. "Does that look professional to you?"

There were dark yellow stains on the rim and little curly pubes, like earthworms after the rain.

"No," I said.

"No. This bathroom is dirty. That equipment room is a mess with food all over the ground—I'm honestly worried about mice getting in there. You look like shit. The fanny pack is—well, that's your call. But that mustache, the tattered shorts?" He shook his head. "Guys said the spreads started off pretty good but took a turn downward as the season went. Nothing you can do about that if you're getting leftovers. Look, I'm glad you stuck to your guns with Mills on the baseballs—that was good. But overall? Subpar, my friend, subpar."

I wanted so badly not to care what he thought. Jake wasn't even my boss and we technically didn't even work for the same company, but his words hung heavy in the bottom of my stomach.

Later in the day, when Jake was out doing his own thing, I went back to that urinal in the coaches' bathroom and scrubbed it down. Muggsy and Mills were talking near their lockers so I tried to sneak in and out without them noticing me.

"Hey, meat," Mills said as I walked out. "We need baseballs. These pitchers need to throw in the off-season and they need baseballs to do it."

"I'll have to ask Jake," I said.

"I'm not asking Jake, I'm asking you. Is this Jake's clubhouse?"

"No."

"No. It's your clubhouse. You're in charge of this place, and I'm asking you for baseballs."

"And I'm telling you I don't know."

"Look, slick," Muggsy said, "these guys need to throw in the off-season. These Latin guys—you think they have baseballs to throw with?"

Whenever I put new pearls in the BP basket, they always disappeared at astronomical rates. Then later in the day I'd see balls sitting on the top shelves of guys' lockers and I'd be tempted to take them back. But I never knew if they were a first strikeout or a milestone home run ball. "So, yeah," I thought, "they probably did have some balls to throw with."

Mills cut me off before I could answer. "And good ones too," he said. "Not those scuffed up ones."

Muggsy made that little click in the back of his sinuses before spitting into a cup. "Really it's no fuckin' wonder we walked so many batters this year: these guys were warming up with oranges all season. They get in the game and don't know what the ball's gonna do."

It was probably my fault, too, that we were 26-46. If Jake weren't there to do inventory I would've told them to take every baseball they wanted—take every fucking baseball in the universe and tell Cal Ripken Jr. to fire my ass for all I cared. "Give me an excuse," I thought, "to never come back here again."

"Yes," I said. "You can have baseballs."

That night, the IronBirds were already down by five runs going into the bottom of the first inning. I watched from the bullpen. I wasn't worried about washing the dishes or doing the BP laundry or anything of the sort: it was the last home game—I'd get it done eventually.

At the top of every inning, someone from the bullpen had to grab two baseballs and open up the padded door next to the right-field foul pole. That player would throw one ball to the center fielder, trying to drop it onto him like a quarterback's throw to a crossing wide receiver, then the player from the bullpen would use another baseball to play catch with the right fielder.

"Here," one of the pitchers said, handing two baseballs to another guy in the bullpen. "You warm him up."

"I did it last inning," the guy said. He scooted away from the baseballs sitting on the bench. Everyone else moved away from them too, like they were live grenades. The right fielder stood there, waiting.

"I'm not doing it. I've already warmed him up twice."

"Someone fucking warm him up!"

"Damn it," someone said. He grabbed the balls and quickly hopped out the door.

Normally any miniscule job—anything to pass time—was coveted on the bench or in the bullpen. But not during the last week of the year.

"I see you guys fighting over warming up the right fielder," I said, "but what I wouldn't give to throw on that field right now."

"Do it," they said.

The Orioles' general manager, Dan Duquette, was in the crowd that night—somewhere behind home plate or in the VIP level sitting with Jake Parker and other Orioles executives. If they found out that the IronBirds' clubbie warmed up the right fielder, they'd find a way to get me fired. All it would take was a conversation with my boss, Jason, and I'd be gone.

Another inning passed and the guys bitched again. Someone else gave in this time and warmed up the right fielder. When he came back to the bullpen, we all sat in quiet, watching the game.

"Okay," I said. "Fuck it. I'm doing it."

I ran toward the clubhouse.

"Hell yeah, G!" someone yelled.

I scrambled through the extra jerseys and pants in the equipment closet. The team was wearing their alternates that game: the cobalt blue with a silver cursive "Aberdeen" across the chest. The only one that fit was a number twenty-five jersey leftover from Jason McCracken, a pitcher who moved up to Delmarva in mid-August. I pulled on a pair of pants: thirty-six-inch waist with the elastic still in so I could wear my socks to my knees, just like I did when I used to play.

Usually, I only wore my blue batting practice cap, so I had to scramble to find a black game cap, seven and three-eighths. I grabbed my mitt, stiff from lack of use, and walked out to the bullpen, feigning indifference.

The guys all laughed.

"That's hilarious," someone said. "What jersey are you wearing?"

I turned around to show them the twenty-five.

"Oh shit, it's McCracken," someone else said.

"Duquette's gonna be up there like, 'I thought we moved McCracken up to Delmarva?'" one guy said.

We all laughed.

I tried very hard to stifle the twitching smile on my face. The bullpen catcher took the baseballs and dropped them into my outstretched mitt and we sat down, waiting for our half of the inning to end. There were a few awkward minutes when we actively rooted against the IronBirds so I could get out on the field.

With two outs, the IronBirds hit a weak grounder to the right side.

"There it is!" someone said.

The second baseman threw over to first for the final out of the inning. Someone opened the padded door and slapped my ass. The bullpen shouted encouragement as I reached my spot: straddling the right-field foul line—not quite on the field, but not quite off it either.

The stadium lights blasted at full power in the twilight, and I was delighted that nobody in the crowd seemed to notice or care that I existed. The center fielder ran straight from the dugout toward his position. Quarterbacking him the ball would be the most difficult throw I'd make. My arms shook as I tossed the ball high out in front of him, but I didn't lead him well enough, so he had to stop and wait for the lob in short center field.

The right fielder jogged to his spot. He squinted toward me, leaning his head in to get a better look.

"G?" he said with a chuckle.

I was amazed at how easily I could hear him. The madness all around us was concentrated at a higher altitude—the fans cheering, the music, the PA announcer thanking local sponsors—so I guess it made sense.

When he realized it was me, the right fielder inched a little closer.

Didn't he think I could make a throw? I compensated by whipping the ball as hard as I could. My first few sailed high, but he made his reaches skyward seem effortless. Behind him sat an expanse of green the likes of which were more terrifying than any ocean. What dangers existed beyond right field if I threw the ball past him? No longer would I be the unseen reliever warming up his teammate, I would become a question to the fans: "Who's that bullpen pitcher who just overthrew the right fielder?" They'd look in the program for number twenty-five, probably expecting to see something like six foot, 160 pounds listed next to it. They'd find nothing, discovering that I did not exist.

But I kept the throws within reach of the right fielder, if a little sporadic. Trek walked along the warning track behind me on a trip between the dugout and the clubhouse. He did a double take.

"Are you fucking kidding me, Greg?"

"Someone had to do it," I said before throwing again.

He stood behind me and watched for a moment. He may have been considering whether or not I actually had a decent arm or whether or not he cared. He probably figured it was the last home game of the season and he was far removed from a time when he gave a shit.

The right fielder gave me a discreet thumbs-up, letting me know he was good. I threw the ball back. He gave me another thumbs-up. I threw the ball back again because I hadn't touched grass all summer—because I'd forgotten how much I missed it until I put on that jersey.

"I'm good!" he said.

The center fielder gave me the international sign for *I'm about to throw you this baseball*: a little shake of the ball near his release point. I gave him a little clap of my glove, chest high—the international sign that I was ready.

The throw got to me on a hop, which I did not catch. I picked it up and ran back to the bullpen. The music had died. The PA announcer sat in silence. The only prominent sound in the stadium, over the constant low mumble of idle bleacher chatter, was the clapping of the bullpen, all on their feet. They opened the gate and I was greeted with high fives. No doubt part of their joy was that I did something they didn't want to do, but maybe they knew how much it meant for me.

"That," I said, "made washing your jockstraps worth it. That might have been the highlight of the season."

A few guys laughed.

"That might be my highlight for the season too," they said.

I called my parents to tell them all about it.

"How did your arm feel?" my dad asked. "You haven't thrown any in awhile."

"It felt fine," I lied.

"Did the guys in the bullpen say anything?" my mom said. "Like good job, or nice arm, or any of that."

My dad laughed. "We're asking him questions like he was pitching in the World Series." He stopped. "But maybe that's how it felt."

"Yeah, I guess. Nobody really gave a shit. The bullpen guys who sort of goaded me into it didn't seem to think twice about it."

Even that was a lie. I only *hoped* no one cared about me warming up the right fielder—or anything else I could ever do on a ball field—because it would only amount to one atomic particle of the baseball universe I'd dreamed of as a child. Because that kid taking ground balls with his dad in central Minnesota would've looked at the man he'd become and said, "I thought you'd be a star." Still, it did feel pretty damn good to get on a ball field again.

• • •

The team came back from their final road trip to Vermont having won two out of three. The IronBirds finished the 2012 season with a 28-48 record. The guys filtered in and out of the clubhouse, packing up to depart for the off-season.

Muggsy was the last one out the door besides me. His hair looked freshly shorn—high and tight—hopefully in preparation for off-season job interviews. At the last moment, as he passed me in the locker room, he looked me dead in the eyes, slapped me on the shoulder, and said, "Good luck, slick," before making a little click in the back of his sinuses.

And just like that the place was empty, devoid of all meaning—as though the season had never really happened. I walked through the clubhouse to see if anybody had left any goodies. The only treasures were in Muggsy's little fridge: a few tall cans of Olde English 800 malt liquor, two forty-ounce bottles of Colt 45 malt liquor, and a few Fat Tires.

I went upstairs to the front office for one last inspection of my mail slot—one check from the gift shop for broken bat sales (which I supplied from our players and took a cut of) and one invoice from food services. My heart sank. I'd had a suspicion that Barkley dude, the head of food services, would try to squeeze me at the end of the season. He never stuck to his original promise that he'd prepare a menu every home stand.

The last time I saw him I was wheeling down a smorgasbord from the VIP level. The leftovers that night happened to be more than enough to feed the team. I bobbed and weaved the food cart between fans walking on the concourse when Barkley saw me. He made eye contact and smiled like, "Gotcha, bitch."

Did he think I was living high off the hog with food? Every night in the top of the seventh inning, when I walked past that frail little lady who stood as the bouncer to the VIP level, I'd ask myself, "Am I gonna get enough food to feed the team?" I hated collecting guys' dues after a home stand when we had shit postgame meals or ran out of food altogether.

On that staircase up to the VIP level was a bit of gray mortar or caulking leftover on the brick wall—it must have held some sign in the stadium's earlier days. It looked like a demented, melting smiley face. I'd always see it on the worst part of my nights—the moment before I'd discover whether I had enough food—but it reminded me to smile no matter how fucked up things got. "I mean look at that guy," I'd think. "Here he is melting to death and he's still smiling."

I skimmed the invoice and saw the figure at the bottom: $1,338.75. That number represented something like 10 percent of what I'd earned that summer. I continued reading. All of the prices were multiplied for forty-five players, which was way too many. And some dates on the invoice didn't make sense—a few of those nights we didn't get enough food.

I called Jake and told him the situation.

"Oh, I live for this shit," he said. "Look, just keep your composure, breathe. I know you're pissed off right now and I don't blame you, but all you have to do is go in there and point out the discrepancies between your figures and his figures. I'd say come in with a counter number in mind—you don't wanna get caught with your pants around your ankles. Don't insult the man for God's sake, but you do have to protect yourself. These food services people, they're always trying to fuck over clubbies—no matter where you go. Ugh, I miss this shit. Okay, sound good? Give me a call and let me know how it goes."

I found two more dates when we didn't get enough food listed on the invoice. I texted Jake.

"Lowball this guy," he texted back.

I clubbie-walked up to Barkley's office behind the first base concessions. He wasn't there. I walked over to his cluttered desk and saw a bill from his food provider: he had an outstanding balance of more than $9,000. I came back later and he was standing outside his office talking to the GM.

"Barkley," I said. "Do you have a minute?"

He said to the GM, "I'll come up to your office in a few minutes. I gotta handle this." He turned to me with a fake smile. "What's going on?"

"I have a few questions about this invoice."

"Go for it," he said, crossing his arms.

"I was just wondering how you got these dates." The invoice shook in my hand.

"Those are the nights that we prepared food in-house instead of getting catered out."

"So those are the nights that we got leftovers from food cooked here?"

"Yes."

"Okay. Because I was just wondering why I was being charged for leftovers when at the beginning of the season you said we wouldn't be charged for that."

"Those are still expenses for us. That's still an expense."

"How? We're eating leftovers. The food is going to waste anyway. Not to mention we often wouldn't get enough for the guys. I know for a fact that nobody prepared extra food for us."

"Really?"

"Yeah. Just off the top of my head, August 31 I went up to VIP and was told they didn't have anything for us."

"So how did you get food?"

"I had to scrounge up leftover hamburgers and hot dogs from concessions."

"See. That's still an expense."

"No it's not. The kids working in the kitchen always told me those leftovers would be in the garbage if we didn't take them. And if that's an expense then why wouldn't you charge us for it every night?"

He stopped for a moment. "So what do you think you should be charged?"

I pulled out a receipt I'd printed off.

"Well, first off, I'd say we had closer to forty guys most of the season, and even that's a liberal estimate. Doing the math, forty players gives us $420."

"Four hundred and twenty bucks? For the whole year?"

I nodded.

"Whatever. I'll rerun the invoice and get it back to you." He walked away. "Four hundred and twenty bucks for the whole year?"

"For leftovers!" I yelled back as he closed his office door.

He never gave me another invoice, but I put a check for $420 in his mail slot before I left town.

• • •

A few days before, when I had told my parents about warming up the right fielder, my mom had asked me one more question before ending the phone conversation.

"How did you do this season?" she said.

"Depends on who you ask."

"Well, were you as vocal and positive as when you played ball in high school? Were you getting guys going in the dugout, cheering, and keeping a chatter going?"

"It's not really like that," I said.

I didn't know how else to explain it. I didn't know how to say that nobody really gave a shit on some level, and, at the same time, how everybody cared about it more than anything else. I couldn't tell her that on the last day in the clubhouse some guys would walk around giving a few hugs goodbye, and some guys would leave as soon as they possibly could. That Mills would have a big smile on his face, saying, "Alright, cocksuckers. Y'all can go back to choosing your friends." That guys would never tell me "See you next season" or "I'll be back next summer," because what would that mean if they were back in Aberdeen next year? What would that say about their career? And even so, I sure as hell wasn't coming back to Ripken Stadium.

I cut off the lights for the clubhouse, my apartment, the season— all of it. I threw my deflated air mattress and Minnesota Twins blanket into the back seat of my gold Caddie.

Before I hopped onto I-95 and skipped town, I bought a can of Grizzly Wintergreen for the road. The Caddie glimmered in the clear fall sunshine—me in the driver's seat, blue IronBirds cap on my head—all the way down to South Carolina, leaving Aberdeen forever behind us.

PART 2

11

Aphelion

I didn't know it was the off-season yet; here I thought I'd simply entered life after my one season working for the Birds. But it turned out that life only mattered inasmuch as it could be sectioned off on baseball's terms.

I shaved off the crusty, black mustache before long, once Nicole decided to stop kissing me if I kept the thing. The fanny pack came off too. Wearing it as a clubbie seemed quirky, funny even, but keeping it on as an unemployed kid going to get groceries was just plain sad. I found myself at a unique time in my life: I didn't have a job, but I had some money and almost no financial responsibilities. What did I do with this newfound freedom? I played video games. I sat on the computer. I went right back to that listless place I'd sunk into after graduating college. I'd taken Muggsy's leftover Olde English 800s and Colt 45s when I packed up the clubhouse. I obliterated those within the first week, but I continued to hit the bottle every night. What did it matter if I slept in? Where did I have to go other than our living room couch to watch *Judge Judy*?

Nicole had picked a great home for us. It was well shaded on a quiet street just off downtown North Augusta. The small backyard would need to be mowed. The gutters required cleaning. We would share the only bedroom, I'd get the adjacent den as an office, and she would use the windowed parlor on the other side of the house as a music room. We were in the perfect position for domestic paradise. But before long, that brick, one-story rambler became another place I needed to escape.

Before working for the IronBirds, I used to eat turkey sandwiches and fruit every day for lunch, but now I couldn't cut a watermelon without being brought back to those stressful afternoons in the clubhouse. I'd have to remind myself that I was in no rush—I didn't have to cut the melon in quick, efficient cubes, and I wasn't depriving anyone else of the spread if I took an extra slice of turkey. I tried to laugh off the anxiety, but it was very real.

Nicole's schedule of teaching high school English and coaching volleyball kept her busy. I only puttered around all day, so before long I was in charge of the housekeeping. Nicole didn't mind clutter. If I weren't there, she'd be happy to let her clothes pile up on the bedroom floor or stack unwashed dishes in the sink. Despite Jake's admonishment of my clubhouse cleanliness, a cluttered living space bothered me. So, for the most part, I swept, vacuumed, did the laundry, washed the dishes, and cleaned the bathroom. I tried to express to her how this felt: I wanted nothing more than to come home from the season and not have to clean up after people anymore. She said she thought I'd been doing it out of the kindness of my heart, not obligation. She thought I knew that she needed my help around the house because she was so busy. She pointed out that even I let my fast food wrappers build up in the den sometimes, so maybe I wasn't as perfect as I seemed to think. I agreed. She worked and I was jobless; the least I could do was clean up.

She came home early one fall afternoon. Usually she was out until the evening doing after-school activities, so I didn't expect her anytime during the light of day. When I heard the metallic grind of her key in the lock I felt like a teenager about to get caught masturbating. I'd told her I was spending my days applying for jobs, but instead I sat on the thrift store couch in the den surrounded by fast food wrappers, the TV blaring.

She walked in. Her soft cheeks were cut at the top with bags under her eyes. Her hair was frayed, pulled back and clipped in an unshowered black cascade down her shoulders—it'd been more than a year since her hair had been her natural blond. I couldn't remember the last time I'd seen her smile. She stopped smiling when I found her old diary one September afternoon and read it out of morbid curiosity, hoping to gain insight into this person who I loved more than anyone, but who I still couldn't seem to connect with deeply. She was understandably still upset about it.

During the season, when things got hot, I'd say to myself, "Come October you'll pray for a six-game home stand." And it was true. If not for the money, then for the simple fact that a six-game home stand would give me something to do.

My dad called me up in late October. He said that their neighbor Bob, whose cataracts required me to be his Seeing Eye dog when we golfed together in Florida, asked my dad for an update on me.

Dad said, "I told him from the best I can tell he's still licking his wounds after a summer of sleeping on the floor and working sixteen-hour days." He laughed.

I forced a laugh too. "I don't know what the hell I'm doing."

By November I actually started sending resumes to Craigslist job postings. I got two interviews: one for a liquor store and one for a Sports Authority. The Sports Authority in town needed a seasonal worker for the holidays. The manager only gave me one prompt in the interview: "Tell me about yourself." I told her that I loved sports, especially baseball, and I had worked as an equipment manager for the Orioles. She seemed only tangentially interested and did not ask me to elaborate.

"Okay, great," she said when I'd finished. "This will be your compensation." She wrote something on a piece of paper and slid it over to me. It was a number eight with a circle around it.

"I'll have to think about it," I said.

The liquor store offered me $8.50 an hour, so I took it, not necessarily for the money—I was still doing fine financially—but because I needed an excuse to shave and leave the house on a regular basis. The job didn't help anything though. The house was still a mess and the cold of winter had started to seep in through the cracks between the brick and mortar. I decided that we wouldn't spend money turning on the home's gas heater and instead chose to survive the winter with only a space heater in the bedroom.

"How do you think it's going," I said one evening as we sat on the couch in sweatshirts and stocking caps, "us living together?"

"That's a loaded question," Nicole said.

"Well, it's not like we have sex or—you don't even let me touch you or anything."

She chewed her tongue for a while before answering. "I've seen you become someone you didn't used to be. There was this motivated, confident guy in college that you haven't been for so long. I'm just disappointed. I'm disappointed that you've done so little to find a job. Do you know how much it hurt to hear you say that you were looking for jobs and then see you start looking under the Craigslist listings for 'Gigs'? What little work you did put in got you a retail job. The worst part is that I know you taking it is the right thing to do. But I'm so frustrated it's gotten to the point that I would think that's the right decision. That I'm with a guy who has a job working at the liquor store." Her movements had become hard and angular. She could barely even look at me through her tear-swollen eyes. "I haven't talked to my old friends, even though I've wanted to, because I didn't want to hear the same advice I would've given them back in college: 'You're better than this. You have to set a limit, a timeline, and if things don't change, then you have to get out.'"

I stared off for a few moments, unsure how to respond. Finally, I said, "I appreciate that—that all makes sense." I forced a laugh. "And, you know, I wouldn't wanna have sex with that guy either."

She looked so beautiful in that moment—dark shadow emphasized her watering fierce green eyes. She said, "We have had this conversation before. You said you appreciated it then and nothing changed. Just do something about it. Please. Because I don't know what the next conversation will be. I really don't."

I spent that night drinking alone in my den while she slept in the bedroom.

$$\bullet \ \bullet \ \bullet$$

I was not good at my liquor store job. Part of it was my attitude (*I have a college degree—what the hell am I doing working here?*), but part of it was my lack of knowledge. I kept screwing up at the cash register ("No, I wanted that charged as a debit card not a credit card. Rerun it") and my coworkers knew so much more about liquor than I did. Nicole and I only drank Everclear, a grain alcohol with an ABV of 75.5 percent and about as much subtle flavor as jet fuel. We'd mix it with some orange juice, and a 1.75-liter jug held up for about a month and a half. My boss, a guy in his midforties with slicked, black hair and a goatee, had a creepy ongoing flirtation with one of my coworkers in her early twenties. Empty boxes and leftover promotion items like key chains and pint glasses littered the edges of the store. The bathroom had a shelf with coffee cups, creamer, sugar, and some granola bars for munching while you took a dump. My coworkers only did what was convenient in any given moment. Hell, I did too; otherwise I wouldn't be working there in the first place. Nevertheless, it made me miss the Iron-Birds. If someone got on their high horse in the clubhouse, I could tell them to go fuck themselves—this behavior was not only allowed but encouraged. In retail you just couldn't get away with it.

After my shift one day, I bought a couple bottles of three-dollar wine with my store discount, walked out the door, and never returned. The next day I went into the local library and started writing. I wrote a memoir about college—not because I had a specific story to tell, but because I felt like somehow, if I wrote it down, then it was all worthwhile. And it didn't hurt that it gave me a chance to relive my glory days.

After the library, I'd hit the gym. I always felt like a big reason I got cut from my college baseball team was because I was too skinny. "Two hundred pounds," I thought, "would look so much better in a game day program than one hundred and sixty." So I set out to put on weight, even though I wasn't playing ball anymore. I cooked heavy meat-sauce pastas. Nicole learned how to bake calzones. I taught myself how to make pizzas. I drank two protein shakes a day. I started powerlifting at the little rec center down the street, grunting in the basement weight room with a dozen ancient exercise machines. Eventually I puffed up to 212 pounds. "If only I were this big in college or high school," I thought. "I would've crushed the ball." My chest bulged out of my T-shirts, but my belly popped out almost as far. My jeans, once loose and baggy, were now skin-tight over my thighs. I'd get winded every time I walked up the stairs to the second floor of the library.

"Winter weight," I thought. "I'll slim down in the spring and it'll be all muscle."

Jason, my old boss in Aberdeen, texted me in early January, asking if I was coming back to the IronBirds that summer. Not because he needed a fat-ass shortstop to hit .091 for the team, but because he needed a clubbie. When I left Aberdeen, I wanted to establish myself with a full-time job or a published book so I'd never have to cut another orange or wash another jockstrap again. Yes, I was still financially independent like I'd always wanted, but I had nothing to show for the winter other than a start to a book, fifty extra pounds, and a relationship on the rocks. I never consulted Nicole about being a clubbie again; I only told her when I made up my mind: "I'm going back to Aberdeen for the summer." She chewed on her tongue, saying nothing, then fell into a weeklong sadness.

Earlier that month she'd told me, "My life goal is to have kids—that's what I've always wanted. My mom used to babysit and have all these kids running around the house playing and doing crafts. Plus she had me and my brother. That's what I want too. But we can't have that yet because we don't have any money . . . and we're not ready in our relationship either.

"I hate that I can't achieve my life goal on my own." She paused. "I just need you to be successful."

I thought she'd be happy I was going back to Aberdeen—I'd be making more money after all. Instead, she started hitting me in bed—not right when I told her, mind you, but the next night, once we were more emotionally removed from my decision. They were little slaps in the arm at first, which I thought were cute, and they obviously made her feel better, so I told her she could hit harder if she wanted.

"I don't want to," she said.

"Go for it. It's not like they hurt."

She reared back and punched me in the arm, enough to leave a nice bruise and a dull ache. I couldn't be mad at her, though—I told her to do it. And, anyway, it's not like I hadn't been relieving my anger through violence as well. On two separate occasions that winter, I'd smashed closet doors in a fit of rage while I swept the house. My anger and sexual frustration had built up. "At least as a clubbie I got paid to clean up after other people," I thought. "At home I don't get so much as a hand job in return." So I swung my broomstick at the den closet, shattering the white shutters all over the floor, and, a few months later, I kicked another closet door off its hinges.

She told me I had to get my shit figured out. "I'm not trying to be a bitch or anything," she said, "but we're running out of closet doors."

She'd grown weary of her teaching job. (The school was so small, invasive, and Christian that she had to keep our premarital cohabitation a secret from parents and students.)

I asked her why she'd wanted to teach high school English in the first place.

"I needed a path," she said. "My grandma was surprised when I told her I wanted to be a teacher. She said, 'I always thought you had bigger plans than that, Nikki.'" She talked with remorse about growing up dreaming of becoming an actress or a singer. Sometimes, after working out, I'd approach our house and hear her keyboard piano and distant voice echoing through the parlor windows in the night. She directed a school play here and there, as well. But other than those small brushes with performance, her dreams were behind her.

Only rarely did she gripe about living across the Savannah River from her hometown, where her parents still lived. She sometimes said her life felt stuck there, but neither of us did anything about it. I imagined if the shoe were on the other foot: if Nicole and I lived across the Mississippi River from my hometown in Minnesota. Just the thought of it was miserable—awkward encounters with old acquaintances, going to my high school's homecoming, being close enough for my parents to pop in. (All that stuff would be great in small doses, spread out over the course of decades, but having it right there on your front step? No thanks.) Sometimes it seemed like she was only with me because she'd already been with me—we were only living there because she'd grown up there. Nothing but the mysterious power of nostalgia glued us together in that location.

• • •

In February, as Major League teams started reporting to spring training, I fantasized about working my way up the Orioles' system. What the hell else was I going to do with my life? Being a clubbie was my only job experience, so why not try to work for the big team in Baltimore? Then one day if they won the World Series, I'd get a ring along with the rest of the team, just like I'd always dreamed of. And when people asked me about it I would say, "I won this with the Baltimore Orioles," leaving out that I was nothing more than a glorified towel boy.

Jason called me in the spring.

"Well," he said, "I've got some good news and some bad news."

"Hit me."

"The good news is that there's a lot of turnover this year. You'll still have to deal with Trek and Mills, but Muggsy, Komminsk, and Cesar are all gone. I don't know much about the new guys coming in, but I've heard they're good. On the Ripken side, pretty much every department was in the red last year, so Cal fired the GM without anyone's permission.

"I was already being stretched thin as it was, plus I got a job offer in DC. I'm gonna take it. So it looks like you won't have to deal with me anymore."

My stomach sank. Jason was a great boss. He was hands-off to the point that he let me fail and learn from my mistakes, but he was there whenever I needed him as well.

"Damn, man," I said. "If that's the good news then I don't know if I wanna hear the bad news."

"The bad news is that the team won't pay for your apartment this year. Trust me, I tried to get them to help you out, but they didn't budge."

"Shit," I said.

"Yeah."

"Well, damn. Aw, it's okay—I'll figure something out."

I'd still have to pay my half of rent and utilities with Nicole while I worked in Aberdeen. I remembered something Jake Parker had told me the first time I met him in Sarasota: that he'd lived in the clubhouse one summer. He got free internet, free AC, and, most importantly, free rent. I'd spent plenty of nights sleeping in the equipment closet during the 2012 season—it wasn't so bad. Living there full time seemed like a no-brainer.

And just like that, I packed my things into the Caddie for the drive north (not too much stuff, though—it all had to fit in the equipment closet). Nicole and I renewed our lease, so I was coming right back there once the season finished. We said goodbye to each other, just like we had so many times before.

Aberdeen had been just a memory. I never thought I'd actually return there any more than I'd return to my youth. But I looked forward to the season in a certain way, like when you do the same things over and over again expecting something to be fundamentally different. Because it's always the next meal, the next fuck, the next Christmas that will finally make you happy—the next baseball season. Because this is all you know how to do. You don't ask the sun why you orbit, you just orbit. You let the gravitational waves of the baseball season pull you in and you surrender yourself, happily. You slap on your faded blue stretch-fit BP cap with the orange cursive "A" on the crown, and you drive your Cadillac from one single-story, brick rambler to another, somewhere just off the I-95 corridor in Maryland.

12

A New Era Takes Flight

Aberdeen had this way of sneaking up on you. The town peeked out of the trees about thirty-five miles northeast of Baltimore and receded back into the woods before you knew it. And God help you if you missed the exit: you'd end up halfway to Philly before you could turn around and get back onto Long Drive, wending your way through the woods to Ripken Stadium.

I'd contacted the new GM, Brad, who would serve as my boss that season, and let him know that it was of paramount importance that I got a key for the clubhouse and equipment closet immediately when I arrived at the stadium. I was still contemplating whether I would let him in on my secret. I arrived after office hours, so Brad hid keys for me under the rumbling AC unit behind the clubhouse.

When I got inside, the place was a disaster. A popcorn machine stood partly disassembled near the washing machines and a deflated bouncy castle lay limp on the floor in front of the dryers—it looked like a goddam traveling circus had stopped to take a breather in the laundry room. The couches were gone from the locker room, and there were only about twenty fold-up chairs. I'd need at least thirty. The coaches' office had no refrigerator or tables. For every absence of a necessity, I only saw in its place another task I would have to complete before the team arrived.

I walked through the darkness of the trainer's room and weight room before reaching the equipment closet. The licorice scent of rosin caught me by surprise when I opened the door. A poisonous nostalgia wafted up my nose and shocked my nervous system into beating-heart panic.

It finally hit me: I was going to live inside a closet.

I assumed when I'd left the previous summer that I would never come back to this place, but now I had not only returned, but I was dug in deeper than ever. In that moment, as I looked around the closet, I wondered if I would come out of this with my sanity intact on the other side.

I blew up my queen-sized air mattress and bedded down for the night, wondering just how dangerous it was to inhale rosin particles for an entire summer.

My new boss, Brad, had worked in the ticket office the previous season. I knew him only as the guy I handed our empty pass lists to before every game. He wore an IronBirds polo, khaki shorts, and stood with the same little slouch as all front office people.

"Any idea what's going on with the laundry room?" I said.

"The popcorn machine and all that stuff? We'll get some interns to clear that out if we need to. The clubhouse kind of turns into storage over the winter."

Something about that didn't feel right. Didn't they know that the clubhouse was a sacred place? They wouldn't use a cathedral as a storage unit.

"Did you find a spot to stay yet?" Brad said.

"Yep. Right here. As long as that's okay with you."

"In the clubhouse?"

I nodded. "Is that okay?"

"I don't really care, I guess. Just don't let HR find out."

I spent that day tearing the equipment closet apart. I inspected mystery boxes from the top shelves, holding little chunks of history that nobody knew existed: IronBirds shirts with holes in them, pots and pans with food residue still caked on, old New York–Penn

League baseballs signed by players long since out of the game. I tossed the crusty old cooking equipment in the dumpster out back, but the signed baseballs were still good, so I threw them in the BP basket. The previous season I worried that someone might get mad if I cleared the place out, but I knew now that I was the only one who cared. This was no longer the equipment closet—it was my bedroom.

I trashed all the excess garbage and kept what might be useful. I ran a long extension cord from the outlet near the double doors, all the way along the wall to the other side of the closet. There it powered my little desk area on the bottom rung of the storage shelves. I cut up cardboard boxes to make containers for dishes, Tupperware, and utensils, fully equipped with old towels to line the bottom for water absorption.

Once I had everything the way I liked it, I went to the Applebee's across the freeway for dinner. I watched the Orioles game by myself at the bar, drinking a Natty Boh and wearing my faded blue BP cap. I could barely stand the sweaty stink of that old cap—I'd have to replace it once the season started. I watched the Orioles game with passive interest, wondering how the Minnesota Twins were doing that season—I hadn't paid attention to them since before I left for Aberdeen the previous year.

The next day, back in the clubhouse, somebody came by and painted over the old side-facing cartoon IronBirds logo on the locker room wall. In its place they put up the team's new logo: a fierce, metallic-looking bird facing straight ahead with jet-like wings extending left and right. The marketing materials for the logo, from articles on the team website to the banners around the stadium, all said the same thing: "A new era takes flight."

13

Started from the Bottom

Alan Mills came strutting into the clubhouse wearing an oversized polo shirt, baggy jeans, and a Bluetooth in his ear. A few players here and there were getting set up at their lockers. Mills went around rapping the chorus of a new Drake song in their faces. He didn't even say "What's up, meat?" when he came up to me—he just got in my face and rapped: "Started from the bottom now we're here, started from the bottom now my whole team fuckin' here." He eventually came back for some proper hellos and handed out books to his pitchers. They had titles like *The Psychology of Baseball* and *The Mental Game of Baseball*.

Players and coaches came trickling in throughout the day in preparation for preseason workouts. I walked into the manager's office to meet our new skipper, Matt Merullo. I knew little more about him than his beer preference, which Jake sent me before the season: "Just Budweiser for Merullo and Trek. Should be easier on you than Fat Tire and Sam Adams." Merullo caught in the Majors for six seasons in the '90s, playing for the White Sox, Indians, and Twins, hitting a .234 career batting average.

Matt had big marble-blue eyes topped with bushy haystacks of eyebrows frosted white at the tips but still hinting at their original red near the skin of his brow. His head was rectangular, his upper body barreled, and his legs skinny. He stood there in his office wearing a sleeveless cutoff T-shirt that he would wear under his jersey every game that season.

Leaning against a bookshelf near his desk was an old Louisville Slugger with the name Lennie Merullo on it—not in the form of a signature engraved into the wood, like a modern bat, but in print, all capital letters: LENNIE MERULLO, the name of Matt's grandfather.

Lennie was a handsome man with thick, dark eyebrows (which sometimes crept together into a singular unit) and a prominent nose, like a better-looking DiMaggio brother. Lennie's baseball career bested his grandson's by one year and six percentage points: seven seasons in the Majors and a .240 batting average. He was also the last living member of the 1945 Chicago Cubs team that went to the World Series.

In 1942, Lennie's second season with the Cubs, his wife went into labor in the middle of a game. Cubs owner Phillip Wrigley got word to Lennie that his wife had been taken to the hospital to deliver the couple's son. After hearing the news, Lennie went on to make four errors on four consecutive plays, a Major League record. In honor of the errors, the newspapers named Lennie's son (Matt's dad) "Boots" Merullo, a moniker that stuck with him for the rest of his life.

Lennie eventually became a successful scout and went on to be inducted into the Professional Baseball Scouts Hall of Fame in 2008. Lennie, the Massachusetts native, spent his postplaying career scouring New England for future Cubs while grandson Matt sat in the front seat of his car packing a tobacco pipe for his grandfather. Lennie would strike a match, set fire to the tobacco, and puff his way through another scouting trip. The smell of his grandpa's pipe cemented itself into Matt's memory, always reminding him of his connection to baseball history.

"You like cigars?" was the first question Matt asked after I introduced myself.

"Hell yeah."

"Here," he said, handing me a stogie. "I got this box of Cubans. Give it a try."

It said Cohiba on the band with Habana, Cuba, written just below it. I looked them up online, and a few forums said these Cohibas were often fakes. But there was nothing phony about Matt. He was one of the first people I'd met in baseball who seemed genuinely interested in learning about me. This was something he learned from Brian Graham, the grim reaper I'd met in my first season. When Matt moved from a scouting role (like his grandfather) to being the manager in Aberdeen, B.G. told him that players don't care about how much a manager knows; they want to know how much a manager cares about them.

But, then again, I wasn't one of Merullo's players.

"You go by any nicknames?" he said.

"Guys just call me G."

"G? G-man."

"Yeah, that works."

"Where'd you grow up, G-man?"

"Small town called Elk River, Minnesota."

"Yeah?"

"Just north of the Twin Cities."

"You a Twins fan?"

"Big time. I saw that you played for them."

He nodded as he sat down in his black swivel chair. "Played for T.K.," he said, meaning sixteen-year Twins manager Tom Kelly. "Learned a lot from him. Even though we weren't a very good team, he made us play the right way. In fact, he's the reason I still wear number twenty-seven." He pointed behind me to his jersey hanging in the locker. "He always said you play the whole nine innings, win or lose, to the best of your abilities. So I wore twenty-seven for the twenty-seven outs in nine innings."

My first thought was that he should actually wear number fifty-four because, yeah, you had to play twenty-seven outs in the field, but you had to bat for twenty-seven outs too. Then I remembered the Twins team he played for in the midnineties—they never seemed too concerned with the whole hitting thing, so I guess it made sense.

In his preseason news conference announcing him as the Iron-Birds' new manager, Matt stressed the word fun, something his father, Boots, ingrained in him. Before every game Matt played, his father would tell him, "Go have some fun." Now, as a manager, he wanted to instill that same belief in his players. He told the press in Aberdeen: "Seeing the kids make progress and feel good about themselves, that's the whole key. This game will let you know how bad you are. Sometimes you need human beings around to remind you how good you are."

• • •

I geared up a new player in the equipment closet. Outside the door, I could hear a familiar monotone voice coming from the weight room. It was my old roommate, Sam Kimmel.

He said to another player: "One of the front office people said, 'I bet you're happy to be back here.' I was like, 'This is single-A—why would anybody want to be here?'"

"I hear that," the other player said in reply.

He walked into the equipment closet. "Greggy," he said, picking me up and squeezing me to crack my back. I handed him his jersey, pants, and caps that I'd set aside, all in his size. He still had his shaved black hair in heavy stubble and his eyes still squinted almost shut when he smiled. Everything about him looked the same, except he might have packed on more than fifteen pounds of muscle in the off-season—almost all in the chest. I'd cut back a bit from my high of 212, but I was still jealous that he'd muscled up without any fat, by the looks of it. He finished the 2012 season with a .282 batting average and three homers in forty-seven games, but if his added weight helped him crush the ball, he might muscle his way up the Orioles' ladder and I'd be out a friend.

Other familiar faces filtered in after Kimmel. Sebastian Vader, the six-foot-four, right-handed starter who weighed 175 pounds soaking wet, was back with the team. He still had that devilish stare in his eyes when he spoke and the sort of laugh that sighs at the end and whispers "Fuck that guy" on its way out the door. He might have been the unluckiest pitcher I'd ever seen. He finished the 2012 season with a 1-8 record, an exceptional number of losses in a seventy-six-game season, but if he'd said he pitched better than his record, it would've been true—his solid 3.71 ERA served as some hard evidence in his favor. (Forget his win-loss record; the true injustice of Sebastian Vader's 2012 campaign was his omission from MiLB.com's Moniker Madness competition for best player name in the Minors.) Even Jorge Rivera was still on the IronBirds after a 1-3 record and 3.26 ERA in 2012—we gave each other an amicable hello when he came in for gear.

I had heard from Jake that a catcher named Jack Graham, B.G.'s nephew, would be on the team. I expected him to be a hotshot—a real douchebag—but when I met Jack he was kind and gentle, and he spoke with this easy intelligence. Jack went to Kenyon College, a private liberal arts school in central Ohio with an enrollment below two thousand students, and graduated in four years with a degree in political science. They played in the North Coast Athletic Conference (whatever the hell the north coast is) and went by the nicknames Lords (men's teams) and Ladies (women's teams). He only played baseball in his junior and senior years, hitting for a career average of .307 against teams like College of Wooster, Hiram College, and the University of Scranton. He was drafted in the thirty-eighth round of the forty-round draft in 2012 and had spent the previous season hitting .118 for the Orioles' Gulf Coast League team.

I tried not to get too attached to anyone because I knew just how likely it was to lose them before the season ended.

• • •

I watched BP from the dugout one day during workouts. I had nothing better to do, so I sat bullshitting with Trek in the shade. A few line drives shot into the stands in left-field foul territory, smacking against the seats between the field and the concourse where a bouncy castle would be erected come opening day. Next to the castle would be a carnival game to test your pitch speed. There would be a fake catcher and batter printed on a tarp that the kids would throw into. Front office interns, all wearing khaki shorts and IronBirds polo shirts, would say, "Nice job, buddy," as a kid handed them another ticket. The radar gun would read forty-five mph, almost fifty miles per hour slower than some of the pitchers for the IronBirds. But the children playing that carnival game would throw with similar accuracy to the IronBirds' pitchers, and with the same furrowed brow, thinking: "I don't care where the ball goes, I'm just gonna throw it as hard as I flipping can." It didn't matter if it was some twenty-year-old IronBirds intern or a forty-five-year-old Orioles executive, they would all say the same thing to the little kid, the player—anyone with a dream they wanted to keep coming back for more: "Oh, that one was really close, champ. Now all you gotta do is . . ."

Baseballs kept whizzing into the stands during batting practice. These weren't any old balls that could be lost without consequence, either. These were pearls I'd just put into the BP bucket because our new hitting coach, Scotty Beerer, had said, "These guys can't practice baseball by hitting oranges." Old, worn-out balls were oranges because they were soft, squishy, and didn't come off the bat real well. So the oranges went into the batting cage buckets and the pearls went into the rolling BP bucket (for on-field batting practice).

Two kids, probably in high school, had somehow made their way into the empty stadium and were harvesting pearls by the armful. If it wasn't for the chance at a foul ball, surely they'd have no reason to come to their local Minor League team's preseason batting practice.

"Oh, for fuck's sake," I said to Trek.

"What?" he said, looking down at his phone.

"I'm hemorrhaging inventory over here."

He looked up in time to see the two kids, obviously friends, scrambling for another ball in the seats. The victor held it up in triumph and ran back to add it to his pile underneath a seat.

"Better find a spot up there and get to work," he said.

I hopped out of the dugout and clubbie-walked around the warning track up the left-field foul line, glancing over my shoulder with every crack of the bat. My first instinct was to ask the kids for the baseballs. I practiced what to say as I walked. "Gentlemen," I'd start. This would give me credibility. But then I remembered I wore a fanny pack. "Fellas," I'd say instead, "we need your balls." Oh, God no. "Fellas, we need *those* balls." Still bad. "Fellas, those baseballs don't belong to you." There you go. "Those are IronBirds property and you need to return them." Much better. That made it seem like I spoke for the whole operation rather than me just being the anal clubbie.

I approached their stockpile, hidden under a first-row seat. There weren't any other fans in the stadium, so the two teenagers were comfortable enough to leave their stashes unattended as they chased another ball. I hopped over the fence from the field and looked down. I considered taking the baseballs from those kids.

But I stopped myself in that moment. "Are you really about to steal baseballs from kids just to keep them in your inventory?" I thought. With them, those baseballs might be magical—with me, they were one of many. I'd pop them out of their plastic wrappers, one by one, like the white pus of a pimple, and throw them into the rollaway BP bucket. They would be smacked around Ripken Stadium until they became oranges, at which point they'd be tossed into the batting cage buckets. And when they became too worn-out even for tee work—when the blue ink that said "Official Ball New York–Penn League" had disappeared along with NY-P president Ben Hayes's signature—then some player might pick it up and throw it to a begging kid. But by then much of the magic would have vanished like the president's signature.

These kids had acquired the baseballs fairly—they didn't steal them, they earned them. If I picked them up, then *I* would've been the thief. Was this what my relationship to the game had become— heartless, transactional? I had accidentally taken my first love and turned it into a business partner—our relationship devoid of all passion, transforming me into the kind of guy who would take baseballs from kids.

A crack sounded from home plate. I turned my head to see a line drive shooting into center field—a white pill cruising along an invisible line out past second base before falling into the outfield grass. I lowered the bill of my cap over my eyes and walked away from the boys' hard-earned treasures, small beads of moisture bouncing off the top of my Under Armour Orioles shirt like ground balls skipping across the infield.

14

Number 75

I cracked open the crab shell, picked the stringy meat from the body and rolled it between my fingers, seasoning it with the leftover spices on my fingertips. I sat at a picnic table with Trek, his son, and his wife—just one happy family, me included. We were enjoying the annual preseason crab feast that the stadium provided the players and staff at the end of workout week. Last year I didn't think I was allowed to join. This year Trek invited me.

"I don't think I can," I said. "I have laundry to do."

Trek shrugged it off, but Mills, who had overheard, piped in.

"It's a team meal, meat."

"I know," I said.

"You don't think you're a part of this team?"

His gaze did not stray from mine and his face didn't betray any hint of jest. Only days before, he'd been in my face about not getting his mortgage bills, saying that if he lost his house it would be my fault since I was in charge of getting mail to the team. I scoured the mailbox for days looking for his mortgage bills until I learned that Trek, unaware of Mills's running joke, had been getting the mail from the front office before me, and Mills had his bills the whole time. With that prank, though, there was always a glimmer in his eyes that told me he wasn't fully serious. There was no such glimmer at this moment.

"Yeah," I said.

"Yeah what?"

"Yes, I'm part of—"

"Who told you you're not a member of this team? Was it a pitcher? If it was a pitcher I'll kick his ass."

I refrained from answering truthfully—that it was none other than me.

"Come on, meat, you like crabs, right?"

"Yeah."

"Then what the fuck?" he said and walked out of the training room and up to the team meal.

So I went up there and joined Trek's family as the mid-June sun set behind us.

"How was it today?" Trek's wife asked him.

"Well, today I popped a cyst in Steven Brault's ear," he said. Brault was a newly drafted pitcher. "It was pretty gross. I loved it. It kinda looked like—well, it looked like some of those crab lungs there. It was the best part of my day—besides hanging out with you."

His wife pressed him for more about the day, but he said he didn't want to think about work right now.

"It feels good just to breathe for a minute," he said. "Once the season's over we can do this all the time, just sit outside and eat crabs."

Trek usually walked around hunched, tight—always under pressure. He didn't laugh much, but when he did it was a tiny release, like his body was a giant ball of rubber bands and each laugh was a single band breaking. He grew up in Minnesota like me, and sitting with his family felt something like sitting with an uncle, aunt, and cousin.

The day before the home opener, I put up our white home jerseys—with the players' names on them—in everyone's lockers. Many of the guys came in from the field and stared in wonder. Jose Figuereo and Alex Santana, both from the Dominican, asked me to take their picture as they held up their jerseys. Alex yelled like an announcer in his accented English: "Now pitching, Alex San*tan*aaaaa!" Even our young, new coaches, Paco Figueroa and Scotty Beerer, were excited to see the jerseys. To the players, a jersey with their name on it was a symbol that they'd survived the grim reaper's visit during workouts.

Sure, B.G. had come around to analyze the new talent, but he also seemed intent on indoctrinating the fresh draft picks on the Orioles' version of life in the Minors.

At the team meeting he said, "I know you wear a jersey for the IronBirds right now—and you're playing in Aberdeen, not Baltimore—but you're all Orioles players. You signed a contract with the Orioles, so if anyone asks you, you tell them you're a player with the Baltimore Orioles." A few guys looked at each other and smiled.

Toward the end of his talk, B.G. mentioned something about how Mills once punched him in the head when he coached for the Kinston Indians and Mills was a twenty-year-old pitcher for the Prince William Yankees. They'd crossed paths for a single-A Carolina League game in 1987 and a brawl broke out. During the brawl, Mills punched Graham in the forehead then spit at the Indians' manager, Mike Hargrove.

Mills shook his head and smiled when B.G. told the story. I'd never seen him fake a smile before.

"Do you remember that, Alan?" B.G. said.

"I'm not gonna answer that."

"Did you punch me in the forehead during a brawl? Answer the question, yes or no?"

Mills sat in silence. He let this strange tension linger in the locker room, full of mostly new players trying to get a feel for the power dynamics at play here.

Kimmel piped up, saying, "Mills, you tell that story every day."

The room erupted in laughter. Later that day, when B.G. took the position players onto the field for drills, Mills talked to his pitchers in the locker room. By then he was used to me sitting in on pitchers-only meetings—he would make eye contact with everyone except me as he spoke, but he never once told me to leave.

"You don't play for the IronBirds *or* the Orioles," he said. "You play for yourself. You play for whichever team is willing to pay you money to play the game of baseball. Maybe you spend your whole career with the Orioles, maybe you don't. But wherever you go, you need to stay in this game as long as you can. 'Cause it's hard, meat—it's a hard game. But you're lucky enough, you're skilled enough, to play it professionally."

Mills was good enough to pitch professionally for more than seventeen years. Almost three years after that fight with B.G., Mills was called up to start the 1990 season with the New York Yankees, compiling a 1-5 record and 4.10 ERA with the big club. He split time between triple-A Columbus and the Yankees for the next two seasons before being traded to the Orioles in February of 1992.

He was assigned the jersey number seventy-five in spring training. Numbers that high were usually reserved for Minor League players and nonroster invitees who were not expected to make the Major League roster. He started the season with the Orioles' triple-A team, the Rochester Red Wings, but after a mid-April call-up he broke out as a middle relief man for the Orioles, filling in at times as a setup man, closer, and even making a few spot starts. He still wore the number seventy-five.

By then Mills had learned how to better control his slider and improved a changeup that complemented his ninety-mile-per-hour fastball. He had also worked on holding runners on base in the off-season, a former weakness of his. His teammates described him as quiet and unassuming, even as he worked his way to a 10-4 record with a 2.61 ERA in 1992. He figured to be a big part of the Orioles' future, even though he had a slight elbow irritation that sidelined him for the last month of the '92 season. Orioles manager Johnny Oates even considered Mills a contender for a starting role coming into the 1993 season.

Mills, by then twenty-six, was still a starry-eyed kid in the Orioles' clubhouse. During spring training in March of '93, he walked around asking former Cy Young Award winners Rick Sutcliffe, Fernando Valenzuela, and Mike Flanagan to sign some baseball cards. "It's kind of awesome," Mills said at the time, "to be in the same clubhouse with three Cy Young Award winners."

But his teammates took advantage of his unassuming nature. The year before, in a road game at Comiskey Park, his teammates in the bullpen arranged to have a police officer come in and make a phony arrest of Mills after goading him into an argument. But Mills took it all in stride. Oates described Mills as being "receptive to new ideas" and said "he doesn't seem to be excitable."

"I'm just happy to be here," Mills said after making the Baltimore roster in '93. "It's a really nice city and the people are really nice. I really like it here."

Fast forward just a few months later to a June 6 afternoon game against the Mariners at Camden Yards. Mike Mussina of the Orioles was pitching against Bill Haselman, the backup catcher for Lou Piniella's Mariners. The Orioles had taken exception to a few inside pitches from the Mariners, so in the top of the seventh Mussina retaliated by plunking Haselman in the arm with a fastball. Haselman charged the mound, and within moments an all-out brawl exploded. Now, like I said before, during a brawl it was customary for the bullpen pitchers of both teams to jog out to the scrum in the infield and find a bullpen pitcher from the other team. They would then hold each other, as if to say, "Boy, if this guy wasn't holding me back I'd be in there fucking shit up."

But Alan Mills, who did not and would not pitch in that game, came out of his bullpen looking to offer genuine help. He calmly jogged to the pitcher's mound and gently motioned a few players out of the way so he could pull out one of his fallen teammates. But something clicked in Mills. Each time the fight would die down, with men exchanging nothing but words, Mills seemed to light it back up again. First, Mills threw a punch at Mariners closer Norm Charlton (who also did not pitch in that game). The two were separated before they could land any solid blows. Then Mills went after

Charlton again. This time Mills hit Mariners primary catcher Dave Valle, though he was aiming for Charlton.

"Seemed like every time I dove into a pile to get a white jersey out, it was Mills," Orioles pitcher Rick Sutcliffe said. "Mills, he's crazy. He was fighting half their team."

Mills said someone took exception to him trying to keep the peace. "That's how it started," he said. "That's all I have to say."

When Mills entered the clubhouse the next day, one of his coaches called him Cassius Clay. To his teammates, he was the star of the fight. "I really don't know what to expect," Mills said to a reporter, referring to a possible suspension. "But I have no comment. You can ask me for days, but I'll still have no comment." He was given a four-game suspension.

The next year, 1994, he went 3-3 with a 5.16 ERA in the strike-shortened season.

In 1995 he went 3-0, but he had a terrible 7.43 ERA and was shut down midseason to remove bone spurs from his elbow.

In 1996 he bounced back nicely after an unexpected re-signing by the Orioles, going 3-2 with a 4.28 ERA. He and the Orioles made a run to the ALCS that '96 season, where they met up with a Yankees squad that was on the front end of a dynasty that included World Series wins in four out of the next five years (including that season). That Yankees team included young studs Andy Pettitte, Mariano Rivera, and Derek Jeter, all of whom made their debut the previous year, in 1995. But the Orioles were no slouches either, with All-Stars Rafael Palmeiro, Roberto Alomar, and future Iron-Birds owner Cal Ripken Jr.

Mills and the Orioles were not impressed by the Yankees. "You can't go out there thinking that the other team is better," he said, "I don't think anybody feels that way." Maybe nobody in the Baltimore clubhouse felt that way, but the rest of the world knew the Yankees were the better team. The Orioles stole a victory in game two, but they were overpowered and outpitched in the ALCS, losing 4–1.

Mills and the Orioles returned to the ALCS in '97, this time facing the Cleveland Indians. They split the first two games, entering game three in Cleveland with a 1–1 tie in the series. Mike Mussina of the Orioles and Orel Hershiser of the Indians both pitched gems, leaving game three knotted at 1–1 in the bottom of the ninth.

Enter Alan Mills.

With two outs and Jim Thome on first, Mills dealt to Indians third baseman Matt Williams. Williams was having a hard time finding his power stroke in the playoffs, but he hit .263 in the regular season with thirty-two homers and 105 RBIs. Mills's tree trunk legs stretched the fabric of his gray road pants as he stood on the mound, ready to throw. He stood in the set and stared over his left shoulder toward home plate. He dropped his black glove from his chest down to his belt buckle before delivering. He bounced a first-pitch slider and got a foul-tip strike before surrendering a single between shortstop and third.

Runners on first and second, two outs, game tied.

Next up was Sandy Alomar Jr., the brother of Orioles second baseman Roberto Alomar. The Cleveland crowd stood on its feet and cheered, sensing an impending victory and a 2–1 ALCS lead for the Indians—the winning run stood on second base.

Mills nearly bounced two more sliders but got a strike on a foul ball. With the count 2-1, Mills left a slider hanging at the knees for Alomar. He swung late, barely glancing the topside of the ball, bouncing it off home plate and sending it sailing into the cool Cleveland night. Third baseman Cal Ripken Jr. glided over in front of the shortstop and caught the dying dove at his forehead. In one motion he swung his right hand, his glove, and the ball into throwing position and slung it over to Rafael Palmeiro at first.

If the throw didn't get to Palmeiro in time, the bases would be loaded with the winning run on third. If he got the runner out, the inning would end and the game would go into the tenth. The throw was on target, and Palmeiro reached with his glove turned down and his left hand trapping the ball for extra safety, but it was too late—

Alomar beat the throw by half a step. However, the first base umpire emphatically called the runner out with a gauntlet throwing punch toward the bag, yielding groans across Cleveland. Mills escaped the jam and left the game having surrendered no runs. But the Indians went on to win the game in the bottom of the twelfth inning.

Mills wasn't so lucky the next night. The Orioles were now down 2–1 in the ALCS as they faced the Indians again at Jacobs Field, before a crowd of forty-five thousand fans. They trailed the Indians 7–6 when Mills entered the game in the bottom of the seventh inning. He worked efficiently, getting Matt Williams on a line out to right, a fly ball to right field from Sandy Alomar, and a Brian Giles groundout to end the inning. The Orioles went quietly in the top of the eighth, as did the Indians in the bottom, with Mills getting the 9-1-2 batters in succession. Then the Orioles tied the game, 7–7, in the top of the ninth.

Another tie game going into the home half of the final inning.

Right-hander Manny Ramirez, who would go on to hit 555 home runs in his career, led off for the Indians. Orioles manager Davey Johnson decided to leave Mills on the mound. Mills got the count to a quick 0-2 but couldn't put the slugger away, eventually walking him on a 3-2 count. "I just didn't get the job done," Mills would say with a look of disgust after the game. "Walking the leadoff man in the bottom of the ninth?" His voice would trail off.

Mills was yanked from the game after the walk to Ramirez, but that run came in to score, tabbing Mills with the loss that sunk the Orioles into a 3–1 ALCS hole that they would not climb out of. This all came as a shock for an Orioles club that fancied themselves the team of destiny, especially after their ALDS sweep of the ninety-win Seattle Mariners.

"Somebody's messing with fate right now," Davey Johnson said after the game four loss to the Indians.

The Orioles closed up shop for the off-season after the ALCS. As he packed his belongings, Mills said, "I believe in fate. But to hell with fate—I want to see the World Series."

Mills never went to the playoffs again as a player after that 1997 season, and the Orioles entered an embarrassing stretch of fourteen straight losing seasons, fueled in large part by their lack of home-grown Minor League talent. (Their situation in the Minors was so bad, in fact, that their triple-A affiliate, the Rochester Red Wings—with whom they had the longest-running relationship between a Major League club and its top affiliate, at forty-two seasons—quite literally fired the Orioles in 2002. Usually it worked the other way around: a Major League team would tell their Minor League affiliate that it wasn't going to work out, forcing them to search for a new parent to latch onto. But the Red Wings were so sick of the continued futility of the Orioles' talent pool that they changed allegiances to a Minnesota Twins team that was facing contraction from Major League Baseball.)

Nineteen ninety-eight brought the famous Yankees brawl in which Alan Mills punched Darryl Strawberry.

Mills said later that '98 "was one of those years you try to forget about. You wish there was a restart." During the last road trip of the 1998 season, Mills was playing cards with a teammate in Toronto's visiting clubhouse when first baseman B. J. Surhoff made a playful comment to Mills as he walked past. Mills stood up and got in Surhoff's face, smiling all the while as he grabbed Surhoff by the jersey and shoved him into a locker. B.J. tried to remind Mills that there were reporters present and this wasn't the time or place. Infielder Jeff Reboulet rolled his eyes, put the cards on the table, and walked over to intervene, the only one in the clubhouse who did so. And with that scene, the lights dimmed on the Orioles' '98 season.

By 2000 Mills was with the Los Angeles Dodgers and found himself involved (at least tangentially) in another infamous brawl. This time the fight wasn't between two teams but between a bullpen and the fans. Mills's Dodgers were playing the Cubs at Wrigley Field, where the visiting bullpen was located in foul territory on the first base side, separated from the fans by nothing but a short brick wall. On the night of May 16, a drunken fan punched backup catcher Chad Kreuter in the back of the head as he sat in the visiting bullpen, stealing Kreuter's cap in the process. Kreuter followed the man into the stands and punches started flying. Before long, other members of the bullpen joined in, along with players from the dugout. It was a dark moment for Dodgers baseball. Broadcaster Vin Scully, as he watched the moment unfold and relayed it to his California listeners, simply said, "This can't be happening here." Frank Robinson, the former Oriole and baseball's new vice president of On-Field Operations, attempted to dole out a record nineteen suspensions to the Dodgers, including three games for Alan Mills. But twelve of those suspensions, including Mills's, were eventually dropped. (Not for nothing, Mills got the win for working a clean seventh inning.)

Eventually, Alan's health betrayed him. He hung up his cleats at the end of the 2001 season, age thirty-four and having struggled for years with arm troubles. His friend and bullpen-mate Arthur Rhodes said, "He shouldn't retire. I told him to come back and pitch, but I don't think it's going to be soon."

Mills did indeed change his mind and tried to come back in 2002, but, in a surprise move, his wife divorced him before the season, so he stuck to his previous decision and walked away from Major League Baseball. I once asked Mills why he really left the game in 2002. He said the main reason was to spend time with his three children, two of whom were just babies.

"No matter how much money you make," he said, "you can't buy that time back."

"Did you feel like you had a couple years left in you?"

"Most definitely," he said.

In retirement Mills continued to work out and maintain pitching form as he coached amateur teams. He kept in such good shape, in fact, that by 2007 Mills, as a forty-year-old man, made a comeback in the Tigers organization.

"Why did you try again with the Tigers?" I once asked.

"Because I no longer had what I retired for," Mills said.

"And what was that?"

"My family."

Mills dominated as a closer in 2007 for the Erie SeaWolves, the Detroit Tigers' double-A affiliate in the Eastern League. He converted twenty-three save opportunities and posted a 2.79 ERA— all while pitching against kids about fifteen years his junior. But the Tigers never made the call to move him up, so he walked away for a final time. He eventually coached baseball for Kathleen High School, his alma mater, in Lakeland, Florida. "My only regret," he said in 2010, "is that I should have kept playing." Then, in 2012, the Orioles—a team on the rise in both Minor League talent and Major League success, about to make their first playoff appearance since 1997—asked him to join the IronBirds' staff.

Mills wore the number seventy-five all throughout his years pitching for the Orioles and Dodgers, the same number he wore during spring training in 1992. In 2012, my first year with the Iron-Birds, Mills didn't mind that I didn't have a seventy-five jersey for him, but this year, 2013, he insisted that I have the team seamstress create a custom seventy-five jersey for him. He demanded this modification even though he had said to me, on more than one occasion, "I'm not a player—I don't wear a jersey."

Sometimes Mills still wore his 1997 ALCS shirt, with an image of the Orioles players' big cartoon heads on little bodies. The armholes had frayed where he'd cut the sleeves off, and the players' images, including his own with the black Fu Manchu mustache, had faded over the years.

• • •

Jonathan, my always-smiling batboy, was back for the 2013 season, barging into my equipment closet on the afternoon of the home opener.

"Is that B. J. Surhoff out there?" he said.

He must've been referring to one of what felt like twenty extra people in the clubhouse—roving instructors, special assignments coaches, weightlifting supervisors. They'd all be gone by the next day, though, or at the very least by the end of the home stand—they never stuck around long.

"I have no idea," I said.

He paused. "I think Al Bumbry was out there too."

I shrugged my shoulders. Jonathan had grown up watching the Orioles and knew their folklore, including the stories behind former players like Bumbry and Surhoff. I couldn't give two shits who these guys were; I was just ready to get the season going.

Before the game, I'd be introduced with the team in front of the whole stadium, packed with 5,281 people. My boss, Brad, the GM, told me I'd be going onto the field first, of all things, even before the players and coaches.

Ripken Stadium had been completely rebranded. All images of the old, cheesy cartoon airplane with a happy-go-lucky smile were gone, and in its place were the fierce, front-facing bird heads with silver and cobalt accents that hinted at the metallic origins of the IronBirds' namesake. I liked the new logo, but I hesitated in donning one of our new caps—I'd been wearing my old blue BP cap as a kind of passive-aggressive defense against the players when they inevitably started asking for extra shit.

"Look at me," I'd say, pointing to my old cap, "I've been wearing this puppy for two years and I don't need a new one."

"That's because you don't play," they'd say.

"And neither do you," I'd say, and they'd laugh and drop the matter entirely.

But if I was getting introduced with the team, I'd have to look the part. I grabbed a black game cap, size seven and three-eighths, and slipped it on. I stood at the front of the line of players on the warning track in right-field foul territory, near the bullpen, waiting to be announced with the starting lineup. Two rows of local children waited for us to jog between them, on a path to the infield. I could feel all eyes in the stadium watching our every move as we stood there. The players seemed to shrug off this attention with ease.

The PA announcer bellowed, "Are you ready to meet your 2013 Aberdeen IronBirds?"

The crowd released a cheer they'd built up since the previous September. Cars driving past the stadium on I-95, if they had their windows open, could surely hear the roar fade in and out quickly as they passed, like screams from a roller coaster.

"Introducing the clubhouse attendant, Greg Larson."

My smiling picture popped up on the big screen beyond right-center field, and I burst between the lines of children, running so fast I missed half of their high fives. I touched second base like I'd been instructed and jogged over to the foul line in front of our first base dugout. A smattering of confused applause trailed me all the way. (They erupted much louder for Merullo, Mills, and everyone else.)

I wore a blue IronBirds polo and khaki shorts, the only nonjerseyed person in the line. A low haze trapped the mid-June humidity, but the evening was mild, comfortable. The smell of cinnamon pecans from the concessions danced around us, even on the field. The stadium buzzed with the energy of anticipation. Out behind the third base seats, on the open-air part of the concourse, bounced the multicolored, inflatable castle, with children hopping as the season got underway.

I removed my new cap for the national anthem and planted my orange-and-black shoes (oversized hand-me-downs from one of our catchers) firmly on the green grass of Ripken Stadium as though I belonged on that field. It was baseball season again and anything was possible.

15

Selling Garbage

The Ironbirds lost the opener then proceeded to drop the next four games: business as usual in Aberdeen. My only regret was the fleeting moment of realization that I was about to spend another season aboard a sinking ship, swabbing the poop deck all the way down. But Aberdeen loved baseball despite the years of losing and the 0-5 start—fans usually showed up in droves, regardless.

What spoke to the power of baseball in Aberdeen more than anything else, even more than the sellout crowds, were the fan phone calls to the stadium, of all things—especially when the forecast showed rain. The Doppler radar and weather forecast plays a big role in the daily life of a Minor League Baseball team. Uncontrollable weather systems decide if a game will be played or not; so when you set aside a free summer evening to head to Ripken Stadium with your kids, you want to make sure there'll be a baseball game when you show up. In desperation people would call the front office asking our new receptionist, Lauren, if it was going to rain or not. Lauren was already overwhelmed with her job by the time the season got underway. The same way the pressures of clubhouse operations filtered through me, the pressures of the front office filtered through Lauren. The constant demands of other people can wear on you very quickly, especially when those demands necessitate that you manipulate the laws of the universe.

"Do you know if it's going to rain tonight?" the calling fan would ask.

Lauren would assure them that she was watching the same radar as them and she had no extra knowledge of the weather patterns.

Early that season I overheard one such conversation when I came up to grab the mail.

"How the hell should I know if it's going to rain?" she said. "Do I look like freaking Mother Nature?"

I didn't have the heart tell her that yes, in a way, she was. We all were. As workers for a professional baseball team, we were gatekeepers to "Something Special"—whether it was easy access to players who might one day be stars, insider knowledge, or, yes, the fortunes of the all-important summer weather patterns. That was the power of baseball to the fans: we knew something they didn't. Despite Lauren's protests, most of us on the periphery of the game wanted to foster this illusion.

Like Don Eney, the manager of Ripken Stadium's gift shop, The Hangar. Don wanted so badly to be jaded. Whenever I went up to the shop to get more caps for the players or to drop off broken bats, he would make a snide comment, something like, "Do these guys even know what a win is?" or, "Let's see if they find a few runs in that cap." Every few months, though, he'd tell me this same story about his days working at the Camden Yards gift shop in the '90s:

During a rain delay Alan Mills and a few other players came up from the clubhouse in full uniform to peruse the gift shop. The jerseyed players caught the eyes of fans, and suddenly a deluge of people overwhelmed the store.

"Alan," Don said, "you guys can't be up here—people are going nuts."

"Don't worry, meat, we're just shopping."

The players quietly made their purchases and walked back to the clubhouse.

Don would hold his hands up, lurch forward, and shake his head when he got to this part, bugging his eyes as if to say, "Can you believe it?" But that was the extent of the story: no point, really, except to let me know he was part of it—that a couple of Major Leaguers did something once and he was close enough to watch it happen.

I'd stop by and see Don in The Hangar some afternoons just to throw a few broken bats his way. Most of the bonus babies' agents hooked them up with custom baseball bats (bonus babies were the coddled early round guys with big bonuses), but the late-round guys, the ones who couldn't afford to buy bats on their own, would have to get team bats from me. They were bone-rubbed Rawlings—made with ash wood—and they were god-awful.

Back in the early days of the game, players used heavy hickory bats that were durable but heavy. Later on in the twentieth century, white ash, which was lighter than but not as strong as hickory, grew in popularity and became the wood of choice for almost all bats. By that 2013 season, though, maple bats had grown in popularity because of their light weight and strength. Maple was popular with players, but Major League Baseball as an enterprise didn't like it due to its potentially dangerous characteristics. Ash bats, when they deteriorate, have a tendency to crack or chip before breaking down. This allows a batter to recognize the damage and switch out to a new bat before the old one completely breaks.

Maple bats, on the other hand, tend to break all at once in explosions of small shrapnel or larger blades of sharp wood. Ash has looser, more separated grains that allow a flex or trampoline effect with a ball's impact on the bat. Maple has tighter grains, making the wood stronger, which creates compression on the *ball* instead of the bat. But because the grains are so tight, the sweet spot on a maple bat is smaller, thus causing more mishits.

In short, when players mishit on a maple bat, they send dangerous shards flying all over the infield.

Perhaps more important than the dangers of maple bats was the price of the wood: maple bats are much more expensive than ash bats. It's likely that MLB teams simply didn't want to dole out the money for the more effective (yet more dangerous) maple bats, so they bought ash for their Minor Leaguers instead. But the Orioles' stinginess worked out just fine for me—the crappier the wood, the easier they broke. Whenever players traded me their broken bat for a new one, I'd slap a piece of athletic tape on the knob with their last name and jersey number. Then I'd bring them up to Don in The Hangar and throw them in a barrel near the wall; he'd sell them for twenty bucks a pop. For every twenty-dollar broken bat he sold, I'd get seven dollars and fifty cents—not bad for selling garbage.

I hadn't been diligent about getting broken bats from players most of the 2012 season (I'd let them get a new bat without turning in a broken one in return), but I set the tone quickly in 2013 that players wouldn't get bats as easily this season. I noticed early on that bats with names like Kimmel, Hernandez, or Vega—relative nobodies—on the knob would sit forgotten for weeks at a time in The Hangar's barrel. But bats with names like Yastrzemski sold fast.

Mike Yastrzemski was the grandson of Red Sox Hall of Famer Carl Yastrzemski. Little Yaz was hardly off the bus in Aberdeen before I realized I could profit from his name. Let's say Kimmel broke a bat and turned it in. Rather than writing "KIMMEL #1" on the handle, I'd write "YAZ #28." Hernandez broke a bat? YAZ #28. Vega broke a bat? YAZ #28. But I didn't want to flood the supply with only YAZ bats, so I sprinkled in our first baseman's name, Trey Mancini, because he was hitting around .275 by late June, which was exceptional by IronBirds standards. The thing was, the fans had no way of verifying who had really broken the bat—they were only going by what the athletic tape on the bottom said, assuming (wrongly) that the clubbie wouldn't dare sell his soul for as little as seven dollars and fifty cents.

As I dropped off an armful of YAZ and MANCINI bats at The Hangar one afternoon, I overheard one of the polo-shirt-and-khaki-pants people from the front office mention that he'd been lucky enough to buy one of Yastrzemski's bats before it disappeared. If

Little Yaz ever made it to the show, he might point to Yaz's image on the television and tell his friends, "I have one of his bats!"

I cringed. That bat could've belonged to anyone.

I was just trying to make a buck or two: the same reason I put out peanut butter and jelly for lunch most afternoons. But that front office worker and the fans who bought garbage bats were looking for a connection to baseball that Yastrzemski's name alone represented. The same reason Don repeated that story about Alan Mills: it made us feel like we were part of something larger than ourselves.

• • •

It looked like we were about to go 0-6 to start the season as we faced off against the Cyclones in Brooklyn. Vader, our ace, had pitched eight innings of scoreless ball, but the bullpen had given up the lead in the bottom of the ninth to tie the game at 4–4, swinging the momentum to the Cyclones.

We led off the top of the tenth with a walk, which eventually scored on a single to center field, giving us a 5–4 lead. The Cyclones went down in order in the bottom of the tenth to give us our first victory of the season.

Extra-inning games stacked up quickly in that early part of the season, along with rain delays. However, one fateful game got delayed for another reason entirely. Just three days after our first victory, the IronBirds closed out the road trip with a game at Staten Island against the SI Yankees. The Yankees led 8–4 heading into the home half of the fifth inning when the lights went out in the entire stadium (the team suspected that it was due to damage from Hurricane Sandy the previous fall). After a delay and several flickering attempts for a comeback, a league official decided to suspend the game. Normally a game like that would be made up with a doubleheader the next day, but since the IronBirds were on their way back to Aberdeen, the teams would have to wait until late July to make up that game. At the time, the flailing IronBirds had no idea how important that half-played game would become.

But most of those early season delays weren't for blackouts; they were for rain.

For me, rain and baseball used to mean falling asleep with the windows open as the Twins played in the middle of a West Coast road trip. A West Coast series meant games started late in Minnesota— sometimes as late as 10:00 p.m.—so I would lie in bed listening to the Twins on the radio. As the game creeped toward midnight, I'd drift into sleep, cooled by the breeze from my open window. In my dream state, I drifted out of my bedroom like a thunderstorm sailing high over the Minnesota plains. During a Twins rally, the voices of radio announcers Herb Carneal and Dan Gladden electrified the air, and with them, I wafted all the way to Oakland or Seattle, where I could see the game their words created in my subconscious, like thick-brushed oil paintings in motion.

Outside of my sleeping body and bedroom window, electricity pulsed in Minnesota's summer air, brewing a storm that couldn't touch the Twins, invincible on the West Coast.

It was one thing to listen to a Twins game in the car or at home with my dad—we could scream, shout, or pump our fists in triumph. But falling asleep with the team meant something else. I could snuggle up next to the players like teddy bears in my own bed, dropping my teenaged emotional guard all the way down into sleep. The crack of thunder rolled across the blowing grass and rain soaked the dry gopher hills of our front yard as I floated away into that omnipresent timelessness of baseball, where boys with a dream and long-expired Major Leaguers orbit forever on equal planes.

• • •

The IronBirds were 2-6, about to play the Brooklyn Cyclones at Ripken Stadium, facing a rain delay of almost an hour. To kill some time as we waited for the storm to pass, I ran over to the visiting clubhouse to see an old acquaintance. When I worked for the Winthrop baseball team in my senior year of college, one of our best hitters was Eddie Rohan. Eddie was a tan-skinned catcher, built like a brick wall: six feet tall and 205 pounds. During his at bats, his legs stretched from the back of the batter's box damn near to the front, spread out at least two shoulder widths. He took violent swings at pitches he liked and tried to absorb everything else into his arms and ribs. He never flinched when pitches hit him, and nobody had to yell out "Don't rub it!" as he took his base. He'd just watch the pitcher release the ball, continue staring as the ball thumped against the meat of his bicep, twirl his bat toward the dugout like a pin-wheel, and take his base. He was one of the sweetest guys on the team, too—always smiling (except when he punished himself with pushups on the locker room floor, shouting, "You fucking suck!").

He ended his senior year in 2011 with a .342 batting average, .492 slugging percentage, and twelve HBPS. On draft day in 2011, one month after Eddie and I had both graduated from Winthrop, I watched the boards to see if he'd be selected.

I hadn't watched the draft that closely since 2007, when I grad-uated from high school. Back then some delusional part of me thought it was within the realm of possibility that I, after hitting .091, might be selected in the draft. "There are so many rounds," I thought, "maybe I could just sneak in there." I also thought about how every team needed a guy who did all the little stuff right, like steal signs and keep a good attitude (just like me!). What I didn't think about was that most of those guys were likely the best play-ers in their states when they played in high school. Elk River didn't attract so much as a college equipment manager, let alone scouts for Major League Baseball teams.

Of course I did not get drafted in 2007.

But in the fiftieth round of the 2011 draft, I got to live vicariously through my fellow Winthrop graduate Eddie Rohan, who was taken by the New York Mets with the 1,512th pick. The Brooklyn Cyclones were the Mets' affiliate in the New York–Penn League, so as we all waited for the rain to subside, I went to the visiting clubhouse to say hi to my old friend. Inside I ran into one of the Cyclones' young coaches making his way to the cages.

"Did Eddie Rohan make the trip?" I said.

"Yeah, we decided to bring him along."

"You know where he is?"

He shrugged his shoulders.

"Oh. I went to college with him and I just wanted to say hi."

The young coach gave me a look that said, "I couldn't possibly give a fuck," and brushed past me.

I went back later. Most of their team was standing around the covered batting cage, trying to stay loose as rain fell all around us.

"There he is," the coach said, pointing at me and smiling. A dozen or more heads turned toward me pulling up in the utility tractor. The young coach hollered, "Hey, dude, I found him," pointing to Eddie.

We weren't even close in college, but since we went to the same school he felt like an ally.

"Eddie, how's it going?" I said as I walked up and shook his hand.

"Good, good. Just grinding along. How are you, man?"

"Solid, you know? This is my second year, so I'm starting to get things down pretty good now. It's a lot different than when I worked for the Winthrop team, that's for sure."

"Oh, for sure, man, for sure."

He kept calling me "man" throughout the conversation, and it hit me: Eddie didn't remember me. I was flooded with memories of Winthrop when I was an equipment manager. I stood at first base on the practice field with a glove on my left hand and a bucket on the ground. A coach stood behind the catchers and flipped baseballs over their shoulders to simulate bunts. Eddie hopped up out of his crouch and charged the ball, scooping it and turning his left shoulder toward me at first. "Inside, inside, inside!" he yelled, letting me know the ball would be thrown on the inside, or fair side, of first base. He whipped the ball to me on a line and I reached out to grab it. Over and over the catchers fielded fake bunts and threw them to me. I dropped them in the bucket behind me, first with an empty clunk then with the soft pat of leather on leather. The catchers always thanked me afterward, but I should've thanked them, I loved it so much.

I felt the same way about shagging for batting practice. I would get out of class in the afternoon and hustle to the stadium as quickly as possible to help catch batted balls during BP, usually with all of the players at class or in the weight room—just me in the outfield, coach on the mound pitching, and someone hitting at home plate. Shagging fly balls by yourself is an impossible task—by the time you chase down one ball, another one has been hit, and if the batter pops it up high enough, you might have to quickly nod back and forth from watching the pill in the sky to watching for line drives on field level. I don't care who you are—Willie Mays, Oscar Charleston, Ichiro Suzuki—nobody (*nobody*) can shag fly balls alone. But I loved it. I wasn't worried about making mistakes or losing my spot on the team, I only cared about having fun and doing the only thing I ever wanted to do: play baseball.

But in Aberdeen I did nothing on the field. Sure, this was professional baseball and the stakes were higher, but there were no real rules to say I couldn't participate with the team's on-field activities outside of games. I guess over time I'd just lost the baseball field, and Eddie jogged my memory of what the field used to mean.

Again, we were never close—I hesitated to even call him a friend—but in Aberdeen, waiting for the rain to subside, bat in hand, he was my connection to that part of baseball I'd lost. The part that gives you an excuse to get grass stains on your shins, rub lotion on your glove, and dab pine tar on your bat, even if you know you won't touch the field in the game. You'll remember that part of baseball, eventually, even if you have to be reminded—even if it doesn't remember you back.

16

Lights Out

We finished June with a 5-8 record. Kimmel was hitting well in the leadoff spot and the Orioles seemed intent on moving him away from playing catcher (in 2012 he had eleven passed balls and allowed forty-eight stolen bases in sixty-one attempts—very poor numbers). The powers that be put him in left field instead, where he was unpracticed and uncomfortable. But he thrived at the plate, hitting .344. I worried he'd be moved up.

Kimmel and I were still friends, but without guys moving in and out of my apartment like the previous year, I didn't connect with other players as much anymore. Instead, I buddied up with the coaching staff. In fact, Merullo and I became something like roommates—I lived in the equipment closet and Merullo, during home stands, pulled the cushions off his manager's office couch and threw them on the floor for a makeshift mattress. Trek, too, sometimes blew up an air mattress in the weight room and spent the night. And over time, our thirty-year-old bench coach, Paco Figueroa, started crashing on the locker room couch. Paco, who had played for Spain in that year's World Baseball Classic, picked up the slack from our absent hitting coach, who left midseason to try to save his relationship with his fiancée (B.G. told him he had to try, even if it meant leaving the IronBirds). So Paco spent late nights writing postgame reports on the hitters, work that Scotty

Beerer would've done if he were present. The Orioles gave the coaches a daily per diem for housing, but Merullo and Paco both preferred to pocket that money and sleep in the clubhouse. Men after my own heart.

Staten Island just left town after taking two out of three from the IronBirds to close out June. I always looked forward to visits from the si Yankees because their coaches liked to drink after the games. I would text John, the Budweiser supplier for the stadium, and let him know I needed a booze infusion. John was a huge Orioles fan and played wood-bat baseball on the weekends, so I threw a few bats his way or visiting team caps, and he'd hook me up with as much beer as I wanted. I'd give the visiting coaches some beer, they'd give me a few more caps, and the cycle would continue, with plenty of surplus beer for me, Trek, Merullo, and Paco. Mills, on the other hand, never spent the night in the clubhouse (he always opted for the hotel room), and for all I could tell, he didn't drink.

It was the night before a road trip, so we were in full sleepover mode in the clubhouse: Paco, Trek, Merullo, and I were all drinking Bud Heavies. They could sleep off their hangovers to their heart's content on tomorrow's bus ride to Dutchess Stadium in Wappingers Falls, New York, home of the Hudson Valley Renegades.

All week Trek kept saying that we needed to grab some beers, crack some crabs, and sit down to bullshit one night, just him and me. So I got us some crabs from the Conrad's guy with the crab truck outside the clubhouse, grabbed a pile of beers from the fridge in my bedroom, and sat down with Trek in his office.

"What kinda music do you listen to, Greg?"

"Got any James Taylor?"

"Yeah, I think I do." He put on "Carolina in My Mind" on his little iPod stereo.

We picked at the crabs with nothing but the music breaking the silence. I could see from his fumbling hands that he'd already been drinking, probably while I'd done laundry after the game.

"You throw this stuff out, right?" he said, holding up the lungs and guts from the body.

"Yes. Please don't eat that shit. Here, you just take off the legs like this and get the meat around these shoulder joints."

"You pick these things pretty good." Trek may have been living in Maryland for years, but he was still a Minnesota boy.

We went silent again.

"Thinking about home?" he said. He meant my home with Nicole in South Carolina.

"Yeah."

"Is your girlfriend visiting at all this summer?"

"I hope so."

"Where the fuck're you gonna go when she does? You can't make her sleep in the equipment closet."

I nodded. Silence—except the crack of crabs and music.

"What do you still want to accomplish in your life?" I said. "What're your goals?"

"My goals? I don't know, Greg. Six more seasons after this one and I'll have twenty with the Orioles, which would be nice. That would get me a nice pension. I'd like to move up to Delmarva and be closer to the beach, but I know that won't happen."

"Why not?"

"I'm too good at my job here. They know I get my shit done. I handle the moves with these new kids coming in and they don't want someone else here."

Silence.

"Who's the biggest asshole on this team?" he said.

"That's tough. Most of these guys are solid. I would say Rivera, but he's almost too much of a child to call an asshole. The other day I called him out for taking half the damn oranges I put out for pregame, but he didn't give a shit. I honestly don't think he even knows any better. But overall this team is pretty good."

He shook his head and laughed. "You know, Greg, most of these guys are just a bunch of fuckin' kids. You can't let them get to you.

If any of them starts to give you a hard time, just remember they'll be outta here soon, one way or another.

"And as far as Rivera goes—those Dominican kids are gonna get more chances than an American, so there's not much you can do about that."

"Why's that?"

"Don't know. More money invested in them, probably."

"Huh."

The anti-Dominican rhetoric of Minor League Baseball no longer shocked me like it used to—I'd bought into the narrative myself.

We picked crabs until our hands were stained brown with seasoning and tiny cuts lacerated our fingers. His iPod continued moving down the James Taylor playlist, to "Fire and Rain."

I've seen sunny days that I thought would never end.

"Can we drink some beers and eat some crabs every night?" Trek said.

Suddenly, Paco and Merullo stormed in through the closed training room door.

I leaned over to Trek and said, "I bet you anything they're out of beers and looking for more," and he cracked a rare smile.

"G-baby!" Paco yelled.

Merullo's cheeks glowed red, pushing up against his unfocused eyes. "You guys sharing the fucking meaning of life in here?" he said.

"Greg's just bitching to me about dealing with the players."

"What is this, Dave Matthews Band?" Paco said.

"You never heard James Taylor before?" Trek said.

Paco frowned with exaggeration and shook his head. He was thirty and grew up in Miami—not exactly in the James Taylor wheelhouse.

"Ahh, these young guys don't know a goddamn thing about good music," Matt said. "Hey, you got anymore beers?"

Trek and I met eyes.

"No, Matt," Trek said. "We tanked 'em."

"What's the deal, G-man? You can't get some fuckin' beer?"

"We had two fucking cases," I said. "We just crushed 'em, that's all."

"Hell yeah!" Paco said.

I had more emergency cases stashed in the equipment closet, but I had to keep something in the reserves just in case. If I brought those out, we'd all wake up with our heads in the toilets.

"I'm gonna hit the hay," Trek said. "You guys keep going if you want, just keep it outta here." He waved us out the training room door.

Paco and Matt walked out, but I didn't follow them. It was time to start my bedtime ritual, too. I laid down a blue tarp in the middle of the tiled equipment closet floor (which I'd just swept at the end of the home stand), surrounded on all four sides by shelves of baseball equipment.

It was most efficient to let my air mattress inflate while I brushed my teeth, so I turned the switch and walked back through the weight room where Trek was inflating his own mattress. Just before I reached the coaches' office, where I had my locker with my clothes, slippers, towel, and toiletries, I could hear the familiar crack of wood against baseball in the cages outside. Intrigued, I walked out into the mild night and heard the buzz of the batting cage lights, another crack from Merullo's bat, and then another sound, like the flutter of an insect's wings, signaling a baseball spinning against the vinyl rope of the cage. Darkness had consumed the stadium around us. The field to our right was the deepest green, almost brown in that sleepy hour, in stark contrast to the life teeming from the bright cage. Matt, who batted lefty, pulled a just-lit cigar out of his mouth and puffed.

"That's good," he said to Paco, who sat on a bucket tossing him balls. "Just bring the ball back easy and release it right here." He waved his hand about thigh high over the plate.

Paco nodded in my direction and Matt turned around to see me.

"G-man," Matt said, "get your ass in here. You want a stogie?"

"Definitely! Let me go grab the one you gave me." I ran inside and passed Trek in the weight room, already passed out, and entered my bedroom, where my air mattress was still whirring, full. I hit the off switch, grabbed the cigar from the pencil drawer, and picked out a bat, thirty-three and a half inches long.

"Here, let me get that for ya," Matt said as he lit my cigar.

I cupped the flame as I pulled in the smoke and then exhaled.

"Nice, huh?" Matt said.

I could've been smoking a tube of pine tar for all I knew. "Hell yeah," I said. "So smooth."

"You coming in to take some cuts or what?" Paco said. He picked up his bucket and moved it to the right side of the cage to accommodate me, a righty batter.

"Let's just shoot a couple back up the middle here," Matt said to me.

Paco grabbed an old orange from the cage-ball bucket beneath him and tossed the ball toward my belt buckle. I swung hard, trying to snap my hands through the ball and drive through with my hips, but everything in my body felt slow. I hit a worm burner to the back of the cage. Paco silently did the same again and I hit a two-hopper.

"Do that again," Matt said.

Paco brought his hand back with a ball. I loaded up to swing when Matt said, "Okay, stop right there."

I froze. He put his cigar in his left hand and used it as a pointer. "See where your front foot is? Wherever your front foot goes, your front shoulder will follow. Now look out on a line from your left shoulder. Where's it pointed?"

I followed the line of my shoulder and pointed to the back right corner of the cage.

"Maybe even more closed than that," he said. "Now, get into your ready position again, but this time let's get your shoulders squared. Move your front foot back a few inches. Even more." He kicked my left foot. "Alright, good. Paco, give him a couple more right at his belt buckle. See if he can get around on 'em now."

My front shoulder felt wide open, but this time when Paco released the ball I whistled it to the back of the cage.

"Alright, G-baby," Paco said.

He flipped me another one, but I was slow again. I felt the light sting of missing the sweet spot on a wood bat.

"We're putting you to work for that dues money," Matt said.

I fisted another one.

"Okay," Matt said to Paco, "what's he doing?"

"He's not getting his hands through."

"Good," Matt said. "G-man, your hips are opening up just fine, but your hands are slow coming through."

"Uh-huh," I said, blankly.

"Here, look." He got into a left-handed batting stance to mirror me. He pantomimed his orange-tipped stogie as a bat in his left hand, trailing smoke in the wake of its movements. "You have your hands up here by your shoulder as you wait to receive the ball, which is fine—whatever feels natural for you—but when you open up your hips your hands are still lagging behind."

"Uh-huh."

"Here, imagine you're taking your hands and karate chopping at the ball. You rear back and come through with both hands chopping at it, wherever it's pitched. Try that. That's how it should feel."

"Ahh," I said.

He turned to Paco. "See how that finally clicked for him? A lot of guys just need it put another way. Rather than how some coaches just keep saying the same thing over and over and it never clicks for the guy. Alright, G-man, let's go. Try it again."

Paco flipped me a ball and I sliced through it with everything— hips and hands—all at once, sizzling it to the back of the cage. I'd never felt so much power with a baseball bat. He flipped me another one and I did the same.

"How's that speed?" Paco asked Matt.

"You're giving him fucking ched. But he's getting around on it just fine."

I cracked another one.

"Damn, G," Paco said, "you wanna load up on the bus tomorrow and play some shortstop?"

"Yeah, no shit," Matt said. "Can't be any worse than who we got there now."

I knew they were only bullshitting—mostly—or at the very least, drunk. Against a professional fastball I'd break more bats than Sam Kimmel. But I let myself believe them. I allowed myself a few moments of fierce-eyed delusion and mental trips on the team bus, suiting up for the IronBirds. Because the illusion that it might happen in some nonexistent future was enough to make me swing hard and fierce.

I eventually made my way back to my bedroom, where I laid down for sleep under a soft blanket, with a forest scene of a panda eating bamboo, which I'd found the year before. Just before I turned off my desk lamp, I noticed the stale and annotated June page of my wall calendar staring back at me. I ripped it off to turn over into a blank July, hit the lamp, and fell quickly into sleep.

17

Children in the Outfield

We swept the division-leading Hudson Valley Renegades on the three-game road trip to start July. Powered by some staunch pitching, we gave up only four runs in three games. The offense provided some key hits as well. Kimmel brought in the first game's lone run with a double in the top of the thirteenth inning, and slugging first baseman Trey Mancini went five for five on July 3. The guys came home with a 9-8 record, just one game out of first place in the McNamara Division.

What was this winning thing?

"You missed some good baseball games," Trek said when they got back from the road trip.

"Yeah, I saw."

"Oh, and we got B.G. coming sometime in the next couple weeks, so just a heads up."

I nodded. "You think he'll keep the core of this team together? So, you know, we can maybe do something here."

"I don't know, Greg. We've never won before."

We won our Fourth of July game. We won again on July 5, beating the Brooklyn Cyclones with a walk-off error in the eleventh. Mancini, the first baseman from Notre Dame with a goofy smile, had raised his average to a team-best .361. Kimmel was hitting .340 as a DH and part-time outfielder. Sebastian Vader, the wiry right-hander, had eased into the ace's role with a 2.96 ERA. Late-inning relief men Jimmy Yacabonis and Donnie Hart had yet to surrender any runs between the two of them. (Hell, even third-string catcher Jack Graham, B.G.'s nephew, was getting in on the fun. He started one game as the DH, batting ninth in the order, and went 0-4. But, on the bright side, he only struck out once, and his .000 batting average didn't even drop.)

The walk-off on July 5 brought our winning streak to five in a row.

The clubhouse had shifted. When I'd watch the closed-loop video feed of the game on the clubhouse television, players always filtered in and out from the bullpen—often sitting down for long stretches to enjoy the air-conditioning. They used to be idle, almost indifferent toward the game or, at worst, hoping for it to shoot by quickly. Now those small batches of clubhouse delinquents cheered at the television whenever we scored.

Our routines and rituals shifted, too. Jersey selection, which was customarily left to the whims of the starting pitcher, had gone from a solitary choice to an entire team's foregone conclusion: we always wore the cobalt blue alternates with "Aberdeen" written in silver cursive across the chest, underscored by the flair of a waving pennant. They were my favorite jerseys: not only because they looked good but also because they were much easier to clean than the usual home whites. For good luck we wore those same blue alternates every game of our growing win streak. And after each victory we played Miley Cyrus's "We Can't Stop" in the clubhouse:

Can't you see it's we who own the night?

Hell, even the food was better. Our postgame meals were now cooked fresh, specifically for us every game—no more leftovers (I had to pay two bucks a head now, unlike the previous year, but it was a small price for guaranteed food). We ate hearty meals of grilled chicken and veggies or pastas with meat sauce, and sometimes a front office person brought down a tray of soft pretzels topped with crabmeat and cheese for the players.

I even shagged fly balls during batting practice.

When the team came back from one road trip in early July, they didn't arrive until 3:00 a.m., so I didn't have their uniforms washed until 6:00 a.m. But since the bus got in so late, they wouldn't start stretching and doing early work in the cages until late afternoon, which would allow me plenty of time to get things done without being bothered. I slapped on some rubber gloves and set up my meal prep station in my bedroom: a fold-up table topped with two white towels (which I kept separate from the regular shower towels that were in constant contact with guys' ding-dongs). Next to the table was a makeshift garbage can I made by lining an old baseball box with a black garbage bag. I got the watermelon and pineapple cut and covered in saran wrap, tossed it in the fridge, and did the same with the orange slices, squirting fruit juices through the air with each slice. Then I cut chunks of granny smith apple and drizzled them with lemon juice to keep them from browning. I cracked open a dozen or so canned chicken containers, tediously twisting my dollar-store can opener until aching pain shot through my carpal tunnel. I mixed the chicken with a bit of mayo, salt, pepper, and Old Bay seasoning. I had the whole pregame spread ready by the time batting practice started.

Only hours removed from their late-night bus ride, the guys ambled out of the clubhouse for BP like college students taking the walk of shame, all in their dry-fit black shirts, shorts, high black socks, and topped with their blue BP caps. Unlike the previous year, I actually hooked myself up with player gear, so I felt like part of the team. The final clicks of cleats filtered out of the clubhouse, with the last guy carrying his fielding glove on his bat through the wrist strap, the same way we've all done it since we were kids— the same way players have done it forever.

I sat alone in the coaches' office in front of my locker, the one in the corner, half intruded on by the Coke fridge I kept stocked with water, Powerade, and all the Diet Mountain Dew Trek could drink. I could hear the cracks and pops of batting practice getting underway outside. I exhaled as I unclipped my fanny pack and locked it in my cubby. I took off my frayed cargo shorts and pulled on my black Under Armour shorts with the cartoon Oriole logo on the leg. I took off my generic black shirt and put on the Orioles one to match the shorts. I grabbed my glove from the top shelf of my locker and stepped out into the July sun. My steps did not click on the concrete because I wore my hand-me-down turf shoes, several sizes too big, and they didn't have cleats. I tried to look as natural as possible as I jogged the twenty or so feet out to right field, where our right fielder was getting his reps in. A few dozen feet behind him were little pockets of pitchers trying their best to stand in places where no ball would ever land. I ran out toward Jack Graham and Mitch Horacek in right-center, not daring to venture any farther. Mitch was one of our pitchers, a Dartmouth man whose blue eyes and light eyebrows made him look like a potential relative.

The other pitchers in right field caught sight of me.

"G-money!" they yelled.

I smiled and kept my head down.

"What's up, G?" Jack said when I approached him and Mitch. "Come out for some BP?"

"Yeah. I got some time, so I figured why not." I shrugged like it wasn't pure ecstasy to be on the field at that moment, surrounded by the peculiar beauty of white baseballs popping against the deep blue summer sky like daytime moons. It'd been so long since I'd been on a baseball field for a full-speed practice that I had forgotten how to read the trajectory of the ball off the bat. Luckily the balls were all going to the other side of the field.

"You've played ball before, right?" Mitch said.

"A little in high school."

A fly ball sailed upward.

"That's all you," Jack said.

The pill was hit high and seemed to be coming in our direction, but once it reached its apex all gravity had been sucked out of Ripken Stadium, forcing it to stay in suspended animation against the sky for a brief moment—an eternity, really. I took a step forward just as it resumed motion, initiating its descent into the expanse behind us. By the time I ran back, it had landed with a loud thump in the grass. I picked it up and threw it on three hops toward the guy with the bucket in center field, protected behind his net.

To my relief, the next ball hit our way was a grounder. It would've been an easy play for the second baseman, but during batting practice there was always a cat's cradle of coaches hitting fungos around the horn from either side of home plate. They did this while the batter hit from a thing called "the turtle," named for its vague resemblance to a large green turtle shell cupped over the top of home plate. The coaches' timing was so precise that whenever they hit a ball to the infielders it would be on the offbeat after the batter had hit a pitch. That way the infielders would never be blindsided by a batted ball. So unless a BP ball was hit directly at them, the infielders let grounders from the turtle squirt through to the outfield so scrubs like me could pick them up, absorb the unwarranted confidence of having bent over and caught a rolling ball in a glove, and stand up to lob them off-target to the man on the bucket.

Before long I realized that nobody was actually watching me or judging me. In fact, the players were happy to have someone who wanted to be out there, since shagging during BP was little more than a nuisance for most of them—especially for pitchers, who would never play a game in the outfield in their natural-born lives. For them, having me run around gaining the confidence to call someone off for a pop fly was just another person to help with a chore none of them wanted to do. I might as well have been enthusiastic about vacuuming or washing dishes as far as they were concerned.

That night our winning streak ended on the sixth game, played on July 6. The clubhouse was despondent afterward, all except Mills. As a coach, he never sat down and formally talked to the entire team or gave motivational speeches; he just walked around and said shit as he went about his business, often sporting nothing but underpants. He intentionally bumped into guys who looked especially sad as he made his way to the spread. He dished himself up.

"This ain't football," he said to nobody in particular. Everyone listened. "You can't win every game. What? Did y'all cocksuckers think you'd win out for July? Huh? Sheeit, meat. This is baseball—you're gonna lose sometimes." He shook his head and walked back into the coaches' office.

• • •

By July 10 we were 13-10 and in sole possession of first place in the McNamara Division. B.G. showed up during the home stand, along with about five other coaches called rovers. Rovers were Orioles instructors (usually former Major Leaguers) who focused on a specialty such as catching, pitching, fielding, hitting, outfielding, or base running. They didn't belong to any team in the Orioles' system; they just roamed from one team to the other—this week in Aberdeen, next week in Delmarva—giving players advice from an outsider's perspective. (However, it always seemed like a superfluous job given the fact that there was already a manager, hitting coach, pitching coach, bench coach, and strength coach on each team who could do the same. I had a strong feeling that these roving coaches were more of a sweetheart deal for old Orioles players like Al Bumbry and B. J. Surhoff rather than an actual baseball necessity. And my pet conspiracy theory was that those roving coaches were meant to spy on the Minor League coaches for the Orioles' front office.)

The arrival of B.G. and others worried our coaching staff more than it worried our players—the pitchers had all been pitching so well that the only direction for anyone to go was up. But losing pitchers meant dismantling our team, and Mills and Merullo began whispering that B.G. was there to gut us as we tacked on the wins.

B.G. came back to see me one of those days during a series against the State College Spikes in mid-July. He walked into my bedroom as I cut up veggies for pregame.

"Hey, Greg, what's going on?" he said, doing a quick visual survey of the room.

"B.G. Just getting after the pregame spread."

"Good, good. Listen, we got Buck Showalter coming in a few days, so just a little heads up."

"Oh, damn. Is there anything specific I need to do?"

He shrugged. "Not really. Things look good in here. Keep it up."

As he left Aberdeen after the home stand, he slapped me on the back and handed me a check for thirty dollars: twenty-one dollars for three days of dues plus a nine-dollar tip. A part of me loved his validation, but another part of me recoiled at my own desire for him to like me.

Jake once told me that winning makes everything easier, and as far as I could tell he was right. We were even getting this visit from Buck Showalter, who had a few days off from managing his 53-43 Orioles during the MLB All-Star break. The Orioles would be represented by five players in the All-Star Game: center fielder Adam Jones, first baseman Chris Davis, shortstop J. J. Hardy, third baseman Manny Machado, and pitcher Chris Tillman. It was the most All-Stars they'd had since 1997, the year they lost to the Indians in the ALCS.

When Buck came by, he poked his head into the equipment closet. The year before, I didn't know who the hell he was, but over my time with the IronBirds I'd seen enough Orioles games and heard enough people talk about him that I felt compelled to stand up and greet him like a dignitary.

I knocked my knees against the fruit-cutting table as I did so.

He gave me a nod and did a quick scan of my bedroom, only his head and upper torso poking in through the side, like he was Mr. Ed. He looked back at me, nodded again, and scooted away so fast I half expected to see a puff of rosin powder where he'd just been.

Buck got to see us win a 3–1 game against the Williamsport Crosscutters, which included another brilliant performance by the pitching staff. But by the time B.G., the rovers, and Showalter left Aberdeen, we lost only one pitcher: David Richardson, who took his 6.38 ERA up to low-A Delmarva.

I went to collect David's jerseys, pants, and laundry loop before he left for the Shorebirds' stadium. Vader, who was D-Rich's locker neighbor, spring training roommate, and best friend on the team, was spitting venom at David as I approached.

"You lucky fuck," Vader said with his lower lip protruded slightly. He stood staring at the top of David's head. "You lucky fuck."

David sat there and avoided eye contact like a child in trouble.

I don't think Vader was mad at D-Rich or even jealous of him, really. I think Vader was mad at the *idea* of someone like David, who was far from the best pitcher on the team, moving up ahead of him, especially with Vader's solid 3-2 record and 3.00 ERA. That was just part of Vader's personality. I'd once seen the lanky right-hander applaud sarcastically from the top of the mound after his shortstop booted a ground ball.

"He's a good pitcher," Mills told me in the coaches' office after Vader didn't get moved up, "but he's gonna always think he's unlucky. He doesn't realize that guys don't wanna try behind a pitcher like that. It's not like guys go out looking to make errors, but when a pitcher shows them up, they say, 'Okay, I see how it is.' So maybe next time they won't dive for that ball in the hole or make that little extra effort on the next play. He thinks he's unlucky. I think he's got an attitude problem. But what do I know." He leaned back. I could see a little poster taped up on the inside of his locker. It had a lifelike cartoon of a businessman sitting in a swivel chair, and it said, "Every day at work I wonder if I'll accidentally scream 'You f***ing idiots!' out loud instead of just in my head."

• • •

My mind always defaulted to thoughts of Nicole whenever the team left town. There were times during the season that I missed her so dearly it felt like life was just a daily countdown to seeing her again. On July 16 the IronBirds left for a long road trip up to

Burlington, Vermont, to play the Lake Monsters and back down through Jamestown, New York, for a set against the Jammers. Nicole came to visit in the meantime.

I took Trek's advice and got hotels for Nicole and me: a couple nights in DC, where I picked her up from the Reagan Airport, before spending the rest of her trip in an Aberdeen hotel. When she came walking up to my car at the airport, it almost felt like watching a celebrity: we'd been together for two and a half years by then, but being apart for those long stretches turned infatuation into obsession, and perhaps twisted love into something else.

She looked bright and healthy, her skin beaming with clarity. She'd taken up this Paleo diet where she didn't eat carbs—only meat and vegetables. She'd even started a blog in the process, a way to create some pressure on herself to continue the diet (or lifestyle change, as she called it).

Some nights, long after Trek and Matt had drunk me out of beer and I was in the equipment closet waiting to fall asleep, I'd read her blog posts, over and over, just as a way to connect to her. I looked at the pictures of her meals and thought, "Wow, that's our kitchen! Holy shit, those are our plates!"

She looked happy and toned as she walked out of the airport toward me in the Caddie. I hopped out and embraced her. She hugged me back, holding tightly, briefly, before breaking the embrace and scooting behind me to the car.

"It's so good to see you," I said. "You look great."

She was already curled up against the center console, hiding from me like she did whenever we'd been apart.

"Mhmm," she said. "How far is the hotel?"

"Not far."

She held onto my arm as I drove, still curled up against the center console. When we got into our hotel room, she stripped herself naked unceremoniously and climbed into bed, facing the wall away from me. I leaned over and kissed her neck. She twitched her shoulder as if by reflex and bumped me in the chin, clacking my teeth with a surprising jolt. She forced a smile to cover for it, but continued facing away. I rolled onto my back, resigned, and stared at the ceiling. She finally came back to me and latched on, getting into her "Nikki pocket" as she called it—the spot in my armpit where she laid her head safely, snuggled up against me.

"I'm just remembering you," she said.

"I know."

I knew she had a hard time sleeping alone in our little house in South Carolina. She kept herself as busy as she could down there, coaching volleyball camps and getting her lesson plans ready for the fall. But I think loneliness can become a habit that's difficult to shake, even when you're with the person you miss.

Her fingers groped around my face—searching my chin and cheeks—finally stroking my upper lip.

"Looking for something?" I said.

"I'm just seeing if you still had that mustache."

"You don't remember from forty-five seconds ago?"

She laughed her little chin-out laugh against the hairs on my chest. "I guess not."

I hadn't worn a mustache since last season, so I didn't know why she asked.

Fortunately, she didn't ask if I was still dipping. I used to do it only when I did laundry, but now I had a dip in when I drove, when I showered, and when I sat in bed waiting to go to sleep. I popped the tiny brown cancerous fibers into that pocket between my bottom front teeth and my gums and felt the buzz that, for whatever reason, made doing 2:00 a.m. laundry fun. I only did it when nobody was looking, though. That way, nobody thought I took up the habit to be cool. I didn't want anyone thinking I was the pathetic clubbie looking for everyone's approval out in the open.

But, of course, I didn't tell Nicole any of that. Although she liked that my clubbie money allowed us to go out to dinners and visit wineries during her trip, she knew me, and she knew the secrets in the depths of my soul. Sure, she squealed with excitement when I told her about shagging during batting practice because she knew that harmless fun would make my job easier. But if she knew that the negative parts of the game had sucked me in as well, it would devastate her.

We explored DC and Maryland like the tourists we were. We snagged official Library of Congress cards with our pictures on them and everything. Back in Aberdeen, we went to a local winery, Mount Felix Vineyard, and did a private wine tasting. In the off-season, when the flow of cash only leaked out of my checking account like a kinked hose, we didn't eat at restaurants if we could help it; when we went to movies it was at the dollar theater; and we sure as hell didn't go to wineries.

I prided myself on being a frugal guy, but when those players went on the road after their home stand and I'd built up the piles of twenties, tens, and fives that made up their dues payments, it was hard not to make it rain with Nicole just a little bit. We made love some nights, we didn't on others, and we spent those days during her trip in a cocoon away from anything else going on in the world, including (and especially) baseball and the IronBirds.

Before I took her back to Reagan Airport, we ate lunch at a Chinese restaurant. She sat there silently. She'd felt closed off—hurt, even—when we'd had sex that morning.

"What's going on?" I said.

"Nothing," she said, staring at the table. "Just thinking about my flight."

I nodded as she chewed on her tongue. I signed the check and took her to the airport with the promise that I would drive down to see her during the IronBirds' long road trip in August.

She hugged me at the departure drop-off then pecked me on the lips. When she pulled away, she gave me a look that said, "You still don't get it do you?"

On my lonely drive back to Aberdeen, I thought, "This must be how players feel with long distance relationships during the season." But I wasn't a player, I was the clubbie—the team mom—

and there was no future for me in this place. And maybe that was all Nicole ever wanted me to realize, from the moment I'd jumped in my Caddie and joined the IronBirds the year before.

• • •

When a Major Leaguer does a rehab assignment with a Minor League affiliate, it's customary for him to buy a postgame meal for the players. It's a way of thanking the team for letting him use their game as a workout. In 2012 we had Orioles second baseman Brian Roberts visit us for what was supposed to be a two-game rehab assignment. After his stint on the disabled list, the Orioles wanted to see if he could return to the big club without undergoing hip surgery.

He arrived at Ripken Stadium just before first pitch that night in 2012, too late to buy the spread, but he told me he'd buy the team Applebee's for the next game. It quickly became the hot topic of that game's conversations.

"Is Roberts getting the spread?"

"Where's the spread coming from, G-baby?"

They hemmed and hawed when they found out he couldn't get the spread that night, but they were giddy with anticipation for the next night.

In the first game, Roberts went 0-4 with two strikeouts and looked overmatched, slow, and downright broken at the plate. The next afternoon, guys sat around the clubhouse, playing cards and bullshitting, as ESPN blared in the background. All of a sudden Brian Roberts was on the screen holding a press conference in Baltimore, telling reporters that he was shutting down his 2012 season to have hip surgery. He didn't need to say it, of course, but he would not be finishing his rehab stint with the IronBirds. The Orioles front office, Baltimore fans, and the rest of Orioles nation were thinking, "Oh shit, there goes our second baseman." Everyone in the IronBirds clubhouse was thinking, "Oh shit, there goes our postgame spread."

So in late July of 2013 when I got word that Orioles pitcher Steve Johnson would be making a rehab start with us, I was as stoked as everyone else for the impending postgame meal. Johnson would absorb the cost of postgame food and I'd still get the players' dues—win-win. However, there was one thing I hadn't considered: I read online once that when Major League *pitchers* did rehab starts with Minor League teams, they used Major League baseballs.

A baseball is a baseball, right? Not so. The biggest difference is that a Minor League ball is easier to pitch with than a Major League ball. Those red stitches, all 108 of them, are bumped up: raised above the white leather of the ball just a little bit higher on a MiLB ball than on an MLB ball. The difference is minute, almost imperceptible (borderline superstitious), but it's an important difference all the same. See, when a pitcher grips the ball, a higher seam means he can gather better traction on his fingers for a breaking pitch.

So the best pitchers in the world are forced to use baseballs with the lowest seams as a way of challenging them—handicapping their abilities so they can't line up their index or middle finger along those raised red railroad tracks to get a better grip. That extra friction from raised seams could turn their already nasty breaking balls into something out of a cartoon, demolishing all competitive balance between pitcher and batter.

The only problem was that I didn't have any Major League baseballs.

I once asked Trek during a rain delay if the team might just play a seven-inning game instead. He said, not hiding his condescension, "This is baseball, Greg, we play nine innings." I always asked Trek these kinds of questions before going to anyone else because I knew my baseball stupidity was safe with him.

"Do I need to get Major League baseballs for Steve Johnson?" I said.

Trek said, "That's a good question, Greg. I'm not sure. Ask Matt."

Merullo said the same thing and told me to ask Mills.

"Shit," he said. "You know who you should check with? Rick Peterson."

Rick Peterson was the director of Pitching Development for the Orioles, and he was in town to watch Major Leaguer Steve Johnson's start. Peterson was a spry-looking guy, especially for a fifty-eight-year-old, and he sported a curly mullet that made him look like he came directly out of 1985. Mills called him Hannibal Lecter behind his back for some reason.

Peterson didn't even know if I was supposed to get MLB baseballs for Johnson's start.

Finally, I texted Jake as a last resort. If he didn't know what to do, I was prepared to just say fuck it and give Johnson some batting cage oranges in a sunflower seed bucket and let him go to work. It didn't come to that.

Jake sent me down to Camden to meet up with the Orioles' clubbies—they'd hook me up. I texted one of them and said I needed six dozen balls for Johnson.

"Six dozen? What? Is he throwing batting practice lol?" he responded.

The Orioles were on the road, so the players' parking lot at Camden Yards was full of their shiny SUVs and cute little sports cars. I pulled my '97, gold Caddie in between two of their cars and met up with the clubbie, who drove me on his golf cart down into the Orioles' beautiful clubhouse.

I was blown away by their lockers. They were made with solid dark wood, and each one had its own chair. In our clubhouse it was a constant struggle (especially when our roster swelled) to get enough chairs for everyone. Best-case scenario, everyone had their own prison-quality metal fold-up chair. Here, every player had a black, rolling swivel chair, like he was the CEO of his locker space.

I saw Adam Jones's white home jersey with his last name on the back. It had that beautiful circular patch on the left sleeve with the crest of Maryland inside the circle and the word "Baltimore" arching over the top and the word "Orioles" dipping along the bottom. A pristine pool table, Ping-Pong table, televisions, and black couches all decorated the room.

"How much do you guys charge in dues?" I asked the clubbie.

"Oh, I don't take care of that. I let Chris handle all the money stuff." Chris was their head clubbie.

I looked at him and he looked back at me. It was a true clubbie answer—it said, "You know I make a lot more than anyone would guess. I know I make a lot. So let's not ruin it by telling the secret."

I just nodded.

"Come on," he said. "Let's bring you out onto the field."

We walked through a hallway into the dugout, where the late July sun shined bright and the field glistened with sprinkler droplets floating down in rainbows.

"Not bad, eh?" he said.

I nodded, standing with one foot on the top step like a manager about to yank his pitcher. It was hard not to be romantic about baseball standing in the first great stadium of the modern era: Oriole Park at Camden Yards. I didn't dare step foot onto the grass, but looking around, I knew that I was part of this. I had somehow, almost by accident, walked myself into a job that allowed me to brush shoulders with history.

Before I left, the clubbie handed me six boxes of baseballs with a smile and said, "Let me know how Johnson's batting practice goes." I put them in the Caddie's backseat and convinced myself it was just for laughs when I buckled them in. I drove with guarded caution from Camden Yards to Aberdeen, anxiously peeking back every few minutes to make sure the baseballs were still safe.

When I got back to my bedroom, I closed the door behind me and locked it. I lifted the cardboard lid off the first dozen baseballs, like a Christmas present. The box design was almost identical to the Minor League baseball boxes I was used to: it had a red cover with the Rawlings logo in the top left corner. The only difference was that it said "Official game ball Major League Baseball."

Inside a Minor League ball box, the balls were all separated by hard cardboard inserts, and the balls came packaged in plastic wrappers. These MLB balls, however, were each wrapped in white tissue paper. The cardboard inserts to separate them were so thin and flimsy—fragile, in a way—that the box bent in my hand when I took the top off. Right there on the front of each baseball were the iconic words:

OFFICIAL

MAJOR LEAGUE BASEBALL

With Allan H. "Bud" Selig's signature underneath.

I swiped one for my ball boy Jonathan and put the rest in the ball bag for the umpires to rub up for Johnson's rehab start for the IronBirds.

Johnson had a low pitch count that night (fifty pitches) and came out in the third inning having given up two runs in two and a third innings. He didn't seem to mind, though. Rehab starts like his were more about process than results, similar to the way a Major League team's front office saw the Minors on the whole. Guys like Rick Peterson weren't worried about how many hits or runs Johnson gave up, they were more concerned with health (in this case, whether Johnson's oblique held up alright) and technique—whether Johnson had a pure throwing motion, his hands and legs moving up and down together in a balanced, fluid delivery.

Johnson sat at his temporary locker in the middle of the game and did the weight cuff exercises that all pitchers in the organization did after they pitched. He had the face and build of some average Joe who played pickup basketball at your local YMCA. I walked up to him and handed him his credit card and the receipt from the spread (he'd bought us all Applebee's).

"Thanks," he said.

"Thank you. I know the guys will really appreciate it. How'd it feel out there?"

"Pretty good. My command was a little off but my oblique didn't split open, so that's the most important part."

"Are you gonna be back in the show this season?"

"Hope so. You never know, though. Just gotta get healthy first."

I nodded. "What's it like being up there?"

"Oh, the standard stuff," he said (his father, Dave, was a MLB pitcher as well). "The butterflies in the stomach, all that stuff." He thought for a moment. "One of my first games, we're playing the Yankees and I'm up there on the mound at Camden and I have no idea what's happening. I see Derek Jeter coming to the plate and I say to myself, 'Holy shit, that's Derek Jeter! I've been watching this guy my whole life.' Then I gotta think, 'Okay, now let's go after him.'"

"Did you?"

"No, he hit a liner to right. Then the next inning I'm facing A-Rod and I got him to strike out. Then I got the next guy to fly out deep to right, and just like that I'm out of the game. I barely even knew what happened. None of it really sank in until the postseason, when I had a chance to really sit back and take a breath and realize I was in the show.

"It was nice up there—food was better, you got guys carrying your bags, you travel on private planes instead of buses. And of course the pay is way better. But at the same time, you're almost so scared of losing it that you don't enjoy it."

I thought of something Mills once told me: "It's hard to get to the big leagues. It's even harder to stay there."

We lost the game Johnson pitched against the Lake Monsters, but the next night we slugged our way to a 14–4 victory to avoid being swept (that game got so out of hand that Jack Graham had a chance to pinch hit in the eighth inning. He walked and scored a run, which kept his batting average snug at the .000 mark).

The next morning the team left for a road trip against Hudson Valley and Staten Island. Utility outfielder Mike Yastrzemski and first baseman Trey Mancini were both holding onto .325 batting averages, our lanky ace Sebastian Vader's ERA was 3.13, and our late-inning men, side-armer Donnie Hart and closer Jimmy Yaca-bonis, were sporting ERAS of 0.75 and 0.48, respectively.

The Hudson Valley Renegades were 1.5 games ahead of us in the McNamara Division, then we went into their stadium, The Dutch, and dropped both games to fall back 3.5. And, as the team made the drive from Hudson Valley to Staten Island, we were poised to drop even more.

During their stay in New York, the IronBirds would finish the game against the SI Yankees that had been suspended due to a power outage earlier in the season. Before the lights had gone out, IronBirds pitcher Austin Urban had been tagged for eight runs in the first four innings (primed for a yank from Merullo). But since his turn in the rotation happened to be up again on this visit, Mer-ullo sent him back out for the bottom of the fifth, thirty-two days, nineteen hours, and twenty-eight minutes after the top of the fifth inning had ended in June.

It's never easy to start your day down 8–4 before you've even stepped foot in the stadium, but Urban, the forty-first-round righty with first-round confidence, sent the Yankees down in order in the fifth and yielded nothing more than a walk in the sixth.

In the top of the seventh, still trailing 8–4, the IronBirds' bats came alive. Second baseman Jeff Kemp led off the inning with a double to right field and moved to third on a groundout. Kemp then scored on a wild pitch to Conor Bierfeldt, our slugging DH who was a Division III first team All-American out of Western Connecticut State (and who'd changed his walk-up song to Miley Cyrus's "We Can't Stop"). After the wild pitch, Bierfeldt launched a solo shot over the left-field fence to cut the Yankees' lead to 8–6.

The IronBirds eventually tied the game at 8–8, and Urban kept dealing until the bottom of the ninth. Merullo gave him a chance to pitch one of the most unorthodox complete games ever, but after a leadoff walk, Merullo pulled Urban. His final line looked like something out of a time when pitchers threw baseballs until their arms had turned to spaghetti noodles and counting pitches seemed as necessary as counting the blades of grass in the out-field. He threw eight innings, gave up eight earned runs, nine hits, six walks, and struck out six. His pitch count, including the first four innings in June and the second four innings in July, totaled a hearty 156 pitches. Side-armer Donnie Hart came in and got three outs in the ninth to bring us into extra innings.

We scored three runs in the tenth, and Hart closed the door in the bottom of the frame, completing the month-long comeback. With that, the IronBirds left Staten Island with a 20-20 record, just two games out of first place.

We approached that hottest part of the summer, the dog days, when Sirius makes its first morning rise on the eastern horizon. Who were we to gather hope this late in the season? Didn't we know we were cellar dwellers? Didn't we know that Aberdeen was a black hole for wins?

Last year we were like the Little Leaguer in right field picking dandelions, just waiting for the game to be over. We heard fans' and coaches' screams echo across the field as fly balls dropped all around us like white meteors. Yet there we sat, wondering why the game wouldn't end already.

But this year, for whatever reason, we looked up from our dandelion picking, saw the baseball floating over our head, and said, "You know what? Let's do this."

Then we dropped the dandelions and sprinted as fast as we could toward the descending baseball, prepared to lay our bodies and lives on the line for nothing more than an outside chance to catch it.

18

Summertime Sadness

N o matter how well your team is doing, there will always be some guys counting down the days once August hits. We were only two games behind Hudson Valley, but Kevin Clark, our strength coach, and Scotty Beerer, our hitting coach (who was back with the team after an unsuccessful attempt to save his relationship), still made gleeful comments about having just one month remaining. Success or failure, sometimes people just want to go home.

The team's success had created an unexpected side effect for me. Every game day, I put out a pass list for the players to get free tickets for their girlfriends, families, cleat-chasers—whomever. Each player was limited, in theory, to two passes per game. But up until our hot streak, that limit might as well have been zero or a million for all it mattered. I'd take the pass list up to the ticket office and one of those polo-shirt-and-khaki-pants people would see just a couple names on the sheet and say, "Nice job, Greg!" as though I'd played some part in deterring people from coming to watch the IronBirds lose.

The product on the field was usually deterrent enough, but with more wins came even more fans. Yes, most of the games were sellouts already, but they were generally season-ticket sellouts, meaning even if the stadium was half-empty, those empty seats had been purchased by season-ticket holders who decided they'd rather catch the Orioles game on TV than watch the Iron-Birds in person.

Now people around town suddenly cared about the Birds. Sometimes at the Aberdeen Wal-Mart, as I stocked up on a full cart's worth of peanut butter, jelly, and bread, the cashiers would ask me, "Do you work for a restaurant?" ("Yes," I thought, "I work for one of the many famous PB&J restaurants here in Aberdeen.") "No," I'd say, "I work for the IronBirds, and it's my job to feed the players." They used to say something like "I haven't been in so long . . . " before trailing off.

But now they asked me how the team was doing and when the next game was. They'd think about it and say, "Huh, maybe I should go to a game." IronBirds caps and T-shirts popped up around town. Players could tell girls at the bar that they played for the IronBirds and it would actually tilt the odds in their favor for once. Now host families asked their summertime children for tickets to the games, filling up our pass list beyond capacity.

When I set out the pass list one afternoon in early August, I added an announcement: "The front office said to keep it to two per guy or they'll start doing standing room only for player tickets."

Mills must have heard the announcement because he came into my bedroom later that afternoon to file his complaint.

"If your girlfriend or your dad visits," he said, "where are they gonna sit?"

"They're not coming to any games this year."

"They'd sit behind home plate if they did, though, wouldn't they?"

Trek and I always had eight home plate box tickets for every game. We saved these for visiting Orioles dignitaries or, yes, if we wanted, we gave them to our loved ones. I put my hands up, defeated.

"Answer the question, yes or no?"

"Yeah, they'd be sitting behind home plate."

"So why are Austin Urban's parents sitting up so high they can't even see their son pitch?"

"Believe it or not, Mills, I'm not actually in charge of—"

"No, see, I don't wanna hear that it's someone else's job. If that guy who's in charge of tickets is fucking up, you gotta go up there and tell him he's fucking up. It ain't that tough, meat. Shit, that's what I'm telling you right now." His eye contact dared me to look away. "The people in the clubhouse—players, coaches—they should have first preference on those seats behind home plate. There wouldn't be anything to watch if it weren't for us."

"Those are season ticket holder seats."

"They should be player seats."

"Look, man, I don't appreciate you coming in here and getting in my face about something that's outta my control."

The whites of his eyes expanded and he leaned in toward me. "You'll know when I'm in your face, meat, and this ain't it." He let his look linger for a second before walking out. In that moment I'd seen a single fierce glimpse—one movie frame—of the man who'd punched Darryl Strawberry, Brian Graham, and damn near half of the 1993 Seattle Mariners.

• • •

We took two out of three from a very good Tri-City team to close out our first August home stand only 1.5 games behind Hudson Valley. I had my schedule down pat so I could get out to shag for BP almost every day. The days were so hot that I could feel the afternoon sun through my shoes to the top of my feet during batting practice.

In the heat of August, pitchers, if they weren't lazy before, took lethargy to a new level. They no longer made any illusory attempt to catch fly balls in the outfield: instead they stood in an execution line against the right-field fence, all the way back on the warning track, hiding in the final slivers of afternoon shade. A few position players grumbled about it, but I liked having the pitchers out of the way: it meant there was more space for me to roam.

On the last day of that early August home stand, I came in from batting practice to change in the coaches' office, huffing after putting in my reps in the outfield. I stared at my flip phone while Kevin, our strength coach, and Mills sat in front of their lockers.

"Do you ever miss your mom?" Mills asked Kevin. "Is your mom a major part of your life?"

Kevin answered him.

Mills nodded and said, "My mom passed away about three years ago. You just miss her sometimes, you know? I think it's just a different relationship with your mom than your dad. I can go and talk to my dad just like me and you are talking right now, but that's as far as it goes. With your mom you can just unwind and she'll care about you, she'll listen to you. My dad—he can get on my ass sometimes."

• • •

The team hit the road before the All-Star break in mid-August. They went 3-2 on the trip, and while they did, I decided to take their extended absence as a chance to visit Nicole in North Augusta. I surprised her by making the ten-hour drive a day earlier than she was expecting.

I pulled into the dead lawn of our one-story home, driving over yellowing newspapers with my Caddie. I picked away at green weeds that had happily sprouted up between the bricks of the porch steps. I pulled out my key to open the front door, but it was unnecessary: the door was not only unlocked but also slightly ajar. The living room chair had apparently become Nicole's depository for mail. On the area rug was her electric-blue bra and an empty wine glass, along with a pile of crumbled crimson acrylic—her discarded fingernail polish. The kitchen table had found a new purpose in life as a dirty laundry hamper, but the nearby parlor, where she kept her piano, was still tidy. Dirty dishes sat piled halfway up the sink, with several clean plates drying on the rack. And in the corner stood a wooden broom, leaning up against the fridge like it was taking a smoke break. Near the broom's bristles on the floor sat a pile of swept dirt and dust.

When she came home from school I said, "I just need you to know that this is the last thing I needed when I came down here— feeling like I had to clean up after another person."

"I know," she said. "But I've been doing better. I just wish you saw that."

I let it go and went about my business of sitting on the couch playing video games while she coached a summer volleyball camp. Whenever she came home, she still huffed at me for sitting on my ass all day. I was employed, though, and the laziness was only temporary. It was just muscle memory, I think—the only way we knew how to relate in that home—the same way our sex life was more tepid midseason during that visit to North Augusta than when she visited me midseason in Maryland.

I couldn't explain to her how lonely it is in baseball. Even if you're just the clubbie, you're still sleeping in the equipment closet. It's a grind, a war of attrition, and you only have little things to look forward to: a nice postgame spread, a funny inside joke with the bullpen, a base hit in the fourth. It's a team game, sure, but it's not like there's passing in baseball, or three-man weaves to set up. Baseball is a series of one-on-one battles—pitcher versus batter, fielder versus ball, clubbie versus pants stains. I didn't have the words to explain how every day felt exactly the same at 2:00 a.m. when you were scrubbing pants with a dip in your mouth—how much I wanted to hold her, melt into her, love her with our most tangible expression. But she just wanted to cuddle.

Her dark strands of hair snaked along my face when we lay in bed at night, weaving themselves into the stubble of my cheeks. Her eyes, her mouth—everything about her hid from me at point-blank range as she rested her head in her Nikki pocket in my shoulder. She touched me, sometimes, in the textbook definition of the word. But I might have been a teddy bear, and she a scared little girl.

What hurt the most was how content she seemed with our intimacy—or at the very least how little we were both willing to work on it. We had talked about us not having sex, as well as our emotional disconnect, but it never came to a resolution.

"Things will be better this fall," she said, "I promise. I'm just overwhelmed right now."

Then my supposed midseason respite in North Augusta ended as though it'd never happened, and suddenly I was driving north to Aberdeen.

By mid-August we led the division by two games, but we were bit by the injury bug and stopped scoring runs. Against the Connecticut Tigers on August 17, we were down 2–1 with two outs in the top of the fourth. IronBirds second baseman and number two batter Jeff Kemp tried scoring on a single to right. He was thrown out at the plate and injured his shoulder on the play, forcing him to exit the game. He was replaced by a six-foot-tall, 160-pound Italian native named Federico Castagnini. Federico, who went by Feddy, went 0 for 2 for the injured Kemp, and we lost to the Tigers, 5–3.

A few of the guys, including Sam Kimmel, went out drinking after the game. Merullo hadn't been starting Kimmel against lefty pitchers (Kimmel being a lefty himself), so with the Connecticut Tigers slated to start a lefty the next day, Kimmel decided to drink late into the night, assuming he'd spend the next day on the bench.

Kimmel was still drunk the next morning, even on the bus from the hotel to the stadium. Merullo called out the lineup to the team.

"Kimmel!" Merullo yelled. "Kimmel Karma, you're starting in left, leading off."

"Fuck me," Kimmel said, laughing. He didn't even know what Kimmel Karma meant.

He started the game with a groundout to the second baseman, which was just as well—it meant he wouldn't have to run the bases. In the second inning he caught an easy pop-up for an out in left. Leading off the top of the fourth inning, he attempted to bunt for a base hit but instead popped out to the catcher. In the sixth, he grounded out to first. The day was shaping up to be a wash for

Kimmel, but things got even uglier for him in the home half of
the seventh.

Yacabonis, in relief, started the inning with three walks before
Merullo had seen enough. He replaced him with Donnie Hart, the
side-arm-slinging lefty. Connecticut led 1–0, and they were ready to
blow the game wide open with the bases loaded and nobody out.

Hart got back-to-back strikeouts before giving up a deep drive to
left field. It was an afternoon game, so Kimmel reacted late to retreat
backward, fighting the sun, the hangover, the ball, and, before he
could notice it, the left-field wall. He never even felt the dirt warning track. He smacked hard into the wooden fence, but he'd securely
caught the fly ball—inning over. Kimmel's hangover absorbed the
concussion, blending the two together imperceptibly, so he stayed
in the game. In fact, it seemed to improve his performance: when
he came up with a runner on second in the eighth, he hit a line
drive single to knot the game at 1–1.

Still tied in the bottom of the frame, the Tigers put a man on
second with one out. Hart coaxed an easy ground ball to Castagnini at second base. Feddy took his sweet time making the play
and "lollipopped the throw to first," as Trek would tell me after
the road trip. The runner was safe at first and the man on second
advanced to third. The Tigers wound up plating three that inning
and pulled out a 4–1 win. But the bigger losses hit us right at the
top of our lineup: the concussion for our leadoff hitter, Kimmel,
and the hurt shoulder for our number two hitter, Kemp.

While the team was on that road trip, my dad came up from
Florida for another visit. As you can imagine, Dad, the man who
hit me ground balls for hours on that dusty field near our Minnesota neighborhood, was an old-school baseball guy—the kind
of guy who, for whatever reason, always had the crown of his cap
perched higher than young ballplayers. I would say that he taught
me everything I knew about baseball, but that wouldn't be quite
right: he taught me everything I needed to know in order to learn
the rest for myself.

By the early 2000s—when I was a middle schooler just discovering the game—he'd been away from baseball for decades. Though he'd been a talented first baseman in high school, he walked onto the University of Minnesota's campus in the fall of 1968 as a dedicated football player. In spring of that first year, on the first play of the first spring game, he dislocated his hip and never returned (when talking about his college football days, he liked to joke that he wore the number sixteen because that represented how many seconds his career lasted).

He coached my brothers' Little League games here and there and played some beer league softball into his forties, but it wasn't until baseball became my obsession that he had an excuse to get back into the game fully. He coached my summer teams, and I was the coach's son who batted leadoff, played shortstop, and pitched. I wore the number forty-two whenever it was available because it was one number higher than my basketball jersey number, which seemed like as good a reason as any.

"What famous Major Leaguer wore the number forty-two?" my dad asked me once when I was a young high schooler.

"I don't know. Maybe Kirby Puckett."

"Nope. Any more guesses?"

"No, I don't know."

"Ever heard of Jackie Robinson?"

I knew the name, and I knew what he had done, but I didn't answer my dad.

"If you're going to wear the number forty-two, you need to know who the hell Jackie Robinson was."

He explained Jackie's significance to the game—breaking the color barrier in the Major Leagues and enduring the ridicule and hatred from people who didn't want him in baseball. The way my dad told it emphasized Jackie's guts, his humility, and his base-running abilities ("Jackie was the master of the hook slide. Guys these days don't know a damn thing about how to slide properly").

And he told me that Jackie's number forty-two was retired from all of Major League Baseball just a few years prior.

"I just picked it because it was there," I said. "It's not like I was trying to make a statement or anything."

"That's not the way it works with baseball. The game's been around for too long. If you choose to keep playing ball, which I hope you will, you'll have to learn something very important: every choice means something in this game."

• • •

Jake Parker left tickets for Dad and me at Camden Yards for two games against the Rockies.

"It says Suite 9," I said when we got the tickets. I gave him a confused look.

We were ushered into an elevator that brought us to club level. Two of the Orioles' World Series trophies greeted us in a glass case outside the elevator. We found our suite, which had a beautiful high view of the field from the first base side. As we waited for the game, we made our way around the club level, exploring the different trophies and pictures. I came across the midnineties team pictures and saw Mills standing with his arms behind his back, the number seventy-five on his stomach, and a black Fu Manchu on his face, mean mugging for the camera.

When we sat down for the game, my dad asked how the Orioles were doing.

"I've been trying to catch most of the Twins' games," he said, "but I don't pay much attention to the rest of the league."

"We're about five games back, I think."

"The Orioles?" he said.

"Yeah."

"The Orioles are 'we' now?"

"Well, I work for them, so . . ."

"Did you give up on the Twins?"

"My allegiance still lies with them, but I guess the Orioles just hold a certain place in my heart now too."

He looked at me like a detective trying to read a suspect's face.

What I didn't say was that I didn't watch any of them, really. I watched the IronBirds, sure, but those games had a direct impact on my immediate well-being: will the game go late; will my friends be happy; will we get into the postseason? I was proud to work in the organization, but I didn't have much interest in watching MLB games any more than I'd want to do laundry in my free time. But, of course, you can't say that to the guy who taught you the game.

· · ·

In the middle of August, kids from all over the world descended upon Aberdeen for the Cal Ripken World Series. On the north side of Ripken Stadium, opposite from I-95, was a complex of youth fields, all made in replica of famous ballparks. They had Fenway Park, fully equipped with a little green monster; a Wrigley Field with ivy on the outfield walls; and a mini Old Memorial Stadium, a facsimile of the Ripken dynasty's place of origin. That side of the complex buzzed with little kids from across the country and around the world—Japan, Mexico, Australia, Korea, Canada, and the Dominican.

On the other side of the complex, in our home clubhouse, Mills could sense his pitchers growing tense during the playoff push. Our pitching staff had been throwing well all season, but they were starting to lose close games. Hudson Valley had fallen back in the standings, and in their place were the Brooklyn Cyclones, trailing us by only one game. With four pivotal games coming up against the Renegades (who were only 3.5 games back), our status as division leaders was precarious. In an effort to relax his pitchers, Mills brought them over to the Cal Ripken World Series one afternoon.

I asked Mills what happened.

"I told them, 'This game is fun, and sometimes you lose sight of that. You get *paid* to play baseball—what all those kids out there wish they could do—and that's special.'"

"Did it sink in?" I said.

"Who knows. They think I'm retarded."

We laughed.

"I need a real job, Greg."

I could stand to learn the same lesson Mills tried to teach his pitchers. Sure, I had to do a lot of degrading shit for this job, but the job was pretty special. Although that was hard to remember on nights like the one I had a few weeks before. Food services had been doing a great job of feeding us with huge postgame spreads, but we started running into a problem I never thought I'd have: we were getting too much food—way more than even forty hungry young men could eat.

At first I enjoyed the surplus—I could put the leftovers in big Tupperware containers and send them over to Tony, the visitors' clubhouse attendant. Tony would then spend the early afternoon putting his little microwave to work heating up our leftovers. He said players looked forward to visiting us because not only did we have the nicest hotel in the league—the lovely brick Marriott right next to the stadium (which was in stark contrast to the bed-bug-infested motels in places like Niles, Ohio)—but also because we fed them. Most other places in the New York–Penn League either didn't feed visiting teams or only gave them PB&J. Instead, we gave them our leftovers, and they loved every bit of it. Guys would come into the clubhouse for the first time in weeks and say, "What've you got for us this trip, Tony?" And Tony would say, "Whatever Greg's whipping up over there," referring to our leftovers (he was slippery, like any good clubbie).

But by late August I was getting so much food that even after packaging leftovers for the visiting clubhouse I was still throwing out piping hot piles of perfectly good grub. Full trays of rice cascaded down into the garbage can. I slopped green beans in after them, and sometimes, if we were at the end of a home stand, I would throw out pound after pound of beautiful pulled pork. At the end of each night, I would take the double-lined garbage bag filled with food and leave it in a cardboard box behind the clubhouse where the stadium janitors would pick it up in the morning.

As I took the garbage out back one night, just a few weeks before our games against Hudson Valley, the bag ripped, releasing a toxic slurry of sloppy chicken, rice, and veggies all over my feet and onto the grass. Mixed in with the sludge was the rest of the day's clubhouse garbage: old socks, dirty athletic tape, Styrofoam plates, dip cups, gum, etc. It was one of those moments when you realize it wouldn't be that tough to take off your rubber gloves, run to your Caddie, and speed off into the night, never to return. But I couldn't leave all this for the janitors to pick up—I had to scoop the waste into a new bag. I grabbed a dustpan and proceeded to get on my hands and knees to regarbage the soupy mess. Guys exited the clubhouse and saw the scene before them.

"Oh shit, G," they said, "do you need a hand?"

"No, no point in you getting in this mess too."

Yacabonis came out and said, "G, what're you doing? Why don't you wait for someone else to come clean that up?"

"I am someone else," I said, taking solace in the thought that his pity might improve his tip.

Garbage cleanup aside, I felt lucky to be a clubbie—it even came with perks, at times. I sat in my bedroom one afternoon in August, just trying to hide out from the players, hoping nobody would come in and bother me. Norah Jones's album *Come Away with Me* played on my computer. I sat in my swivel chair at my minidesk, staring at the ground, waiting for the day to end. I heard a knock on the door and my stomach sank. I couldn't stand another guy coming in asking for gear he didn't need. "My cap was stolen," they'd say, when what they really meant was, "I looked for my cap for seven seconds and it didn't turn up. Give me a new one." And if I gave away too many, I'd have to get more from Don in The Hangar. He'd give me that look with his penetrating blue eyes, a look that said, "What, you can't say no to these kids?"

I couldn't. Even though I was older than all of them, I still wanted them to like me. So I gave in to their childish demands for a new cap or a new pair of shorts just to be accepted. I guess part of me knew how pathetic that was, so I cringed every time I gave in.

But it wasn't a player coming in to ask for something, it was Merullo carrying a bat.

"G-man," he said as he came in, "love the music."

"Norah Jones."

"Makes me think of sitting in bed on a Saturday morning with some chick bringing me breakfast in her panties."

I laughed. "Hell yeah."

"Here. Got a little present for you."

He reached the bat out to me and I sat up straight. It was 33.5 inches long and 30.5 ounces heavy with a black handle and a naked barrel with the label burned on, not just painted on like our shitty ash Rawlings bats.

"Maple?" I said.

"Yeah, yeah."

"Wow. Thank you so—"

"You're welcome—don't mention it. Now you can come out and take some BP with us sometime."

I looked up at him, but before I could say anything else he walked out, saving us both from whatever embarrassment would follow.

I looked closer at the label:

PROFESSIONAL MAPLE

IRONBIRDS

MODEL D-13 33.5

D5855 7-28-2013

IRONBIRDS, it said. The team name was plastered all over the stadium on shirts and caps and plastic beer cups that anyone could buy, but this particular collection of those nine letters—I-R-O-N-B-I-R-D-S—was special. It had been bestowed upon me by Matt Merullo, the manager.

"Here," the bat said, "in case you didn't realize it before, you are indeed a member of this team."

• • •

Some players liked to come back to the equipment closet just to hang out or chat for a few minutes whenever they got sick of the other guys in the locker room—Kimmel did this sometimes, and Mills too. But Conor Bierfeldt, our home run–slugging DH and outfielder with the dimpled chin of a cartoon superhero, was not one such player. In fact, Bierfeldt almost never asked me for anything, so I knew he really needed gear when he came by the day after Merullo had given me the bat.

"Hey, G," he said, "can I get some new socks?"

"Here."

I tossed him a pair, and he caught the plastic package against his sternum without looking, eyeing my new bat leaning against the equipment shelf. He walked over and picked it up.

"Damn this is some good wood. Whose is this?"

He was doing that thing players do when they pick up a new bat for the first time: he got into his full batting stance and stared down an imaginary pitcher who existed beyond the confines of the room, then he took a couple of testing chops, belt high, just to the front of the plate.

"It's mine," I said.

"Really? If this wasn't a 34 I'd take it from ya," he said, smiling. "I'd be all over a 33.5."

He held the bat out to a contact point with an imaginary ball. I grabbed the barrel and pulled it out of his hands.

"It *is* a 33.5," I said. "Anything else I can help you with?"

He raised his eyebrows, shook his head, and walked out as I put my bat in a safe, hidden place between my desk and the concrete wall.

Bierfeldt got one of the team's seven hits as we took the first game of a late-August series against Hudson Valley, 5–3, but it was obvious that this lineup would suffer without Kemp and Kimmel. Just in time for our next game on August 20, we got a shot of life: our first-round draft pick, Hunter Harvey, moved up to Aberdeen from the GCL. Hunter was all of eighteen years old but had just been inked by the Orioles for a $2 million signing bonus. Most of the players on our team were later-round guys just trying to survive on their $1,250 a month salaries (during the season)—they could hardly imagine getting that kind of money.

Harvey was six foot three and 175 pounds. He had a silly little mustache that had the exact inverse of its intended effect, subtracting about three years from his already boyish face. He'd been pitching well in the GCL, owning a 1.35 ERA in five starts, so only two months removed from graduating high school, Harvey came to us in the middle of a pennant race.

He started the next night, and it was immediately evident why the Orioles had drafted him in the first round: he popped the catcher's mitt with fastballs in the midnineties and a nasty curveball in the low-eighties. He worked quickly, and his windup featured something like a quick, three-step, soft-shoe dance as he rotated and turned toward home. He pitched four and a third innings and only gave up one unearned run, but that run was enough to beat us, 1–0. Still, the team was heartened by the arrival of even more pitching help.

"He looks like he's fourteen, but he pitched like he was thirty-four," Merullo told the press after the game. As he spoke to the reporters near his manager's office, the clubhouse echoed with somber music. Miley Cyrus marked a victory, but Lana Del Rey's new song, "Summertime Sadness," signaled defeat. It was pure melancholy, and she sang it in a low range that reminded me of a singer out of the '60s:

Like the stars miss the sun in the morning skies.

As the season bumped along, "Summertime Sadness" eventually made its way onto the clubhouse stereo whether we won or lost.

The next morning, before the team hit the road for two games at Hudson Valley, I found Trek passed out in his office. He'd woken me up throughout the night, walking into my bedroom to grab more Bud Heavies from my fridge.

He'd stumble in, hunched over and drunk, unapologetically saying, "Greg, I'm coming in to get some beer."

I locked the door after his first visit, but I forgot he had a key.

"Didja miss me?" he said.

"No."

"What'sa matter? You got somewhere to be?"

"No. I'm just trying to sleep."

"Well, if yer goin' to sleep, just make sure I get up by nine tomorrow."

I sat up on my air mattress. "Are you really gonna wake up, Trek, or are you gonna be an ornery bastard and get pissed at me?"

"I'll probably get pissed at ya, but just kick me if you have to."

The next morning he snapped at me like a drunken bear.

"Goddamnit, Greg, gimme fifteen minutes."

"I'm not your alarm clock," I said, walking away.

The drunken night I had with Paco, Trek, and Merullo—when Merullo had given me batting advice in the cages—was a thrilling novelty, but the guys had been taking it too far. Paco wasn't even staying in the clubhouse anymore, at least in part because Merullo and Trek were getting toasted every night. And the thing was, they didn't even drink *together* anymore—Trek sat in his office drinking Bud Heavy, and Matt sat in his office drinking Bud Heavy, like a married couple watching the same TV show in different rooms. I'd recently learned the team's nickname for Merullo: Buttermaker. They called him that after Walter Matthau's character in *The Bad News Bears*, the Little League coach who had an unquenchable taste for Budweiser.

I slid Trek's training equipment underneath the bus, which was loaded with players, all waiting for the coaching staff.

"Wake up, Trek!" I yelled when I went back to shove him. "Trek!"

He stirred. "Iza bus 'ere?" he said, barely opening his eyes.

"The bus? Dude, everyone's already on the bus waiting for you."

He popped up. "Are yew fuckin' kiddin' me, Greg? What time's it?"

"It's nine fifteen."

"I told you to wake me up at nine. D'you ferget?"

"I didn't forget. You—"

"Is all my 'quipment loaded on the bus?" He sat there looking at me through his bloodshot, beady little eyes, his head wobbling.

"Yes, Trek, I loaded your shit."

He fell back down onto his blow-up mattress. "Then tell 'ose fuckers to wait fifteen goddamn minutes." He closed his eyes and fell back to sleep immediately.

"I already gave you fifteen."

Mills and Merullo were still in the coaches' office—Merullo was hungover, but he seemed to be in solid shape, wearing his polo shirt and golf shorts. They both had their travel bags slung over their shoulders.

"Where the fuck's Trek?" Merullo said. "We gotta get outta here."

"He's passed out in the training room," I said.

Mills dropped his bag and strutted past me, grimacing. He turned on all the lights in the training room where Trek slept.

"Wake the fuck up! Bus is leaving." He stomped in Trek's direction, shouting loud enough to rattle him awake. "You need an alarm clock or something?"

Trek stood up just in time, before Mills got close enough to do whatever his next step would have been.

"Don't drink so much if you can't handle it," Mills said. He strutted out of the training room, grabbed his bag without missing a beat, and walked with Merullo out of the clubhouse and onto the bus. I stood there while Trek got his shit in order.

"Damn it, Greg. You see what you did?"

"What *I* did?"

"I thought I told you to wake me up. Now I got Mills fuckin' chewin' my ass."

"I did wake you up. You said just fifteen minutes."

"We don't have fifteen minutes, Greg." He shut his computer, loaded it into his bag, and stormed out of the office. "The fucking bus is here."

I chased behind him, trying to make my point. He loaded his drunk ass onto the bus, and I could hear the sarcastic round of applause through the open windows as the door shut and they rumbled through the stadium parking lot. They drove away to play Hudson Valley in Wappingers Falls, New York, where I could follow their every pitch and at bat through the MiLB.com website. But despite that thread of connection to the team as they traveled, the moment they left Ripken Stadium, they felt so far away they might as well have been in—well—Wappingers Falls, New York.

• • •

The guys split their two games against Hudson Valley to hang onto their 1.5 game division lead over the Brooklyn Cyclones. When they came home there was no laughing, smiling, or bullshitting: everyone just dropped their gear at their lockers and went about their business. It was almost 3:00 p.m. on a game day, and they had just arrived nearly *twelve hours* after they were supposed to.

Mills came in with sleepy eyes and a slower-than-usual gait toward the coaches' office.

"What's up, meat?" I said.

He shook his head. "You could kick my ass right now, Greg. I'm dead."

I walked up to Kimmel, who was still on the DL with a concussion from his fight with the left-field wall in Norwich, Connecticut.

"The fucking bus lit on fire," he said. "Like ten minutes from Hudson Valley."

"What?"

"Yeah. And then the replacement bus they gave us broke down on the way here."

Yacabonis walked past. "It was a fucking shitshow, G."

(Kimmel once told me about a road trip to Brooklyn the previous season when the AC on the bus went out. Almost everyone took their shirts and pants off—a Coach bus filled with professional athletes wearing nothing but their boxers. "We didn't even have water," Kimmel said. "Some guys would take turns poking their heads out the top of the emergency exit.")

After returning from their road trip at nearly three o'clock that afternoon, the IronBirds looked lethargic in an 8–2 home loss to the Connecticut Tigers. The clubhouse cleared quickly after the game.

Some clubbies traveled with their teams, some didn't. I couldn't discern any larger logic to the decision other than precedence—I'm sure Jake, as the first IronBirds clubbie, finagled it so he didn't have to travel, so no future IronBirds clubbie would either. But there was this growing sense of guilt inside of me whenever I collected dues at the end of a home stand. Sure, I felt the primal surge of dopamine that accompanied the bulging front pocket of my fanny pack (I started keeping a few dozen ones and fives for change in the back pocket closest to my body while sticking the player payments in the front pocket. That way I wouldn't have to flip through the big bills looking for change, which gave players the impression that I was flush with cash. I'd also started keeping track of not only who paid their dues, but how much they tipped, as well. That way I knew who to take care of when it came to extra goodies).

But there was something else adding to my guilt. I'd been in Aberdeen long enough to see how much most of these guys made. Sure, there was Hunter Harvey with the first round multimillion-dollar signing bonus, but most of them didn't get seven figures from the Orioles—a lot of them barely got five. Here was the weird thing: after they got that signing bonus, everyone made the same $1,250 per month their first year in Aberdeen (again, that was before taxes and only during the season). Then they had to pay me dues—seven bucks a home game—which was essentially another tax.

Even guys like Vader, who was drafted out of high school and got a $150,000 signing bonus, would have to make that money last *a long time*. How many years until Vader made it to the Majors? He was 5-3 with a 2.72 ERA, he had a pitcher's build at six foot four and 175 pounds, and he had that serial killer's stare that somehow fit the job description. But he was twenty-one—certainly not old for short-season, but not on the fast track either. Maybe he'd make it in five years, maybe never. Take away thirty-some percent of that bonus for taxes, then spread it out over the years it might take him to reach the Majors, and six figures suddenly doesn't look like very much. And then, what if he didn't make it?

It wasn't uncommon for guys to get drafted straight out of high school like Vader, so part of negotiations with teams was whether or not they'd pay for him to get a college degree after his career was up, but that wasn't offered to everyone. Even the guys who did get that extra bonus might be ill-equipped both socially and financially to handle the college experience after years in a locker room making dick jokes and playing poker. And the teams that did add school tuition to a player's signing bonus often gave them tuition for a school much worse than the ones they could've attended on a baseball scholarship. (Of course there were guys like starting pitcher Mitch Horacek, who spent his late August afternoons on my laundry room couch, whenever he wasn't scheduled to pitch, studying for his upcoming fall classes so he could continue work toward his hybrid engineering and economics degree from Dartmouth. Guys like that were going to be successful no matter what, whether it was on the field or off. Let's just say that sort of academic determination was rare in the clubhouse.)

So I guess what I'm getting at is this: after learning all that shit about their financial situations, taking their dues just seemed like an extra kick in the dick to these poor guys. Yeah, I provided them with services for those dues (mostly food), but I sure as hell did not need all of that money to cover the spreads I bought. And then there was that pressure to tip. Guilt didn't allow me to hassle them about tips, and even though I kept track of how much each guy gave me, I still had too much pride not to do my job well no matter what. Yeah, I worked my ass off, but so did they. They didn't get hardly *any* off days—I got tons of them, and I knew for a fact I was making way more money. But, then again, our situations weren't exactly analogous: I technically worked for the IronBirds and, by extension, the Ripken empire and its mysterious patriarch. The players were employees of the Baltimore Orioles.

People's perceptions of the IronBirds players usually swung one of two ways. The fans and the polo-shirt-and-khaki-pants-wearing front office people projected a stronger connection between the players in Aberdeen and the Orioles. I think of the usher who shared his theory about Merullo moving Yaz around all the outfield spots: "They must be grooming him to be a utility outfielder for the Orioles," he said. I didn't tell him that sometimes the regulars are just too hungover to play. On the other hand were fans who saw *no* connection between the IronBirds and anything else. They'd get an autograph or a picture with a player and, trying to be nice, would ask if he thought he'd ever make it to the pros. The player might respond with something snide—"We *are* pros"—or they'd infer what the person meant to say, and respond with something like, "I sure hope so."

The truth was somewhere in between those two—in the middle of glamour and bleakness. I knew Kimmel, an eighteenth rounder, got a nice $50,000 signing bonus, but he spent the off-season at his parents' house in order to save that money (and spent his first summer in professional baseball sleeping in his clubbie's apartment living room). It was a little more difficult for the lower round guys to improve their game at the same pace as the bonus babies because most of those later draft picks (and even midround picks) had to work other jobs in the off-season. Many players led baseball clinics for kids. Jack Graham, who had a degree from Kenyon College, worked at a Starbucks in the off-season. (His game had taken a shot of espresso in recent weeks: he had hits in back-to-back at bats on August 11 and August 16, raising his average to a healthy .111.)

The Dominicans seemed to have the hardest time managing their money—always coming in with new Gucci pants and shiny Ed Hardy shirts—but who could blame them? Most had come from nothing in their country and were handed what might as well have been a small fortune. There was no evidence that the team made any effort to acclimate them to American life either. Jake had warned me that the "coños" would cause the most trouble in the clubhouse and tip the least, but it had gotten to the point that I didn't fault them—I mostly just felt bad for them.

I didn't always feel that way. Earlier in the 2013 season, I remembered that two players who had come up at the end of the 2012 season still owed me dues money. They were the pitchers Santana and Severino. Santana and I had become something like acquaintances: he would help me with my Spanish and I would help him with his English.

Jake advised me to get the money they owed, which was forty-nine dollars each. They complied without question, both remembering that they'd failed to pay in 2012. I didn't need that money, even though it was technically owed to me through some ancient clubhouse tradition. Surely once the off-season came along and Santana was playing winter ball in the Dominican, he would need that money more than me. But at the time I rationalized it, telling myself that he and Severino would have just blown that cash on clothes anyway. As time went on I wasn't so sure about my perceptions. Like when the American guys bitched at the Dominicans for taking so much food from the spreads—the Dominicans probably weren't trying to be selfish, they were just hungry and getting their money's worth.

For me, the season was an opportunity to hoard enough cash to sustain me for an entire year. But for a lot of players, Americans and Dominicans alike, it was a struggle just to stay afloat, both financially and athletically. I got to play make-believe like I was really part of this team, but in reality I didn't have to make the same sacrifices as them. Some of these guys were gladly giving everything to the game—their education, their body, their youth—yet most of them would never see a return on their investment.

• • •

"I think we're going home," Trek said as we talked in his training room office.

I didn't know if he was saying what he expected to happen or what he hoped would happen. It was August 28 and we kept trading half-game division leads with the Brooklyn Cyclones, with us currently trailing. Hudson Valley, who snapped at our heels from third place, was coming into town again, this time having won five of their last six. Kimmel had been officially shut down for the season, but Kemp, our second baseman, was scheduled to come off the disabled list for game two against the Renegades.

"I think Hudson Valley's gonna win this thing," he said, "and we'll all be home by September 5."

I nodded: the only thing I could do when he got cynical like that.

"Anyway, that's what I think's gonna happen."

Everyone else was hungry for the playoffs, which was a first for the IronBirds. Mills talked to the pitchers before that big home game against Hudson Valley. He had grown a Fu Manchu mustache, the same kind he used to sport as a pitcher, the kind that was technically against the Orioles' facial hair rules (no mustache past the corner of the lips).

"You always wanna do well on a personal level," Mills said, "but you know how you get people's attention? You win. It's not rocket science. I'll tell you what, though: ain't any other teams in this organization that're gonna make the playoffs this year. And there's no better feeling than when you come into spring training and they give out those rings," he chuckled for effect. "People notice. They look around and say, 'Lemme see what you got.'"

Austin Urban, the sneering pitcher with the cool confidence, calmly took his 1-5 record onto the mound in Ripken Stadium and shut down the Renegades for six scoreless innings. We only got three hits all night, but one of them was a Conor Bierfeldt line drive in the bottom of the second. He turned on a ninety-four-mile-per-hour fastball and ripped his eleventh homer of the year over the 378 sign in left-center. Yacabonis and Hart—our setup man and closer combo—came in to close the door for the final three innings, bringing their ERAs to 1.63 and 1.64, respectively. We won 1–0 to remain a half game out of first behind the Cyclones with only five games left in the season.

Luckily, we'd have a chance to decide our own destiny: we were about to go on the road for a two-game series at their home, MCU Park in Coney Island.

"Trek," I said. "Can I come with on the road trip to Brooklyn?"

He looked up at me and thought about it. He shrugged. "Yeah," he said, "I don't see why not."

19

The Team of Destiny

I was in the middle of the strangest pissing contest of my life. I guess, technically, it was a kissing contest. We were barreling north on the I-95 corridor, a few bored hours into our trip between Aberdeen and Brooklyn. Kevin Clark decided to challenge me for some reason, turning around from the seat in front of me, saying, "Shit, I bet G won't even kiss me." Kevin had once asked me if I could switch out the Brut body spray in the coaches' bathroom with Axe—he said he was sick of smelling like a member of a barbershop quartet. Now, the stink of Axe—a prepubescent stink like flavored bug spray—seeped out of his pores as I leaned my head over the seat between us.

I closed my eyes and pursed my lips. He did the same, both of us inching toward each other over his seat. The air blowing out of his nostrils was close enough to tickle my lips. I peeked out of one eye and saw his lips protruding cartoonishly, like a boy going for his first kiss—all exaggeration. Was this some kind of strange hazing ritual? Did everyone have to kiss someone else before he could be fully accepted into the fraternity of the IronBirds? I couldn't imagine my seatmate—the team's goatee-sporting, five-foot-nothin' TV broadcaster, Paul Taylor—kissing anyone, man or woman. And yet he was still allowed on the bus.

Kevin and I hovered there, our lips twitching only inches apart. There was a silent anticipation of more than thirty men, all with the same collective thought: "How the hell are they gonna get outta this?"

I broke the silence and said, finally, "I went 90 percent, Kev. You gotta go at least 10."

The bus erupted in relieved laughter. But for the rest of the two-day road trip I couldn't win a single locker room argument without being bested with: "Well, at least I didn't kiss Kevin."

"We didn't kiss," I'd say. "But if we did, it would've been strictly platonic."

Still, it was the closest thing I'd had to a real kiss in three weeks, back when Nicole pecked me on the lips before I left North Augusta. I checked my phone obsessively on the bus to Brooklyn, but she hadn't responded to my texts in days. Maybe she was nervous in anticipation of my homecoming and assumed an off-season of laziness, already closing herself off to me.

When we unloaded at the stadium, Paco asked me if I wanted to throw. I put on my shorts and cap, grabbed my glove, and went out onto the field.

"How's the arm feel?" I said as I stepped farther and farther away from him.

"Good," he said. "Never felt better." Paco still looked like he could play. He had a strong chest and a whip for an arm.

Merullo walked over and stood next to Paco on the foul line as we threw long toss. Merullo said something to Paco but I was too far away to hear.

"Hey, G!" Merullo yelled.

"Sup!"

"You wanna take BP?"

My stomach dropped. "Hell yeah!"

When batting practice started, I went into the clubhouse and grabbed my bat from my travel bag—the one Merullo had given me, with the black handle and naked barrel. I carried it into the dugout and stroked the handle with a Mota stick. I then dabbed it with the pine tar rag and patted it down with rosin. Mills was throwing BP, so I stood off to the side to time his pitches. "Who knows?" I thought. "Who knows what happens if you hit well off of Mills here." I ran through a scenario in which I crush the ball in batting practice, then Mills taps me on the shoulder and says, "Shit, meat, I didn't know you could play," and I shrug like I couldn't give two shits. Then the coaches put me in the game as a joke and I go 4 for 4 and get a contract with the team. I shook the thought as I walked inside the turtle.

Mills stood on the artificial pitcher's mound, about forty-five feet away, looking down at me behind the L-screen. Sweat glistened on his temples and cheeks. The white in his eyes was striking, scary even. I could feel the muscles in my legs failing me as I waited for his pitches.

In baseball there are plenty of young men who hurl the ball toward the catcher with exceptional velocity but lack the precision to get it over the plate consistently. They're called "Throwers." But once they add precision and intention to their pitches, like a singer focusing their vocal runs, they're finally called "Pitchers." Alan Mills was a Thrower until 1996, when he got hurt as a twenty-nine-year-old and lost his velocity. Before his return he fine-tuned his slider, and he came back as a Pitcher. Mills was deceptive on the mound—all good pitchers are.

Baseball, in general, is a liar's sport. You trick the runner into thinking you're going home before you pick him off. You throw a fastball and changeup with the same arm motion so they look the same coming out of your hand. You tell your wife or girlfriend that you'll always be there for her before you disappear on some bus or plane to Pawtucket, Kansas City, or Brooklyn.

A *Baltimore Sun* sportswriter once said Mills's three best attributes on the mound were his fastball, his slider, and his stare. For god knows what reason, Mills the forty-six-year-old was giving me all three as I stood in the batter's box at MCU Park.

I started off by squaring up to bunt just like every other hitter at the start of his BP round.

"Get that shit outta here," he said. "Swing away."

I'd hardly pulled my bat back before he pumped a fastball on the inside corner. I swung and missed. He threw me another one to the same spot and I fisted it short of the pitcher's mound. The sting of the hit reverberated through my bare hands. I tried to remember Merullo's advice from that night in the cages: stay square and karate chop the ball. Mills dropped a slider on the outside corner and I whiffed, predictably, much to the amusement of everyone in the outfield.

Here was Mills: a man who over the course of his twelve Major League seasons had struck out Derek Jeter, Alex Rodriguez, Mark McGwire, and Dave Winfield, among others. Who knows? Maybe Mills was just eager to add "Greg Larson" to that illustrious list of victims. Each one of those pitches I swung on and missed whispered to me as it went past, carrying a message from Mills. I couldn't hear the message until one ball blurred past me with a *thump* against the green tarp of the turtle. The ball rolled to a stop and said, "You know you don't actually belong here, right?"

He had made his point, so he put the sliders in his back pocket and continued pumping heavy fastballs into the strike zone.

"Come on, G," Paco said from behind the turtle. "Just like in the cages. Relax."

I thought to myself, "Just swing a split second before you think you should."

He released the ball. I started my swing before I could even see where the ball was going. If he'd thrown that pitch into the upper deck, I would've still taken my cut right through the meat of the strike zone. Instead, he threw a strike, the baseball found my bat, and I slapped a hit between second and first. Something like a half-assed cheer went up from the guys shagging in the outfield, as if to say, "Hey, there you go! Now let's move on."

But Mills and I weren't done. I slapped another to the right side, a worm burner straight at an infielder. At that moment there was no cat's cradle of ground balls around the horn, so he bent over and held his glove motionless on the ground and let the ball roll in. He gave a little underhand roll back to the ball bucket near Mills.

"Relax, G," Paco said.

I chopped a couple more to the right side and Paco stopped cheering me on. I hit a weak, blooping pop-up down the right-field line, like a beach ball served harmlessly over first base. While it still floated midair, Mills said, "Alright, meat, move it along." I helped pick up the balls in the infield before grabbing my glove and going into center field.

I heard Bierfeldt talking to someone in left-center. "I'm sure there's a stadium usher somewhere who hasn't gotten any cuts yet—when's he taking BP?"

I looked toward home plate and saw none other than the hunched figure of Trek standing at the dish. Unlike everyone else, Trek wore a helmet for his BP session. He probably figured if he got knocked on the noggin there'd be nobody to treat him but himself, so he better stay protected. He swung just the way I expected him to: with stiff legs, all upper body, and about half a second too late on every pitch. By the time he took each cut, the ball would've been halfway through its journey back to the pitcher if a catcher were back there.

Guys in the outfield started yelling "Now!" when Mills released the ball, goading Trek into swinging earlier. Mills looked like he was still pumping hard fastballs into the zone. Trek fouled one straight up into the turtle and the guys gave another half-assed cheer for making contact.

After batting practice, I went in with everyone else to get ready for the game. I made a few burger runs for small tips, which I used to buy my own lunch, and I sat eating as I waited for the locker room to clear before heading to the dugout. For every road trip, I packed an extras bag with belts, socks, shorts, jerseys, pants, and laundry loops in case new players joined us on the road or someone's pants busted in the middle of a game—or, in this case, if the clubbie decided to suit up.

Vader, the starter, now 6-3 with a 2.64 ERA, chose to wear our favorite blue alternates for the game. They paired with gray road pants that sported a matching blue stripe along the outside of the thigh. Of course I still liked those blue alternate jerseys for their looks and easy cleanability, but I wouldn't have to do any cleaning that road trip—the Brooklyn clubbie would take care of that.

With surprising nerves, I put on a full IronBirds uniform. I could've easily passed as a deceptive righty coming out of the bullpen, or a light-hitting second baseman that came off the bench to pinch run with the game on the line. I admired myself in the mirror, a little too excited to be wearing a jersey. Luckily I'd packed a pair of pants that fit me—thirty-six-inch waist, twenty-nine-inch inseam—perfect for high socks.

I pulled my black game cap onto my head: first positioning it against my forehead, then sliding the back down over my cowlick. My dad taught me this as a kid: you put your cap on front first so the pressure is built up against your forehead. This prevents your lid from sailing away when you chase after a fly ball. The new logo on my cap faced me in the mirror. Long gone was the cheesy, side-facing cartoon airplane with a smile and a "golly gee, we're twenty games out of first place" attitude. This new logo stared me dead on—a fierce bird saying, "We're the Aberdeen fucking IronBirds, and we will not be denied our destiny. Let's do this." I snapped a picture in the mirror and sent it to Nicole—she'd think I looked sexy in full uniform.

I nodded to myself in the mirror. "So this is as close as you're ever gonna get, eh slick?"

If I were a real player, I would've walked over to Brooklyn's dugout during the pregame lull and said hello to Eddie Rohan, my old classmate from Winthrop. Fraternizing with opposing players was a status symbol, as if to say, "I know so many goddamn people in this industry that I even have friends on other teams"—but not on that night. These assholes were the only thing standing between us and history (or as close as you could get to it in the New York–

Penn League). You don't shake hands across the galactic divide of a battlefield, so you don't say hello to your old classmate on the other team.

The sun's light fell behind us to the west, and in its place, popping up like fireworks in the darkness, were the neons that marked the permanent county fair that was Coney Island. Each bank of lights illuminating the field was accented with a neon circus ring surrounding it like a halo. Out beyond the right-field foul pole, between the park and the Coney Island Channel, stood the Parachute Jump: a defunct fossil leftover from the World's Fair in 1939, the same year the New York–Penn League was founded. It no longer operated, but the 250-foot-tall dandelion-shaped structure still blazed with an ever-changing rainbow of colors.

Vader was lights out on the mound. He held the Cyclones scoreless in the first, and we got out to an early one-run lead with a line drive over the right-field fence, right toward the Parachute Jump.

Between innings, the Cyclones cheerleaders, called the Beach Bums, stood on the dugouts throwing out T-shirts and doing dance routines to Usher songs. I snuck away to the locker room during one routine to check my phone. Nicole still hadn't responded to my picture.

I went back to the dugout and stood with my arms hanging over the railing talking to Alex Murphy, who had just been called up from the Gulf Coast League in Sarasota. This was his first game with us.

"This is so different from the GCL," he said, watching the action around him. His eyes were pale blue and he smiled with a reverence that I hoped would never fade. "Down there it's about a hundred degrees and like eighteen people come to the games."

I nodded and looked out on the field. Vader was rolling untouched through the middle innings, still up 1–0.

"Do this many people come to our home games?" he said. The announced crowd that night was 8,447 in attendance, about two thousand more than Ripken Stadium could hold.

"Sometimes," I said. "Depends on if there's fireworks or not. Depends on if we're winning or not. Last year we'd sell out games but nobody'd show up. I think it was just season ticket sellouts or something."

"Man," he said, shaking his head, "it feels pretty damn good to be up here."

Up here, I repeated in my head.

We led 3–0 by the bottom of the eighth, and Nicole still hadn't texted me back. I worried about her—about us.

"I've been married three times," Mills once told me. "And you know what was the main culprit for the end of those relationships— the common denominator besides me? Baseball."

Nicole never responded to the picture.

We won the game, 7–0; Vader's record jumped to 7-3 and his ERA lowered to 2.43 after seven scoreless innings. And just like that, we were officially a half game ahead of Brooklyn in the McNamara Division.

After the game, the coaches and I all sat around drinking beers in our private locker room. The conversation shifted from the game to our batting practice.

"Thanks again for letting us get in there, meat," I said to Mills.

"No," Paco said. "Thank you. Having you guys in there is good for the team—it keeps them loose. It lets them see how hard it is."

Mills took a sip from his water bottle. "Hitting," he said, "is the hardest thing to do in sports. You gotta hit a round ball with a round bat squarely. Sometimes pitchers forget that. They forget how difficult it is to hit, and they go out there and try to over-throw the ball. It's not tough—the best hitters still fail 70 percent of the time. Having you guys out there hopefully clicked with a few of them that, hey, this shit isn't as easy as it looks from the bullpen or the dugout." He bulged his eyes at me. He'd once complained to me that Trek, who never played professional baseball, did too much bitching in the dugout about players' performances.

Trek shook his head. "I couldn't get turned open to save my fucking life."

"You didn't even use your lower half," Merullo said. "You were all arms."

"I felt so fucking tight, I was worried about doing something stupid and tearing a muscle. Then I had Mills throwing me fucking ched."

"I turned it up on you a bit and you had a hard time keeping up." Then Mills pointed at me while still looking at Trek. "He kinda got this look in his eye when I cranked it up on him—he said, 'Okay, now I gotta turn it up too.'"

"Damn right you did, G-baby," Paco said, pounding my fist.

"I'm glad you've loosened up, meat, because last year you were as green as that grass out there."

Trek allowed a little laugh.

I'd planned on waking up early the next day to go to the Museum of Modern Art before our 5:00 p.m. game, but instead I got hammered with the coaches and Paul Taylor, our broadcast guy. Paul eventually dragged me to Times Square, and I could barely keep the vomit in my mouth as the New York subway rolled me underneath the city.

In the locker room the next morning, I put my shades on and lay my head down on an equipment bag. I dropped my cap over my eyes to shield them from the fluorescent glow of the locker room. Guys trickled in (some in similar straits) and gave me words and looks of approval, like we were in high school again, congratulating each other for drinking alcohol. Then I remembered that Hunter Harvey, our starting pitcher for that night, was eighteen years old and probably still thought a hangover meant you had an unseen badge of popularity, when in reality all it meant was that you'd swallowed your own puke on the Q train.

Harvey decided to go with our black jerseys, the ones with no buttons and a blue cursive "A" over the right breast, trimmed with orange. For some reason, the black seemed like a perfect fit for the day. September clouds had eclipsed the sun, like the billowing steam of a squelched summer. I sent Nicole another picture of me in uniform, and again she never responded.

Yaz led off the game with a double to center field. Jeff Kemp, acting as DH, came up to the plate and hit a ground ball to the shortstop. Yaz made the aggressive move and broke for third, but the shortstop whipped the ball to the third baseman, who tagged Yaz out on a headfirst slide. Kemp stood on first with a fielder's choice. With one out and Mancini batting, Kemp stole second. The catcher's throw went into center field and Kemp advanced to third. The next two batters struck out to end the IronBirds' half of the inning. Kemp's advance to third base was the closest either team would get to scoring until the sixth. Harvey shut the Cyclones down for four and a third innings, giving up one base hit (which was erased by a double play) and one walk.

After we blew a scoring opportunity in the sixth, the game was still scoreless in the bottom of the seventh. One of our bullpen guys came in to pitch out of a jam: men on first and second, one out. The Brooklyn batter grounded to third base for a force out—two down, men still on first and second. The next batter hit a single up the middle. The Cyclones runner on second rounded third. The throw to the plate sailed away from our catcher, allowing the first run of the game to score. We got a strikeout to end the inning, but we now trailed 1–0.

Kemp led off the top of the eighth by getting hit by a pitch. Trek jogged out to check on the already-injured DH, but Kemp shook him off and stayed in the game. With the slugging Bierfeldt at the dish, Kemp broke for second, where he was caught for the second out. Bierfeldt proceeded to launch a fly ball to center field. It floated over the fence for a solo home run to tie the game. We cheered in the dugout, but our excitement was tinged with regret.

"We should be up 2–1," someone said.

"Why do you send Kemp with our best home run hitter at the plate?" someone else said, not expecting an answer.

The homer was the big righty's twelfth of the season, setting an IronBirds record.

Our half of the eighth ended, and we went into the bottom of the frame tied at 1. The Beach Bum cheerleaders climbed onto our dugout and threw out T-shirts, hopping and dancing to the music. Jorge Rivera watched, holding a handful of Dubble Bubble in twisted yellow wrappers.

"Morena!" he called to a Latina-looking Beach Bum. "Morena!"

She gave him a bored look over her right shoulder. Rivera held up a piece of gum and smiled with his crooked teeth and high, freckled cheeks. She tossed her last T-shirt into the stands then turned back to Rivera and held out her hand. He threw her the gum and she mouthed a thank you before running off with her fellow Beach Bums. The interaction reminded me of a moment earlier in the summer when Mills had come into the clubhouse before a game.

He walked up to a couple of his pitchers. "There's a kid out there that'll give you candy for an autograph," he said. A couple guys gave an excited "Really?" and gathered their gear in a hurry before hustling out the clubhouse door. I wondered if the kid had any idea that he'd elicited a child's response from the players. Hopefully not.

We struck out the 9-1-2 batters in the eighth to head into the last inning still tied and the season on the line.

We loaded the bases in the top of the ninth with one out. The stadium pulsed with noise—*Boom, boom, clap. Boom, boom, clap.* The Cyclones were a double play away from getting out of the jam. Yaz came up to the plate with a modest .268 batting average, but he always had a knack for finding his way on base. If he could just squeak one run across the plate, we had side-armer Donnie Hart getting hot in the bullpen, ready to finish the game.

Yaz ripped a double to left-center that scored all three runners, bringing us out in front, 4–1. The stadium fell silent except for our dugout. I always wondered what it felt like to be on the visiting team that silenced a ballpark. Our cheers felt like a middle finger to the fans: *How dare they root against the team of destiny?*

Jeff Kemp worked a full count with Yaz still on second after his double. The next pitch, ball four, got away from the catcher and Yaz broke for third, another potential base-running gaffe for the Birds. The catcher picked up the ball and proceeded to gun it into left field, which allowed Yaz to score, giving us a 5–1 lead going into the bottom of the ninth.

Left-handed side-armer Donnie Hart jogged in with his 1.64 ERA. Donnie had been zeroed in all summer except for back-to-back bad outings in mid-August where he gave up three earned runs in three and a third total innings. Unfortunately, on this night, the Cyclones had his number.

They started with back-to-back singles to put runners on first and second. The next batter hit a ground ball to third. Our third baseman fielded it cleanly, but he had trouble on the transfer out of his glove. He rushed his throw, which short-hopped Mancini at first. The ball skipped past him and a run scored. Men on second and third, no outs, IronBirds 5, Cyclones 2.

The crowd threw cheers back in our faces and we sat in the dugout, silent to each other save a few forced claps. With the infield back, the next batter hit a ground ball to short. We took the easy out at first, which allowed another run to score. Man on third, one out, IronBirds 5, Cyclones 3. A line drive single to right field scored the runner on third. Man on first, one out, IronBirds 5, Cyclones 4.

The winning run came to the plate. All that work for nothing. We were going to split the two-game series and go back home in the same position as we had come in, a half game behind Brooklyn, but now we'd only have *three* games to make up the deficit. The team would find a way to blame me in some joking way—"Maybe if G weren't bad luck"—but those jokes would bounce around my mind like pinballs. The Cyclone at home plate would find a way to round the bases, I just knew it, and in doing so, he would nullify our win the previous night. We might as well have ripped open a black hole on the field and thrown in August 31 and September 1, 2013, erasing them from the calendar of the universe forever.

The batter popped up toward Feddy, our backup second base-man. It was just a chance. I could feel myself in his shoes—the skinny, no-hitting second baseman who truly did not belong. I could feel him forcing himself to pretend like it was all so routine, like he didn't give a shit that the second out snapped inside of his mitt. The next batter hit a fly ball to right field. From our angle, on the third base line, for just a split second, it might have had that cosmic power to erase time, and the cheers behind us signaled the same. But it died well short of the fence and found its way harm-lessly into Yaz's glove for the final out.

We won, 5–4, and we were about to leave MCU Park with a 1.5 game lead over Brooklyn with only three games left in the season.

I walked confidently from the dugout into the tunnel con-necting the intestinal works of the stadium. I felt a jolt as though I had personally helped win the game. And why not? I did about as much as Jack Graham. I could sit on my ass and enjoy a baseball game just as well as him or any of our other benchwarmers.

I was still wearing my jersey when I walked past a group of the Beach Bums in the concrete tunnel under MCU.

I looked directly at one of the girls and said, "I love you."

I knew immediately that it wasn't the right call. I could see Nicole chewing her tongue if she knew. Or maybe Nicole would pretend that she didn't care—I didn't know. I just figured that I'd give one "I love you" to someone who might accept it.

The Beach Bum looked up at me and beamed. "Thank you," she said, giggling. She was all shine, tan, and glitter.

I sauntered on, a walking jersey, as the group talked in my wake. In the locker room, I changed into my street clothes with the play-ers. Every few minutes someone would shout something like, "Let's go home and take this shit for good." Paco came by to grab a towel from the players' locker room and told me I was the team's good luck charm.

"Fucking right he is," someone said.

I wheeled Trek's training room box through the tunnel toward the team bus. I ran into the Brooklyn clubbie, who I'd met the day before.

"How're your guys doing?" I said, thinking they'd be despondent after the sweep.

"Oh, they couldn't be happier. Yeah, most of them were ready to go home anyway, so they were kinda quietly celebrating." I gave him a quizzical look, but he only responded with, "Good luck in the playoffs," and shook my hand before peeling off into a clubbie-walk out of sight.

I continued outside to our team bus, which was surrounded by Cyclones fans seeking autographs. It was dark out now. Groups of children and adults alike crowded around Trey Mancini and Mike Yastrzemski especially—they were our position players with the best chances of making it. I walked through the crowd, ignored, toward the open undercarriage of the bus. Before I could reach it, though, a little boy popped in front of me and asked for my autograph.

"You don't want my autograph, slick. I'm the clubhouse attendant."

He looked up at me and said, genuinely, "I don't care," and shoved his program into my chest. I looked down at his face, as bright as the neon all around us. He was me ten years before, at the Minnesota Twins spring training workouts—spending all day at the stadium just for a chance to talk to the players. All we wanted—this boy and I—was a connection with someone who was part of this thing we loved.

He held his program in one hand, black Sharpie in the other—both reached out for me. My eyes flickered down to him momentarily before finally looking up over his head and brushing past him toward the bus—not because I was too cool, but because of something closer to the exact opposite. He didn't say a word behind me; I wouldn't have either when I was his age.

• • •

Merullo spoke loud enough to wake half the bus on our way home from Brooklyn. It was just after midnight and we were crawling south on the empty interstate.

"Jesus Christ," he said to our driver, "at this speed we'll miss our game tomorrow night. When's opening pitch, seven?"

"The GPS says we'll arrive—"

"You're going sixty fucking miles an hour."

"I'm going almost seventy," the driver said.

"Look at the road. We haven't seen a single car in an hour."

"But if we get pulled over—"

"Oh, step on the fucking gas and send the ticket to Cal Ripken Jr."

The driver was overmatched on this by about forty to one. He'd already lost his credibility in the previous few weeks, what with the bus catching on fire and him hitting a car on a back street in Coney Island. (He went out to exchange insurance information and the owner of the other car nearly fought him. Mills hopped off the bus to cool things down. When Mills came back he said, "You all wanna sit in here and laugh at him, but he was about to get his ass beat. Then how the fuck are we gonna get home?")

The driver turned off the cruise control and stepped on the gas. Throughout the bus, heads leaned back to resume their slumber— even the two guys sleeping in the aisle.

We pulled into Ripken Stadium sometime in the early morning, and I was immediately back to work scrubbing pants and washing clothes. By 4:00 a.m. I was finished and blowing up my air mattress in my bedroom. By then I'd grown fond of the licorice smell of rosin powder in the air—it signaled home. I wondered if I would ever miss that once panic-inducing smell or the hum of the giant industrial refrigerator.

We got word the next day that the Brooklyn Cyclones had lost their early game, which meant if we won that night, we'd clinch the division and a trip to the playoffs for the first time in team history. Our excitement built throughout the afternoon. We'd all seen videos of big league teams spraying their teammates with celebratory bottles of champagne in a tarped clubhouse—they'd all be wearing swimming goggles, spraying with reckless abandon.

I called Jake Parker.

"What do I do?" I said. "Are we allowed to have champagne? I mean, a third of these guys can't even drink legally."

"That's a good question," he said. "We never won when I was there, so we never ran into that problem. Ask Brad."

I talked Brad, the GM, into buying some bottles of sparkling cider, while I tried to scrounge some real booze together. I went out and used my own money to get three bottles of cheap champagne, and lucky enough, I had nearly two cases of Bud Light and Bud Heavy leftover from my last trade with John the beer guy. Still, it wasn't enough for a full team.

"G-baby!" Paco said as I hustled around the clubhouse. "You getting us hooked up for the playoffs, man?"

"I'm trying. Front office isn't keen on buying booze for underage guys."

"What, they can't afford to buy a few bottles of champagne, and after all these guys have done for them? How much extra money will they make if we get into the playoffs? And they can't buy us some fucking champagne?"

Kev overheard us. "We're not getting any bubbly for the game? What the fuck, G?"

"Look, I don't know what to tell ya—"

"Tell us you'll do the right thing," Paco said. "This is professional baseball. You get a champagne shower if you make the playoffs."

Later, Brad came to me with a big case in his arms. I got excited until I looked inside: it was only half-full with apple cider and a couple bottles of real champagne for the coaches.

"They just need a little something to spray," he said. "It doesn't really matter what it is."

It did matter, though. But we had to win the game first.

It was September 2, and the twilight of summer faded fast behind us. The only thing ahead, less than two hundred feet beyond the outfield wall, was the I-95 corridor. If we won that night, the Iron-

Birds, the southernmost team in the league, would load up our bus and ride that freeway north to the playoffs.

A few front office interns helped me tape plastic tarps over the lockers to protect the players' stuff from a possible champagne shower. I put the beers on ice in the coaches' office and a small bucket of cider and champagne in the locker room.

Steven Brault was on the mound dealing for the 37-32 IronBirds against the 40-30 Lowell Spinners. Kimmel; our strength coach, Kevin; and I sat in the clubhouse watching the game on closed-circuit TV. I, of course, usually spent a lot of time in the clubhouse during games. Kev always seemed more interested in getting a lift in or Skyping with his girlfriend in the coaches' office rather than going to the dugout. As for Kimmel, Trek had made him stay off the field ever since he ran into that wall in Connecticut. We had to keep the clubhouse lights off because they were too harsh for Kimmel's concussed brain. So the three of us sat there sprawled out on the couches in the dark as we listened to the anxious voice of Paul Taylor call the game.

"The game looks so easy on TV," Kimmel said.

I nodded as though I knew.

Yaz led off the first with a double. Mancini followed up with a double of his own to score the game's first run. Mancini wound up scoring on an error to give the IronBirds a quick 2–0 lead. Four walks and another error in the second doubled the lead to 4–0.

Brault only pitched three innings, but he held the Spinners scoreless. We led 6–3 going into the top of the eighth.

I ran back to my bedroom to drop off my wallet and cell phone so they wouldn't get drenched in the ensuing festivities. Kimmel came in behind me.

"Hey, Greg," he said in his monotone voice. "Can I have a helmet?"

"You thinking you might get an AB?"

"No. Trek just told me that if I'm gonna do something stupid I should at least wear a helmet while I do it."

I took a medium off the shelf and slapped it onto his head.

"Gracias," he said.

We hurried out toward the bullpen and Kev stopped me, shoving his phone toward my hands.

"Hey, G. You think you could record me and Kimmel running out to celebrate on the mound? Just like a sick video—you running alongside us capturing this insane moment. It'll be awesome."

Kimmel gave him a look.

"What?" I said. "Dude, no. I wanna celebrate, too."

We went out to the bullpen, where Yacabonis was just hopping off the mound. One of the guys held open the right-field door for him and a few of us slapped his ass as he streaked past, running out onto the field.

"Fuckin' shut these guys down, Yac!"

"Let's go, boy!"

"Yacaboney! Yacaboney!"

Yacabonis quickly gave up a single to the first batter. We all craned our heads toward the scoreboard in center field, as if to remind ourselves that yes, we were still winning by three. The next batter grounded out, but Yacabonis threw a wild pitch to the next man, allowing the runner to advance to second. Our cheers came out strained and nervous.

"You got this," we said, so quiet that Yastrzemski in right couldn't even hear us.

He got another ground ball and a pop-up to end their half of the eighth. We struck for one more run in the bottom of the frame to make it 7–3, and Yacabonis came back to try and close the game. The bullpen bounced in anticipation. Someone slapped Kimmel's helmet in happiness.

"Hey!" I said. "Don't fuck with Kimmel's brain."

Yacabonis got a couple of quick outs and we were giddy with anticipation, everything moving up an octave. Yac jammed the next batter with a fastball inside and he fisted it into foul territory behind first base. Trey Mancini angled back for an over-the-shoulder catch. The ball landed in his mitt for the final out of the game and he threw his hands into the air. We opened the bullpen door and sprinted toward the growing mob near the pitcher's mound. The crowd cheered as we ran through the outfield. Music blared over the stadium sound system. I laughed deliriously as our bullpen group collided with everyone else in the infield. We hopped, slapped, and threw cups of water at each other because we didn't know what else to do—all facing each other, smiling, laughing.

Once our ecstasy died down, we walked off the field toward the coaching staff standing at the foul line, waiting to greet us. Each of them gave us a fist bump as we walked past. Merullo smiled at me.

"G-man getting in on the action," he said.

Trek said, "Nice work, Greg," with a straight face.

Back in the clubhouse we sprayed each other just like the videos we'd watched since we were kids, the ones with big leaguers clinching playoff berths and winning the World Series. I bounced in the middle of it, celebrating with my team. Then somebody got a little too excited with one of the bottles and it shattered on the ground. I walked back to the laundry room, grabbed a broom and dustpan, and elbowed my way back into the middle of the celebration. Miley Cyrus's "We Can't Stop" blared over the clubhouse stereo. I swept up the broken glass as the party continued all around me.

I ran into the coaches' office and hugged everyone. Mills gave me a high-cheeked smile and a one-armed bro hug.

"Congrats, dude," I said with a hint of sadness. The Orioles loved Mills—it was kind of a given that he'd be moved up to a new team in 2014. "I'm gonna miss you next year," I said.

"G-baby!" Paco said. "You got us hooked up tonight."

"Damn right."

"G with the MVP move," Kev said. "MVG."

We laughed.

The party eventually died down and the clubhouse cleared out except for Merullo, Trek, and Shawny, the game host, all talking over beers.

"You better get this crowd fucking goin' for a playoff game," Trek said to Shawny.

"What day's that happen?" Merullo said. "Haven't even looked at the schedule yet."

"They'll give us an off day on the fifth. Then we'll play on the sixth," Trek said. "But I don't want these guys coming out here to some fireworks crowd that doesn't give a shit about the game."

"Oh, no," Shawny said. "We're ready for it. The whole Flight Crew is—"

"Look at me," Trek said, holding up his right hand. "You see this? By the end of this season I want a fucking ring on my finger."

I sent Nicole a one-word text: "Playoffs."

She responded immediately: "Congrats." Her first response in days.

"You all good?"

"Yes and no."

"Please talk to me. I love you."

No response.

"Is everything okay?" I sent. "I really have no idea what's going on with us."

"I've just been taking time to think things through."

"Think what through?"

"I've been trying to think and reflect on where we've been compared to where we are. And looking forward it seems clear that we want different things. I'm just really frustrated and I'd rather talk about it in person than over the phone."

The clubhouse was a disaster. Trek and the boys were heading to bed. My batboy Jonathan, who usually helped me clean, went home early for school in the morning. Champagne dripped from the ceiling, and the smell of cheap beer, like sour yeast, dominated the clubhouse.

"Just be straight with me," I sent back. "Do I need to find a new place to live this off-season?"

"We'll talk about it when you get back."

I felt an odd sense of peace at this. I rolled the metal food warmer—big like a refrigerator—up to the VIP kitchen, now dark for the night. I sat in the club level seats watching the sprinklers water the field in the darkness of the stadium. I called her.

"I don't know where all of this is coming from," I said. "I mean, we haven't talked in days. Are you breaking up with me?"

"It's the same thing as always, and that's what hurts. It's always the same argument, the same worry, the same concern: that you're not going to have a steady income and nothing is going to change this off-season. I mean, it sounds so cliché, but you're not the same man you used to be."

"But I feel pretty good."

"That's the problem. You've been complacent. You didn't do anything last off-season, and you didn't have any choice but to go back to Aberdeen. And secretly, I think you wanted to."

"Well, sure, I've made good money here."

"It's more than that. Like you dressing up, it's like you're still trying to play baseball. Like you're still stuck in the past."

I told her I knew I wasn't a ballplayer, Mills showed me that in batting practice. I told her I'd just been rubbing elbows with the guys for better tips. I told her things would be different that off-season—I didn't need baseball. I lied to her. I lied to her, and neither of us believed me.

20

IronNuts!

Jake walked into my bedroom and did a visual scan. The floor was swept, the equipment was all neatly organized on the shelves, and I'd removed the excess equipment-room rubbish left over from years of apathy. His eyes followed the extension cord running along the wall—from the outlet near the door all the way to my little makeshift office on the other side of the room. He smiled.

"Now this shit takes me back," he said. "So how was it living in the clubhouse this year?"

"It was a no-brainer."

"Mhmm. And how'd you make out this season, financially."

"Probably a little less than last year, just with food and stuff, but it was worth it knowing I'd have enough for postgame every night. Plus guys didn't really tip that well most of the season."

"What're you charging down here again?"

"Seven a day."

"Right. Yeah, that's a lot for this level. That's probably why you weren't getting much in tips.

"I don't know if you've heard about Dewey, the clubbie in Delmarva, but he fucked up quite a bit this year with money stuff. At one point he showed up with a new stereo system. Guys asked him how he paid for it, so what does he say? 'Yeah, I'm making hand over fist here.' And guess what happened next."

"Tips went down."

Jake nodded. "He was giving those guys shit spreads and taking too much off the top. Then he decides to open his mouth, and it cost him. You've probably heard me say it before: you live like you're poor and you'll be alright."

I reached into my pocket and pulled out my flip phone. Jake laughed and nodded in approval.

"But what about Brad or anyone else in the front office," I said. "If they ask, should I let them know how much I'm making?"

"Fuck no. How much money you make is your business. I promise you, if anyone up there finds out, they'll all have their hands in that pot in no time. Broken-bat money, free drinks, detergent—all that shit will suddenly disappear."

I nodded.

"But look, I appreciate you keeping everything in order here.

"You want a piece of advice?—well, a couple pieces of advice? Clean the coaches' shoes every night, even roving coaches. And take coaches' clothes off their loops and hang 'em up in their lockers. That's just one less thing they'll have to worry about. Keep making those small adjustments every year and pretty soon you'll be solid.

"Hell of a job this year. The Delmarva clubbie is usually the last one to get an invite to spring training, but since he basically shit the bed this season, I thought I'd extend the invitation to you— even if you can only come down for a week."

I imagined being at spring training with the guys and standing in the sunshine of Sarasota, Florida, getting presented with New York–Penn League championship rings. Having everyone on the field clapping for us, including the Orioles players.

"I would love to," I said.

• • •

We'd already claimed a playoff spot with two games left against the Lowell Spinners. I made the mistake of implying that we had nothing left to play for until the postseason. Merullo overheard me.

"We got about two and a half hours of bus ride to play for," Matt said. He explained that Lowell could still win their division if they beat us in the last two games, in which case we'd play them in the playoffs. "I'd rather take the four-and-a-half-hour trip to Tri-City than the seven-fucking-hour trip to Lowell," he said.

We won our final two games, ensuring the shorter bus ride to Tri-City. We would play the ValleyCats in a best-of-three series in the four-team playoffs. The winners would go to the championship for another best-of-three series for the New York–Penn League title.

Before the playoffs, which would start with Ripken Stadium's first postseason game, we had an off day that we used for an afternoon practice. The clubhouse was loose. Guys laughed and joked around like normal—no hint that anyone was nervous for the playoffs.

The coaches let the team photographer, Bob, hop into the turtle to take a few cuts during BP. Bob was Mills's age, but looked about half his size, with chicken legs, a thick gray mustache, a few graying teeth, and a constant smile and "hey how are ya?" attitude. He always brought a giant bag of Skittles to put on the bench for the players. This man had probably watched every single pitch Mills threw for the Orioles, so Bob still had that star-struck gaze whenever he interacted with him.

Bob swung and missed badly at the first offerings from Mills. Bob's technique was something like Trek's—all upper body—but Bob had certain compensations in his swing that hinted at significant practice. The players around the field all laughed. The other coaches behind the turtle yelled to Bob.

"Keep your weight back."

"Watch the ball."

Bob whiffed, again and again. Mills stood on the fake mound between pitches, square to the plate, arms hanging heavily at his side—one ball in his right hand, three in his left. He wound up, turning, but not quite as fully as he would on a real pitch, and delivered toward the plate. Bob swung and missed, cursing himself but still smiling.

Then something happened: like a flash from Bob's camera, Alan Mills channeled some ghost from his past.

"Boooo," Mills bellowed.

Another swing and miss. "Boooo. Not as easy as it looks, is it, meat?"

Bob smiled and shook his head. Swing and miss.

"Not as easy as pointing that Nikon, huh?"

The pitchers in the outfield laughed.

Swing and miss.

"You suck," Mills yelled from behind the L-screen.

Swing and miss.

"You suck, Mills," Mills yelled to himself.

Swing and miss.

"You'll never make the Majors, Mills."

Bob finally made contact with one pitch before Merullo told him to get out of the turtle.

I took BP with the first group—Kemp, Yaz, Mancini, and me. They all passed around this extra-large black practice bat that was about thirty-eight inches long and thirty-eight ounces heavy. They crushed the ball with it. When my turn came up, I stepped into the turtle with one of Kimmel's old bats, a thirty-two-inch, twenty-nine-ounce, black Louisville Slugger. Mills didn't heckle me (or himself), thankfully, but he did start me with the same routine as before—gas inside then sliders over the outside corner. I still whiffed on the sliders, but I was able to slap a few fastballs to right field before moving out of the cage.

"Look at the bat G's using," Kemp said. He motioned for me to hand it over, and he laughed. "Oh my god. This thing's like a toothpick after swinging the big bat."

Mancini grabbed it. "I don't think I could even swing this right now."

It felt plenty heavy to me.

After BP, I took ground balls at third base. Merullo wound up and hit me a three-hopper. I fielded it cleanly, but I ate shit on my throw to first, slipping on the grass with my oversized orange-trimmed Nikes.

"Can't you get yourself a pair of fuckin' cleats?" Merullo said.

I tried another grounder and did the same thing. Almost in a single motion I slipped, tumbled, popped up midjog and let my momentum carry me off the field. They continued while I stepped down into the dugout for a drink.

Bob sat on the bench with his camera around his neck. "Man," he said, "Mills was coming in hot back there."

I nodded.

"Just when I started to get it figured out, they called me outta there."

I nodded. Bob played town baseball on Sundays, and it was anyone's guess how this story would be relayed to his teammates at the next game. I stood facing the water jug, rehydrating.

"Hey, meat," Mills said from somewhere behind me. He had that admonishing tone I hadn't heard in a long time.

I dumped the last bit of water on the ground, suddenly filled to the gills, and turned around. He was sitting on the bench with his cap turned upward on his bald, sweaty, black head. He pulled his lips back and spit out brown tobacco juice.

"You talking to me?" I said.

"Yeah, you. Come over here." He stared forward as I sat next to him on the ledge above the bench. "What were you talking about after we won that game the other day?"

"What?"

He still stared straight ahead. "Don't play dumb with me. You remember what you said."

I shook my head.

"You said, 'You're getting fired this year.'"

"I said that?"

He looked over at me. "Yeah. You said it sucks you're gonna be fired next year, or something like that. You don't remember?"

I shook my head. "I usually have a good memory with this stuff, but—are you sure it was me?"

"Ain't nobody ugly enough to mistake for you." He forced a chuckle. "What do you know?"

"I don't know anything."

"You know something."

"The hell are you talking about?"

He stared at me. "You really don't remember, do you, meat?"

"Millsy, I have no clue what this is."

He shook his head. "Old man. Old man memory. I used to be a clubbie, too, you know. You hear things. I'm gonna find out eventually."

I sat there trying to think, shaking my head, wondering what he could be talking about—what conversation he was referring to. Normally he would've told me to get lost, or I would've walked away from his interrogations, but I sat there for a few moments, silently, because for the first time since we'd met, I felt sorry for him in that moment.

He stared forward out onto the field again, where Merullo went around the horn with ground balls off his fungo bat. I kept my eyes forward too, but unfocused, watching Mills in my peripherals. I could only see his lips pulled back and hear the hiss of tobacco spit shooting through his teeth.

In the silence between us, I found a memory: me hugging him in the clubhouse after we clinched. I looked at him and said, "I'm gonna miss you next year."

My stomach dropped. He didn't realize it'd been a compliment, saying he'd be gone because he'd be promoted. He thought I meant I'd miss him because he was getting fired.

"Alright," Merullo said on the field, looking around. "Where's Mills? Mills! PFP."

Alan lowered his cap to his forehead and grabbed his fungo bat. He walked into the sunshine with his head down—the bill of his cap casting a shadow over his face—before looking up. Alan

Mills—the guy who always said, "I need a real job"; the guy who had a poster on his locker that said, "Every day at work I wonder if I'll accidentally scream 'You f***ing idiots!' out loud instead of just in my head"; the guy who pitched twelve seasons in the Majors—was afraid of losing his job as the pitching coach for a short-season single-A team.

He took up his orange fungo bat and hammered ground balls to the pitchers the same way he'd done thousands of times before, because what the hell else would he possibly be doing in that moment?

We were the last two in the coaches' office after practice. We sat at our lockers in silence, taking off our shoes and sweaty socks to shower up.

"What do you think's gonna happen in the playoffs?" he said.

"Me?"

"Yeah, you."

He'd never asked for my opinion before. "I think if our pitching is as good as it's been all season it'll just come down to hitting. It seems like that will—um—be the difference maker."

He didn't respond.

"What about you?" I said.

"What do I think will happen? I think the first team to win four games will win the championship. That's it. Not any more complicated than that." He shrugged his shoulders, stood up, and walked into the showers.

• • •

That night, lefty Zach Britton got the start for the Orioles against the Cleveland Indians. He lasted only two and a third innings and gave up four runs on six hits and two walks. The start pushed his ERA to 5.45 to go along with his 2-3 record. The Orioles were three games out of a wild-card spot with three weeks left in their season. Buck Showalter didn't want Britton to end his season with that bad outing (and he certainly didn't want Zach risking their playoff hopes pitching for the big club) so he sent Britton to us. We were the last Orioles affiliate still playing and, of course, despite the fact that we were in the playoffs, our sole purpose in life was to serve the needs of the Baltimore Orioles.

"That's another good thing about having clubs in the playoffs," Showalter said about sending Britton our way. "I'd like to get that taste out of his mouth if I could."

If we split with Tri-City in the first two games, Britton would start a deciding game three of the series. In other words, we faced the exciting prospect of having a Major League pitcher at our disposal against single-A players.

Except we didn't want him.

"I'd take fuckin' Vader or Harvey over him any day of the week," Merullo said to the other coaches. They nodded.

"If you can't throw strikes in the Majors," Mills said, "you can't throw strikes at single-A." (Britton had seventeen walks and sixteen strikeouts on the season so far.)

Merullo said, "B.G.'s gonna try to talk some sense into Buck— tell him, hey, these guys want to win, and they want to win with our own guys."

Players asked me what was going on with the Britton thing.

"Looks like if we make it to Sunday, he'll start for us," I said.

They deflated. They didn't even care when I told them to look on the bright side: he'd probably get us a nice spread.

I didn't take BP or go out shagging fly balls on the afternoon of our first playoff game. I sat in the back cutting up more pineapple than I ever had. I usually only bought two because they took so long to cut (with my butcher's knife, long since dulled over the season) that I couldn't afford the time to prepare any more. But pineapples were the guys' favorite, so I got ten of them that morning and spent the whole afternoon dicing them up.

After BP, Austin Urban came up to me with a plateful of yellow pineapple and gave me a thumbs-up.

"Clutch move, G," he said.

Mills walked past us toward the spread. He made a PB&J before every game. He turned to me, holding up a jar of creamy peanut butter.

"We won the division with crunchy peanut butter for every game. And you bring out creamy for the playoffs?" He shook his head with mock incredulity.

The guys laughed.

"Mills, I put out both kinds before every—"

"If you put out crunchy peanut butter and grape jelly all season, you put out crunchy peanut butter and grape jelly in the playoffs. You don't fuck with what works. Our clubbie with the Orioles put out pretzels before a playoff game—he never put out pretzels before. One of the guys knocked 'em over he was so mad. You know what happened in that game?"

"You lost."

He bulged his eyes. "If we lose tonight, I'll know who to find."

The guys sort of laughed.

On the wall near the coaches' office was a whiteboard with a corkboard on its right, where Merullo had pinned the day's BP schedule. Underneath the schedule was a picture of Yaz, Mancini, Yacabonis, and catcher Austin Wynns at the New York–Penn League All-Star Game. The picture had long since been defiled in the expected ways—patches on eyes, penises in mouths, etc. On the top right corner of the whiteboard was Trek's phone number, which had been there all season. On the other side someone had written:

Tri-City Starting Pitcher:
Feliz (RHP) 69.0 IP 53H 13BB 78K

Underneath it said, "Who wants it more? Is it Tri-City?" Then someone wrote "IronNuts!" and circled it with red marker.

On the bottom, Merullo wrote: "Great job playing with heart + balls—the Ws will come if we play that way." Someone drew a cartoon heart and cartoon testicles over heart + balls.

Vader started the game for us. The six-foot-four righty with the pointy ears and nose and wild eyes had continued his campaign as a legitimate ace for the IronBirds. He finished the regular season with a 7-3 record and a 2.43 ERA. He'd get the first start, Harvey would get game two in Tri-City (the shiny new first-rounder, who seemed bored at all times in the clubhouse, was 0-1 with a 2.25 ERA in three starts since moving up), and Britton would get game three in Tri-City, if necessary.

Steven Brault, the handsome, dark-haired lefty with a 2.09 ERA in twelve starts, wasn't slated to start any of our first-round playoff games. Instead, the vocal performance major from Regis University sang the national anthem before our playoff opener at Ripken Stadium. He stood in street clothes on the grass behind home plate, facing east along with the rest of the crowd, toward the flag in center field. His teammates lined up in front of our dugout, the ValleyCats in front of theirs. Inches behind Brault's feet was a newly painted insignia saying "Postseason" with the new IronBirds logo at the top. His tenor voice rang through the stadium with control that vibrated off into a falsetto on the higher notes. When he finished, his teammates welcomed him into the dugout with high fives and ass slaps before he walked up into the stands to chart pitches with the other starting pitchers.

The crowd was a light 2,736. School had started up, and the Orioles were at home in a playoff push, diverting attention away from us. Stars and Stripes bunting lined the stadium the same way they had on opening day, signaling a new season. Everything that had already happened only mattered inasmuch as it brought us to this moment. The day was clear, bright, sunny, and topped out in the high seventies. But when the sun dropped behind home plate, the coolness of early autumn snuck up on us, unprepared and jacketless, sending a shiver up our spines that said, "How could you forget this was going to happen?"

Vader and Tri-City pitcher Michael Feliz were both perfect through the first two innings. We led off the bottom of the third with a single to left field, but we only got a runner as far as second base before Yaz struck out to end the frame.

Tri-City's leadoff man started the top of the fourth with a line drive double to left field. The next batter moved him over to third with a ground ball. Tyler White, their third baseman, lined a shot to the right side, but it found the glove of our second baseman for the second out. The threat ended with a ground ball.

After that inning, nobody got a man past second base through the eighth, but the crowd couldn't have been more tense if it'd been tied 9–9 instead of 0–0. It was the kind of game that you can only truly appreciate in the playoffs—a pitchers' duel in the middle of July just doesn't have the same sex appeal.

Feliz, the big righty from the Dominican, was absolutely filthy on the mound, striking out guys with his fastball in the midnineties and an unhittable slider. He struck out eight and only gave up three hits before being taken out in the bottom of the eighth.

Our righty, Vader, pounded the strike zone and changed speeds with his low-nineties fastball mixed with a split finger—he let the hitters get themselves out.

I watched the game from the bullpen.

"Come on," we said, "just one run."

In the eighth inning, we had Donnie Hart warmed up, ready to come in when we ran into trouble, but Vader worked out of a jam with men on first and second. Now, going into the top of the ninth, Hart stood on the bullpen mound, waiting again to get the call to relieve Vader. The call didn't come, so Vader walked out of the dugout with his head down as the crowd cheered its approval—Merullo was giving his starter a chance for a complete game shutout.

Third baseman Tyler White, their number three batter, lifted a fly ball to left field to lead off the inning. The entire stadium sunk into the ground as we helplessly watched the ball drift through the darkness. Perhaps in the warmth of mid-July, that ball would've landed in the visiting bullpen, but on that early September night, the cold air knocked it down on the warning track, safely into Bier-feldt's glove.

Merullo had seen enough. He came out to yank Vader, who walked off the field to a standing ovation. Hart came in to face the four and five batters, both lefties. His ERA had ticked up by late August, but Hart still finished the regular season with a 3-1 record and a 2.25 ERA.

He got his mideighties fastball over the plate for strike one to the ValleyCats' cleanup hitter. With the count 0-1, the hitter thought Hart might come back with something off-speed. He sat back, waiting for it. He was right. Hart's Frisbee slider broke away from the cleanup hitter's hands, cutting directly into his swing path. The ball jumped off his bat, towering high toward right field.

The drive was timeless: early September, mid-July—no change in season or weather system could keep that ball in Ripken Stadium. We in the bullpen refused to watch as it flew over us and hit the top of the grounds crew shed with a violent *clunk*. It rolled down to the bright green, artificial grass next to the picnic tables between the bullpen and the shed. I peeked over my shoulder to see the ball sitting there, white against the green turf, with the grounds crew guys all facing forward at the picnic tables.

The next man reached on an error, and Hart left the game without retiring a batter, meaning his playoff ERA was infinite, incalculable—a mournful number that could not be topped: he'd given up one run in zero innings of work. Another reliever came in to finish the inning.

We went into the bottom of the ninth down 1–0. Bierfeldt hit a one-out single to center, bringing the winning run to the plate. The ValleyCats had their right-handed closer, Gonzalo Sanudo, on the mound. He'd only spent part of the season with Tri-City, but he had eight saves in eight attempts with a 0.00 ERA.

Bierfeldt led off first base as the righty Sanudo came to the set. Our six-foot-two-inch, 220-pound slugger had four stolen bases in six attempts on the season. He had the green light to go and broke for second on the pitch. If he was safe, he'd be in scoring position as the tying run. If he was out, it would stop any and all momentum we'd built against a shutdown closer.

The catcher threw him out by a mile.

Our batter followed up with a single that yielded something closer to a groan than a cheer from the crowd—*what could have been*. Sanudo got a strikeout for the final out of the game.

Hart, who gave up the game-losing homer, didn't punch or scream at his locker. He only shook his head and sighed occasionally in big huffs. Vader, the starter, talked to reporters near the clubhouse front entrance.

"I pitched probably the best I've ever pitched in my life," he said. "Whether they had a runner in scoring position or not, I was just thinking, 'They can't score.'"

B.G., shirtless with jeans on and a towel slung over his shoulder, slapped Vader on the ass as he walked behind him during the interview. I didn't even know B.G. was in town. No music played in the clubhouse—no Miley Cyrus, no "Summertime Sadness," no "Can't you see it's we who own the night?"—only light chatter and the incessant muffled boom of unearned fireworks.

The fireworks eventually stopped, and the fans seeped out of the stadium, not likely in sadness, but perhaps a childlike lack of concern that signaled the coming of football season and MLB playoffs— real playoffs.

The lights of the stadium died and silence fell like a black veil over the empty field. The metallic clank of the rolling fridge-sized food warmer cut through the quiet stadium as I pushed it through the clubhouse door. I leaned into it, head down, as I rolled it toward the concourse ramp. Just as I walked over that long slab of concrete outside the clubhouse, I looked to my right to make sure Jonathan, my batboy, had taken the water cooler in from the bullpen. He had. But something caught my eye a few dozen feet beyond: there sat the home run ball from the ValleyCats, untouched in the black of night. I stopped pushing and stood up straight, looking at that blemish, barely visible on the artificial, green grass between the bullpen and the grounds crew shed.

I considered it for a moment. I could walk over and pick up that baseball and nobody would ever know it was me. I'd throw it into the BP bucket and—no. *Not this one*, I decided. Instead, I placed my hands back onto the warm steel of the food warmer and continued pushing up the ramp, pretending, like everyone else, that this baseball had never existed.

• • •

I traveled with the team to Joseph L. Bruno Stadium in Troy, New York, for game two against the ValleyCats. I suited up again and rode the pine, same as I did in Brooklyn. Same as I have my entire life.

We had another pitchers' duel through six innings. Young Hunter Harvey struck out seven batters and only allowed two base runners (both in the fourth, both on hit by pitches). The Orioles' front office put him on a limit of five innings or seventy-five pitches, whichever came first. The five innings did, and he left the game in a 0–0 tie.

Our reliever worked a clean sixth inning, but the wheels fell off in the seventh. A double to left field. A throwing error. Another double: 1–0. A wild pitch. A single: 2–0. We went into the top of the eighth down by two, which was an astronomical deficit on a night like that.

Their starter had us groping our way hopelessly to the end, only allowing five hits in seven innings. Their closer, Gonzalo Sanudo, blanked us in the top of the eighth. Yacabonis came to the mound for the IronBirds in the bottom of the frame. The ValleyCats scored another run to make it 3–0, but it could've been infinity to zero the way we hit. Their closer slammed the door in the ninth and we packed up the bus to head home—season over.

The next day, guys trickled in and out of the clubhouse, grabbing their things and loading onto a big van destined for the airport. Mills packed and left so fast he almost walked out without saying goodbye.

"I'll see ya later, meat," he said, giving me a one-armed bro hug. I walked into the coaches' office to see three of his jerseys in his locker: the gray, blue, and black. He'd taken the white number seventy-five with the Mills nameplate on the back. I could only laugh.

"Of course he did," I thought.

Trek walked out of the training room with a duffle bag over his shoulder. "Are you gonna be at spring training?" he said.

"I hope so."

"Me too."

We shook hands.

"Text me," he said. "Let me know."

I sauntered around the empty clubhouse picking up little scraps of trash, folding up the occasional metal chair. Merullo came out of his office.

"Hey, G-man?"

I was crouched next to a locker trying to scrape off a piece of athletic tape with my fingernails. I stood up.

"I'm outta here," he said. "I left an envelope in my office with the last home stand's dues. I also threw in a couple coupons I had leftover—you might be able to use 'em."

"Oh, thanks."

He walked over to shake my hand.

"Hell of a job this year."

"Thank you."

"Let me know if you want a recommendation for spring training. I'd be glad to give it."

He walked out, and just like that, it was all done—the clubhouse empty. I would soon pack up my stuff in the equipment closet; hand the keys to my boss, Brad; and shoot back down the coast in my gold Cadillac Deville to North Augusta, South Carolina—where Nicole awaited my arrival, eagerly or not.

I walked into Merullo's office, now empty, and found the envelope on his desk. He'd written "G-man" on the front, and there was a little IronBirds logo in the top left with the address for Ripken Stadium: 873 Long Drive. I read the letter, written on Iron-Birds stationary:

G-man,

Thanks for all your hard work and the great attitude you had each day! You were a big part of our success, keeping the boys happy—not an easy job! Great season!

Hope to see you soon!

Will always remember the night in the cage w/ you and Paco—fun stuff.

Matt

I was surprised he remembered the night in the cages—for some reason I didn't think it would mean that much to him. But for me, it'd been a reminder that we were really here—in professional baseball—even if we were just scrubbing the toilets in one way or another. I pulled out the rest of the envelope's contents: a fifty-dollar bill for dues, a coupon for dollar-off hoagies from the local gas station, and an ice cream coupon that had expired in August.

I thought I would go to spring training. I thought Nicole and I would be better that off-season. I thought I would come back to the IronBirds the next summer. But winter passed, and nobody called me to come down to Sarasota. Spring came, and nothing changed between Nicole and me—we split up by mid-May. Then summer arrived unannounced, and I didn't return to Ripken Stadium. I let my days as a clubbie drift into the finite past along with every other dead baseball season, fading into distant memory for everyone except those of us who were lucky enough to be a part of it.

I left Aberdeen with a pocketful of cash, a few memories, and this bad taste in my mouth, like I had taken something from these kids other than their dues money, and they had stolen something from me other than two summers and some baseballs.

The sky blossomed like blazing flowers on a midsummer evening
on the Chesapeake. The lush green of the field at Ripken Stadium
awakened a youthful freedom in me—a remembering, of some
sort. I don't know exactly when this was—2012 or 2013—and, to
be honest, I don't think it matters: it could've been any time at any
Minor League game across America.

I took a seat in foul territory near right field, enjoying a midgame
break from my laundry duties. Ripcord and Ferrous, the mascots,
danced on the dugouts and children smiled from their seats, begging for their attention—a high-five, a wave, anything. The Iron-
Birds' first baseman threw lazy ground balls to his infielders. They
scooped them up with ease and lobbed them over to his mitt, which
he flicked out with a lazy pawing motion and a step forward. The
pitcher threw his final warm-up pitch, a strike, and the catcher
hopped up and threw to the right side of second base.

And everything was right from there—the sun was setting, the
breeze was light, and the heat of summer had lifted for the day. I
was surrounded by pointing fathers, young couples laughing, cold
beer, hot dogs, Cracker Jacks, and the palpable hope for a foul ball
or even a wink from one of the three-hour gods on the field.

I sat, quietly amazed by the team's uniforms, of all things. I
couldn't spot a single stain on any of them. Just as the thought
crossed my mind, the batter sliced a fastball high over my head
and the faces around me all turned to watch it fly toward the clubhouse. They had eager looks in their eyes, as if the ball might take
a lucky two-hundred-foot bounce off the green clubhouse roof and
come back to them. No such luck.

To my surprise, I found myself wishing for a foul ball. I realized,
on a logical level, that I had access to hundreds of the exact same
baseballs in my equipment closet. I could just walk back there and
grab one if I wanted it so bad. But this wasn't a logical desire—it was
baseball. And my dream for the day was to catch a foul. The pearls

in my equipment closet were just baseballs, but the one that sliced over our heads had the dust of magic on it: it had been blessed by touching the field of play in a professional baseball game. But, just like always, a foul never came my way.

I couldn't get over their jerseys. I'd spent hours scrubbing them after every game, seemingly to no avail. But from that vantage point, up in the stands, their uniforms looked as white as the last flashes of dying stars.

Acknowledgments

I'd like to thank:

Nikki Van Noy, for lighting a fire under my ass when I needed it the most.

Emily Howell, for helping me realize I was the main character of this story.

Mrs. Prody, for teaching me that writing could be simultaneously funny, serious, and something I could do for a living.

Jesse Sussman, for challenging me on everything.

Lamar Giles, for guiding me in the early query writing process.

Joe Jackson, for guiding me in the early proposal writing process.

Blake Bailey, for teaching me how to interview and edit with equal parts compassion and ruthlessness.

Mike Pearson, for inviting me to study at Old Dominion University, for always keeping my ego in check, and for teaching me how not to shoot a three-pointer.

My dad, Rick Larson, for introducing me to baseball and for always reading my tomes of first drafts.